Our Contentious Universities

Our Contentious Universities

A Personal History

Neil L. Rudenstine

The American Philosophical Society Press
Philadelphia

Published by
The American Philosophical Society Press
Philadelphia, Pennsylvania 19106-3387
www.amphilsoc.org

Printed in the United States of America on acid-free paper
10 9 8 7 6 5 4 3 2 1

Library of Congress Cataloging-in-Publication Data
Names: Rudenstine, Neil L., author.
 Title: Our contentious universities : a personal history / Neil L. Rudenstine.
 Description: Philadelphia : American Philosophical Society Press, 2024. |
    Includes bibliographical references and index. | Summary: "This book
    describes the current state of American higher education. It is partly a
    memoir, and partly a personal history of Neil L. Rudenstine. The current
    volume considers whether the substantial nature and scale of university
    changes during the past half-century or more indicate that we have
    entered a new era when the probability of frequent protest and disruption
    is more likely than before"— Provided by publisher.
 Identifiers: LCCN 2024017665 (print) | LCCN 2024017666 (ebook) | ISBN
    9781606180075 (hardcover) | ISBN 9781606180082 (epub)
 Subjects: LCSH: College environment—United States. | College students—
    Political activity—United States. | Protest movements—United States. |
    Education, Higher—Aims and objectives—United States. | Rudenstine,
    Neil L. | College teachers—United States—Biography. College
    administrators—United States—Biography.
 Classification: LCC LB2324 .R84 2024 (print) | LCC LB2324 (ebook) |
    DDC 378.1/980973—dc23/eng/20240620
 LC record available at https://lccn.loc.gov/2024017665
 LC ebook record available at https://lccn.loc.gov/2024017666

Hardcover ISBN: 978-1-6061-8007-5

eBook ISBN: 978-16061-8008-2

To David, Zina, Mary, and Dan

Contents

Acknowledgments

This book was initially written during the high Covid period of 2020–21 when there was ample time to read, think, and compose. Since then, events on many university campuses have become more divisive, even as national and international affairs have grown more inflamed. Several rewritings were therefore required. Indeed, the "final" pages were about to go to the printer when Hamas invaded Israel, so production ceased while yet another chapter was added in late December 2023.

The volume that follows draws on incidents and ideas that range from the 1950s to the present. Many individuals (not all of whom are still with us) contributed significantly to the views and sentiments that inform the manuscript. Robert Goheen and Aaron Lemonick (both from Princeton), and Reuben Brower and Douglas Bush (both from Harvard), were instrumental in that respect. They made irreplaceable contributions to my convictions about the nature of universities, of teaching and research, and of the centrality of the liberal arts and sciences in higher education.

More specific, the staff of the Seeley Mudd Manuscript Library in Princeton were exceptionally helpful in my search for documents relating to many Princeton University incidents dating from the late 1960s to the late 1980s.

Meanwhile, advice from a number of individuals made a great difference to my views of Harvard as an institution, as well as many other related matters. These associates have included Jack Reardon, Marc Goodheart, Jackie O'Neill, Dennis Thompson, Margaret Marshall, William Kirby, Robert Kasdin, and John Rosenberg.

Laura Kaye, my invaluable assistant, has been responsible for shepherding the entire manuscript through its several changes to publication.

I owe a very great debt of gratitude to Peter Dougherty, former director of the Princeton University Press, and current director of the APS Press. He helped to shape significant parts of the entire manuscript and provided indispensable suggestions for improvement from start to finish.

Finally, Angelica Zander Rudenstine was more than discerning and patient through change after change, and page after page.

Neil L. Rudenstine

Our Contentious Universities

Chapter 1

Beginnings

Few people doubt that the last decade and a half have been highly contentious in American higher education. Students have been more activist than at any moment since the 1960s. Many politicians, the media, and large sections of the general public are—in various ways—critical of our colleges and universities. The institutions themselves are often internally divided or fragmented, such that different individuals and groups are sometimes at odds with one another. As a result, the task of leading and administering these institutions is simply far more difficult than it was not long ago.

The recent issues are manifold in nature: Climate-crisis demonstrations in favor of university divestment from fossil-fuel stocks; the creation of new graduate-student unions; the attack in the courts on "affirmative action" and diversity; various controversies in admissions concerning the practice of so-called "athletic admits," as well as broadsides against alumni "legacy" admits (and the children of major donors); the campaign to erase from their universities the names of several figures labeled imperialist or racist (such as Cecil Rhodes, John Calhoun, and Woodrow Wilson); the desire of some minority-group students to have "trigger warnings," "safe spaces," and analogous protections to guard them against potentially offensive speech and actions; the high cost of college attendance, and the heavy burden of student loan-debt; the frequent shouting-down of conservative speakers on many campuses; the continuing effort to eliminate instances of sexual assault; the generalized attack on "elitism" (including especially those institutions that are highly selective and well endowed); the possible threat of increased government intrusion in higher education; and finally, the extraordinary protests since the very recent Hamas invasion of Israel.

In addition, there have of course been well-publicized attacks on DEI (diversity, equity, and inclusion) programs at institutions across the nation; Governor DeSantis's recent move to transform New College (in Sarasota, Florida) is perhaps the most conspicuous effort of this kind. He placed several of his own chosen candidates on the college's board of trustees, and they promptly organized to do away with the institution's DEI program. DeSantis also opposed the introduction (in Florida) of the College Board's Advanced Placement program in African American studies, and of course led the way in banning books in libraries. Analogous actions in other states have been less prominent but nevertheless similar. At the same time, one should add that the pressure to use DEI standards can often be at times problematic: A candidate for a UCLA professorship was very recently denied the position for failing to respond "correctly" to questions about diversity and its value.

The preceding list could easily be expanded, but it offers at least a reasonable synopsis of what has been happening on many American campuses. We have entered a new era, with a broad spectrum of divisive issues at hand, including some that have affected not-for-profit institutions beyond the academy (including several museums).

Not all readers may—quite understandably—be familiar with examples of the protests that have been taking place. A small sample may therefore be helpful. For instance:

- Approximately fifty students staged a sit-in outside the office of Rutgers University's president to oppose the invitation (in 2014) to Condoleezza Rice as commencement speaker. They regarded her as a chief instigator of the Iraq War. Students carried signs such as "War criminals out." Following the protest, Rice withdrew from the invitation to speak.
- The Federalist Society recently (2023) invited a conservative judge to speak at Stanford Law School. Students loudly booed the speaker's attempt to give his talk. The DEI officer made remarks that tended to side with the student point of view. "In this school," said the speaker, "the inmates have gotten control of the asylum." There

were no official disciplinary actions against the students, although the DEI officer was relieved of her duties.

- African American students affiliated with the Black Lives Matter movement protested an event (in 2017) at the College of William and Mary. They rushed the stage and prevented the ACLU guest from speaking. The students shouted "You protect Hitler too" and "Shame, shame, shame." A student took the microphone to read a statement. Then the entire event was canceled.
- The dean of Harvard's Kennedy School recently refused a fellowship to a candidate for his alleged anti-Israel work for Human Rights Watch. The dean's move was protested by many students and faculty, which led the dean to reverse his decision. The candidate criticized the Kennedy School for its apparent unwillingness to tolerate any criticism of Israel.
- Two protests (2022) at two law schools—Yale and University of California College of the Law, San Francisco—were aimed at conservative legal speakers. At UC Law SF, the speaker was unable to proceed at all because of shouting; at Yale, students chanted continually, often interrupting the speaker because of his apparent anti-LGBTQ+ views. No disciplinary action followed.
- A recent festival celebrating Palestinian art and culture at the University of Pennsylvania included some speakers who were accused of being antisemitic. The university administration condemned any such speakers but did not cancel the festival. The university itself did not sponsor the event, but some faculty departments and student groups participated in it. Wealthy Penn alumni condemned the university and its administration for failing to stop the celebration. Then, after the Hamas invasion of Israel in October 2023, they faulted the Penn president for not having opposed the invasion forcefully enough. Wealthy Penn alumni (and at least one trustee) then withdrew from supporting the university, and some demanded the resignation of the president.

The forces aligned against higher education are now variegated, and they make it more difficult for our institutions to function effectively as places of vital and humane learning. Indeed, a recent survey suggests that this situation may be taking a toll on the length of tenure characterizing college and university presidents. In 2006, the average length of a president's service was 8.5 years; in 2022 it was 5.9 years. One inevitable question that arises from our current predicament is why (and how) it has come to pass. What major changes, for example, have taken place in our system of higher education—and in our nation—to create the current conditions? If we examine the significant events that have occurred at many of our colleges and universities not only recently, but since (for example) the 1950s and 1960s, does the pattern help us understand the similarities—and the differences—of our very recent situation? That pattern of change is not a simple one, but if we are able to illuminate it, we may be in a better position to comprehend our present predicament more fully.

In the following pages, I have described my own views of what has happened, based partly on my personal experience as a student, faculty member, and administrator since the 1950s. Because my experience has been primarily at two private well-endowed universities—Princeton and Harvard—it is obviously limited in a number of important ways. At the same time, many of the most contentious events at these institutions mirrored to a great extent what was happening elsewhere in the nation's higher education system. In addition, I have of course relied in this volume on research, reading, discussions with colleagues and students, and visits to a number of colleges and universities. In effect, this book is partly a memoir, and partly a personal history. Although it does take issue with some views recently put forward to characterize the protests of the 1960s and early 2000s, it also deals with several other significant developments that did not bear directly on those disruptions. For example, some chapters are devoted to education in the 1950s, and others to the struggle of many small colleges to avoid bankruptcy. In short, not everything in the following pages concerns "contentiousness," although that is obviously the central focus.

Indeed, a major question that the current volume poses is: Given the substantial nature and scale of university changes during the past half century or more, have we entered what is in effect a new era when the probability of frequent protest and disruption is more likely than before? Many of our universities are simply larger and—very important—highly decentralized; more composed of a large number of semi-autonomous parts (such as programs, centers, institutes, departments and schools); highly diverse in political, ethnic, racial, sexual, geographic, and other terms; and consequently more likely to give rise to conflict because there are simply far more actors in a complex drama in which any one of a number of individuals or groups may find themselves at odds with others, or with the institution itself.

Each semi-autonomous part of a university may seek funds—and may accept them from the wrong kind of donor. Each director or dean or president may make a decision or statement that antagonizes one group or another. Each invited speaker may be shouted down by a group that disagrees with the speaker's point of view. Each athletic coach may recommend the wrong kind of admission decision for the wrong reasons. In other words, the possibility for error or serious misjudgment is far more likely when there are so many centers of power with such a diversified population as now comprises so many institutions of higher education.

In addition, the nation and world in which these institutions function are themselves riven in ways that are contentious. So long as there are deeply serious political, economic, social, and other divisions and disturbances in our own society—or in international affairs—it is likely that some or many of our students will be affected by them and may be moved to protest in one form or another. As a result, the possibility of intermittent if not continuous contention and disruption may simply be part of our current and future college and university situations.

Perhaps there will be one or more future episodes (as happened after World War II) that will somehow unite much of the nation (and perhaps higher education) so that contentiousness will greatly lessen or virtually disappear for a period of time. Perhaps not. If not, we may be compelled to live indefinitely with something like our recent and current state of affairs: exceptionally difficult; far less than ideal; mirroring to some extent the current state of our domestic political and other problems, as well as the *world's* problems.

Chapter 2

Constant Change and Beyond

MAJOR CHANGES IN POSTWAR AMERICAN HIGHER EDUCATION

Because this volume focuses partly on a number of the far-reaching changes that took place in American colleges and universities since the late 1940s (and especially the 1950s), a few statistics may help us to understand some of the early developments. The information can offer a particularly vivid sense of the pace and scale of certain significant transformations. For instance, in 1940, about 5 percent of American youth had a college education. By 1960, 50 percent had finished two years of college, and 32 percent had four-year degrees. In 1960, there were 3.6 million college and university students—a huge increase over the prewar era. But by 1970, the figure had swollen to 7.9 million students.

Part of this growth was sparked by the so-called GI Bill, passed by Congress in 1945 at the strong urging of the American Legion (as well as many educational institutions that had suffered from a lack of students during the War). The Bill offered most returning veterans a free year of college or other training for every year of war service.

The initial projected demand for the program was estimated to be in the range of perhaps 150,000 to 700,000 veterans. Instead, about 2.6 million chose (over the course of several years) to go to college, and more than 5 million entered professional training programs.

Clearly, there was an enormous unexpected pent-up demand for advanced education. Before many years had passed, the idea of "going to college" became the goal of untold young people—products of the postwar baby boom—and their families. In response, the federal government and individual states led the way in creating the world's largest and most inclusive system of higher education.[1]

This astonishing development was rapid, expensive, and national in character. It represented a massive shift in the nature of American culture and aspiration. It contributed substantially to the steady economic prosperity of the nation. And it ultimately—decades later—bore witness to a formidable change in the intellectual equipment that began to define an educated person. Well before the turn of the twenty-first century, undergraduate "majors" in specific fields of study were dramatically different from those of the 1950s and the 1960s. Indeed, by the year 2010, it was no longer the case that most American college students were experiencing a broad education in "the liberal arts and sciences." A very different conception of career-related education had come to pass. Few (if any) changes—among the very great number that occurred—were more profound.

Another major development was highly consequential: the extraordinary increase in the number of new PhD candidates, and ultimately new faculty members, that occurred by about 1970. In the late 1940s, there were approximately 4,000 PhD candidates nationally. By 1970, there were more than 26,000. The number of faculty members grew from about 200,000 in the 1950s, to approximately 500,000 by the end of the next two decades. The implications of this growth were enormous. New fields of knowledge and new methodologies were introduced. On another front, the balance of power between the administration (and trustees) on the one hand, and the faculty on the other, was altered—in favor of the faculty. Control of the curriculum and of faculty appointments shifted strongly in the direction of the professoriate and its expertise (as well as its greatly increased numbers). The president (and far less, the trustees) still retained power to evaluate and turn down faculty tenure appointments, for example, but this began to happen much more rarely than in earlier eras.

Under these conditions the role of the president also began to change. In an earlier era—let us say from Charles Eliot's forty-year presidency at Harvard (1869–1909) to that of Columbia's Nicholas Murray Butler's forty-three years (1902–1945)—the president and trustees were substantially in charge. This was, in effect, the age of so-called giants. But the institutions were quite small and malleable, and many faculty were junior and untenured. Harvard had scarcely 600 undergraduates and many fewer graduate students during Eliot's early years. When he later wanted to appoint the formidable Christopher Columbus Langdell as dean of his Law School, the faculty was split precisely 50-50 on whether to approve Langdell. It was the president himself (since he was a university-wide professor) who broke the tie. The final tally was two votes in favor, and one against. It was never easy to be a giant, but institutional diminutiveness and malleability certainly helped a great deal.

Indeed, when Edward Ross, a Stanford faculty member, published a book on immigration and railroads that offended Jane Stanford, co-founder of Stanford University, Ross was forced to resign (in 1900). Such actions were far from implausible. This time, however, the incident left a lasting mark. By 1915, John Dewey (of Columbia) and Arthur Lovejoy (of Hopkins) had created the American Association of University Professors (AAUP). It immediately began to champion the cause of the faculty, of tenure, and of academic freedom. The professoriate was on its way—though only modestly at first.

By the 1950s and 1960s, faculty power had greatly increased and few if any "giants" remained. When Clark Kerr gave his Godkin lectures at Harvard in 1963, he introduced the term *multiversity* to describe the huge new public institutions—with tens of thousands of students and a multitude of faculty—to describe the University of California and similar institutions (such as Michigan and Wisconsin). Their presidents were viewed as *mediators* by Kerr (a term he later regretted). Although he was describing the presidents of multiversities, he left the impression that nearly all presidents of major institutions were in situations that were at least somewhat similar to those of mega-institutions:

> Power is not necessary to the task [of mediating], though there must be a consciousness of power. The President must police its use by the constituent groups, so that none will have too much or too little or use it too unwisely. To make the university work really effectively, the moderates need to be in control of each power center. ... When the extremists get in control of the students, the faculty, or the trustees with class warfare concepts, then the delicate balance of interests becomes an actual war.[2]

Only a few universities were true multiversities, and not all presidents—by any means—became mere "mediators." But Kerr was uncommonly candid in his book, and he often talked in terms of an institution's realpolitik rather than its propaganda. This was in many ways refreshing, if not always sufficiently accurate or complex. It did, however, compel his audience to think about the dynamics of university power relations and some of the actualities of university political life. Moreover, Kerr's worry about possible campus "warfare" was certainly not—in 1963—far off the mark. Within two years, Berkeley found itself in unremitting ferment and student turbulence.

Another of the most significant postwar developments had its origin in November 1944 when President Roosevelt wrote to Vannevar Bush, his science advisor, posing a set of questions related to the continued development of research in the natural sciences following the end of World War II. The scientific objective was to make certain that the nation's capacity to develop new talent and produce major innovations in basic and applied scientific research should continue during peace time, because Roosevelt was convinced that there would be an indefinite need for such work in defense-related activities, in medicine, and in analogous fields. Bush produced an extraordinary report (recently republished) called *Science: The Endless Frontier*. He recommended a formidable government investment—reaching indefinitely into the future—related to national defense, health and medicine, and the public good.

Some government support for work in such fields existed before (and during) the war, but the rapid acceleration and immense expansion of the effort took place following Bush's report. The renamed National Institutes of Health (NIH) were consolidated in 1948, and the National Science Foundation (NSF) was created in 1950.

Although the nature of the mandate and the very great level of funding were certainly critical, the most significant element of Bush's recommendations was that the faculty of the nation's universities—rather than investigators at a set of free-standing government institutes (as is the case in some countries)—should carry out nearly all the research. Individual faculty members would apply for grants, and funds would be awarded based on merit. The recommendation was in many respects controversial, primarily because it would make the universities heavily reliant on the government for very substantial funding. Depending on the nature of the particular government in Washington, or on the climate of opinion in the nation, or the state of the national economy, one could easily imagine government funding rising or falling unpredictably. One could also imagine the possibility of future government intrusion into the affairs of those institutions that had until then been essentially private, but would now become partly public because of this new source of major financial support. The recent Supreme Court decision barring the use of race in college and university admissions is an obvious example of such intrusion in higher education because of partial government funding.

At the same time, there was no other means of major research funding that could even begin to approach that of the federal government. So Vannevar Bush's proposal represented an immense opportunity for the universities. The new system would enable American higher education to create—over time—the most formidable single research capability that existed anywhere in the world. That potential alone made the idea irresistible—indeed, it seemed impossible for universities to turn down. So a complex and risky bargain was made: mainly positive, but at times fraught with difficulties and potentially serious consequences.

Research at hundreds of institutions was eventually so much enlarged and enhanced that it became a major mission, affecting the balance between research and teaching, and altering the nature of the American university. It also tended to change the balance between the sciences—which then seemed very wealthy—and other fields of study, especially the humanities, where grants scarcely existed. Clark Kerr's analysis of this situation (in *The Uses of the University*) is an interesting point of reference, but the literature on the entire subject is of course vast.

In short, within a quarter-century after World War II, the entire system of American higher education had grown dramatically, both in terms of the number and size of its institutions, and the number of students attending them. The nature of the faculty had changed in size, status, and power. The role of the president (and trustees) had begun to diminish: "the day of the monarchs has passed," said Kerr.[3] The research mission of universities became far more intense and imposing. Altogether, a new creation had come into being: higher education in the United States was, by 1970, a very different phenomenon than it had been in either 1945 or 1950.

Even this first phase of change and development in higher education created problems that would, in the coming years and decades, lead to major difficulties. For instance, the growth in the number and size of some institutions (and of some state systems) was very rapid and substantial, with insufficient attention paid to its likely consequences. Colleges and universities have many of the attributes of communities: the ability of students to know a good number of their fellows reasonably well and for faculty and students to have sufficient contact in classes—not simply in lectures. These are important aspects of undergraduate collegiate life (as well as graduate student life), and they help to create the sense of genuinely human and humane environments in which serious learning can flourish.

Nevertheless, some of the publicly funded universities (especially the "multiversities") grew well beyond such human dimensions very quickly and laid the groundwork for future student discontent and protests. In addition, American higher education responded to pent-up student and family demand by expanding without sufficient concern about the possible long-term costs of such a system. The heady postwar years, and the nation's economic growth, led people to believe that a large tuition-free public education system could not only be created but sustained indefinitely through financial down-turns, political headwinds, and other forms of adversity. But this, too, proved to be a grave mistake: Free tuition disappeared decades ago; costs at public institutions have risen dramatically; political backlash curtailed much state funding, and the debilitating educational effects of some of our largest institutions were catalogued at least as soon as the early 1960s. At Berkeley, for example, the total endowment is only about $6.8 billion, compared to figures in the $30 to $50 billion range at major private universities—in addition to the fact that Berkeley is facing a deficit of $82 million in 2023.

Once the large-scale structural changes—described earlier—had occurred, there was of course a multitude of other important developments that took place in the following six to seven decades. The "conformist" fifties yielded swiftly to the student protests and turbulence of the sixties. The Civil Rights Movement helped to usher increasing numbers of African American undergraduates into our colleges and universities. Not only African American studies, but also Asian American, Latino, Judaic, and women's studies found their place in the curriculum. And by the 1970s, almost all all-male—and many all-female—private colleges and universities had become coeducational. In addition, "stagflation" induced a very rapid rise in tuition and fees in the 1970s and was followed by a substantial shift in student "majors"—away from the humanities toward some social sciences, life-sciences, and subjects eventually referred to as *STEM (science, technology, engineering, and mathematics)*.

The advent of (mainly) continental "theory" in the 1960s and 1970s may have helped—with its philosophical complexities—to hasten the decline of the humanities, while also leading to the culture wars of the 1980s. By then, the hegemony of "Western civilization" had long since been challenged, and the continued curricular demise of many dead White males coincided with the introduction of new courses, new methods of learning, and a general relaxation of departmental requirements in humanistic studies.

By the beginning of the twenty-first century, the well-established goal of "diversity" had expanded to include not only race, geography, religion, extracurricular talents and other categories, but the full range of LGBTQ+ students; additional minority groups; more first-generation undergraduates; and an enlarged socioeconomic spectrum designed to enroll more students from severely disadvantaged backgrounds. These developments made our colleges and universities more accessible than ever before, but they also brought, not surprising, a greater share of problems. Conflicts among some groups led—as suggested earlier—to calls for "trigger warnings" and "safe spaces," as well as strong protections against sexual assaults on women. Fair adjudication of these and other matters proved more than difficult to achieve. Simultaneously, in an altogether different sphere, technology made its presence increasingly felt. Computing "centers" gave way to desktop models, and they in turn witnessed the unleashing of hand-held devices. The internet and big data enabled research (among other things) to spring forward, whereas the advent and then pervasive presence of social media presented higher education (and society at large) with new opportunities, new perplexities, and some serious new problems.

Other protests—as suggested earlier—also arrived: divestment demands (especially from fossil fuel stocks), decolonization pressures (in some museums as well as higher education), the consequences of war in Israel, swollen admissions applications to "elite" and other institutions (partly a result of a new "Common Application" form) leading to anxiety and upheaval in much of the entire college admission process.

In other words, the new post-2000 era had arrived. Its protests were more intermittent and sometimes—not always—less virulent than those of the sixties, but nevertheless very difficult to manage, and at times literally turbulent. Nevertheless, American higher education continued to rank first internationally. Whether that leadership could be sustained well into the future was open to question, but it was not yet greatly endangered despite the substantial extent to which it was questioned, criticized, and partly disrupted.

If we step back for a moment from the developments just described, a few additional points are important to mention.

First, the presidency (and some other important administrative positions) in American universities is highly unusual in its ambitions and
expectations. At least since the nineteenth century, many presidents were
major builders and change-agents who sought to move their institutions
forward.

Indeed, the tendency to expand was often present throughout American society itself. When Harvard once constituted a special committee to
help alter aspects of the institution's programs, Joseph Story (a Supreme
Court Justice) was appointed the committee's chair, and his recommended
innovations were preceded by the following statement (dated May 4,
1824): "In a society, like ours, which is continually expanding and embrac-
ing more elevated objects of research, the nature and extent of an University
education, and the methods of instruction, must in some degree be liable
to change, so as to be adopted to the spirit of the age."

This nineteenth-century tendency was only heightened after World
War II, when so many new institutions were created, and when others
grew. Indeed, *growth* and *innovation* became the implicit watchwords of
the time, and they were so ingrained in the system—and in the concept
of the American university presidency—that they persisted as habits of
mind and action even after the immediate postwar period.

In short, the president was often expected to lead his or her institution
to new heights and a new future. Those expectations almost always meant
the introduction of new ideas, new initiatives, new programs, new buildings, and often a new fund-raising campaign. Indeed, the test of a president's success or failure became, de facto, what new ideas, ventures, and
resources were forthcoming. One scarcely needs to cite evidence in support
of such a statement. One relatively recent president has been commemo-
rated as follows:

> During [his] tenure, [the] endowment grew. ... Applications to [the]
> College grew from fewer than 11,000 to ... 28,975. ... Under [him], ...
> the largest building and renovation program took place since the
> 1930s. ... [He] vastly expanded the ... campus ... and worked to
> improve the [university's] relationship with its local workers. ...

The list carries on. Meanwhile, to step slightly aside, a recent director of
her university's museums was highlighted for the fact that under her

> leadership, [the museums] experienced remarkable growth and trans-
> formative change. Her efforts to expand access to the museums [led

to] a groundbreaking new free admission policy. ... She also [led] a
robust strategic planning process. ...

In short, university presidents—and other important administrators—
are almost always known for what concrete results they have achieved.
The implications of such a view are only too clear: in general, American
universities tend to expand, and they tend to increase the number of new
programs or other entities that become part of them. Over time, from one
dynamic presidency to the next, institutions become, not simply larger,
but more decentralized, more complex, more variegated, and more difficult
to lead as single unified entities. Indeed, the many institutional parts
may scarcely know much about one another. Humpty Dumpty doesn't
necessarily have a great fall, but keeping him intact may become increasingly difficult.

No individual book can hope to deal with more than a fraction of
the transformations and difficulties that have occurred in American higher
education since the 1950s. Any major alteration of a system (or "non-
system," as David Riesman called ours) will inevitably have a multitude of
consequences, many of which are ultimately unfathomable. To understand
even part of the significant changes—and the disruptions—that have happened in higher education, and especially *why* they happened, is one hope
of the pages that follow. If they can shed some light on a portion of the
most important transformations since about 1950—and help to explain
our current time of student protests—they can perhaps serve as a useful
footnote to the substantial amount of illumination that has already been
provided by so many others.

SCHOOLING IN THE FIFTIES

In the next few pages, I have focused partly on my early schooling and
college years, mainly to offer a sketch of small-town public school—and
very modest boarding-school—education in the very late 1940s and early
1950s, leading to four years of college at Princeton from 1952–56. More
broadly, I have described the work of several writers who attempted to
characterize important aspects of American society and higher education
during the fifties. This is mainly useful as a means of helping to understand
the movement from the 1950s to the contentious 1960s.

My grandparents entered the United States, passing through Ellis
Island, just after the turn of the twentieth century. They had escaped lives

of penury and, in my father's case, the constant threat of brutal pogroms. They came with nothing, and many of their numerous children had only a highly abbreviated education that stopped short of high school. At the time, such families needed the means simply to live, so they all worked together—from the youngest to the eldest—to survive and make their way in a new land that was completely unknown to them. Little wonder that each family huddled together with others who spoke the same language, ate the same kinds of food, and went to similar houses of worship: in my mother's case, the heritage was Italian Catholic; in my father's, Russian Jewish.

Colleges and universities were inevitably foreign to many immigrant families. For my own parents, education was eventually seen as the way to escape their plight: not for themselves, because that was impossible, but for their children. They encouraged their children to be diligent and—extraordinarily—to follow wherever our interests might lead. They had married in 1934, when my mother was barely 20. It was the depth of the Depression, and my father became a federal prison guard: There were few jobs available and even fewer for people with only a minimal education. My mother, meanwhile, became a waitress. We settled in Danbury, Connecticut, where there was a new correctional institution. Danbury was a small one-industry town and was known locally as the (men's) *Hat City of the World*. Those were the years before President Kennedy's style intimated that men's hats were unfashionable and unromantic. In the late 1940s, nearly all aspiring men wore felt fedoras and looked like FBI agents, until handsome windswept hair won the day, putting the town's demoralized factories out of business, one by one.

At the time, our schools were (at least in Danbury) models of peace, quiet, probity, and predictable behavior. Classes were rather small, and the universal assumption was that we would all be silent and studious. Our desks were bolted to the floor, aligned in rows that were uniformly straight and narrow. There was nothing remotely informal about our arrangements: collaborative or project-based learning, with group assignments and informal chats, could scarcely have been further from anyone's most fertile imagination. We raised our hands dutifully in order to ask a question or respond to one. And although Danbury had a Black community, there was only one Black student in our entire "middle school" (as it was called); where the others were, no one seemed to know—or thought to ask.

Meanwhile, our curriculum was steadfastly "core": English, history, math and geography. Science was impractical because of the need for implausibly expensive equipment. I was rather in awe of the British Empire: Our classroom geography globe displayed every imperial part in glowing pink, and it seemed to me that there was scarcely any color visible *except* pink. Little did I know that the Empire was swiftly dwindling to near-microscopic proportions. Even Winston Churchill had declared, in a war-time speech at Harvard, that the empires of the future would be "empires of the mind." Not entirely accurate, but nevertheless prescient.

Our school's principal was tall, thin, and stern, with a reputation for abruptness and a short temper. As a result, our hallways breathed an atmosphere of uninterrupted authority. Then suddenly, in my eighth grade at age 13, my entire life changed. The principal, Mr. Maginley, called me to his office one day in the spring of 1948 to ask whether I would like to go to a boarding school. He was a man of few words, and I could scarcely muster even fewer. I did not know what a boarding school was, but I thought that my principal—who was in fact a kind man—would not lead me astray. So without quite saying yes, I did not say no. My parents were also puzzled, but decided to learn more. John Verdery, headmaster of the Wooster School—a small private boarding school just outside Danbury—was seeking a candidate to hold a newly created scholarship, and I had been recommended. Boarding schools were obviously not part of our universe, and no one in the family knew whether or not I should enter this new world. My mother was especially anxious. She and my father had several meetings with the headmaster to discuss the subject. If I did not do well at the school, then what would happen? Would I go to Danbury High School? Would I ever have a chance of going to college? What if I did not like Wooster—an environment foreign to us all? But my parents were deeply impressed by John (as we came to call him), so we finally accepted. Nothing was ever the same again.

Wooster was barely twenty years old when I entered in 1948. Founded in 1926, it was one of many such schools that sprinkled the New England countryside—especially Connecticut and Massachusetts— intended for children whose families wanted to ensure some version of an Ivy League education for their offspring. The schools usually included an accommodating version of post-Puritan Protestantism. Some of their leaders (such as Frank Boyden of Deerfield) were outstanding persons and educators, and many were well-disposed capable clergymen who believed that the Deity was either a moderate Democrat or a liberal Republican. Sin and hell were scarcely mentioned, since the whole point of schooling after World War II was to prepare one for life in an America that was on the way to becoming a brighter and more prosperous land. The idea of possible damnation for any member of a well-groomed boarding school would have struck an unimaginably odd note in the midst of so much bounty and benevolence.

But Wooster was in many respects different from more established "elite" institutions: not different in the general optimism of its ethos, but in the relative impoverishment of its facilities and the nature of its Spartan regimen. Its founding headmaster was a minister, and he launched the new institution with precisely two buildings: a three-story farmhouse converted into a dormitory, a set of classrooms, and even an infirmary. And a traditional New England red barn whose original purpose was no longer pertinent. It would now serve as a basketball court and a locus for other feats of physical prowess.

I was part of a fortunate generation whose market timing could hardly have been better. Higher education in the United States was still extremely underdeveloped when I entered Wooster in the fall of 1948. Consequently, we had the benefit of very talented teachers who, a decade later, would almost certainly have decided to earn PhDs and join the faculty ranks of America's rapidly expanding college and university system. So I learned from an early age that teaching could be ennobling, and that it could take many forms, because our classroom instructors were also our athletic coaches, extracurricular leaders, and dormitory housemasters.

Those parents who sent their children to boarding schools were far from misguided: In the late 1940s and 1950s (as well as much earlier), Ivy League institutions were populated largely by the graduates of such institutions, so the chances of going to Dartmouth, Princeton, Brown, Yale, Penn, or Harvard were infinitely greater if one had graduated from Groton or Exeter or Lawrenceville or even Wooster than if one had applied from Danbury High School. It rarely occurred to people that prep schools or Ivy-type colleges and universities were improperly exclusive, or reprehensibly "elitist," or objectionably expensive, even though few people could attend them. Scholarship aid was not plentiful, but it existed and was generally regarded as "meritorious" in a positive sense of that word—something to be prized if one was awarded it. Simultaneously, tuition at publicly funded higher education institutions was free and was beginning to be seen as the natural alternative to private expensive institutions—especially when, following World War II, nearly all states were rapidly expanding educational opportunities for literally hundreds of thousands of individuals. Indeed, by the 1950s, there were beginning to be two alternatives in higher education: private institutions that were financially beyond the reach of most people, and publicly funded colleges and universities where tuition was free and the only real expense was the fairly modest cost of room and board.

By the time I arrived at Wooster, the school had grown to ninety students and nine or ten faculty—a scale that might have seemed immense to its founder, Aaron Coburn. Not surprising, the school's curriculum was similar to that of other institutions, and it had a significant impact on me. The humanities were still very strong in the immediate postwar period and Wooster required four years of history (from ancient to modern), four years of literature (from Shakespeare to Faulkner), two years of Latin and two of French, four of mathematics (taught almost as a branch of logic), and one of largely nonexperimental physics. Language, literature, and history accorded with my natural bent, so Wooster powerfully reinforced my desire to be immersed in the humanities—though the concept as such was not part of my mental equipment, any more than the idea of the "social sciences." But I knew instinctively that the works I was reading taught me much about ideas, perceptions, and feelings—developing my capacity to think more consciously about myself, about a wide range of people, and about the possible meanings of the life that I was only beginning to live.

Wooster also persuaded me that a residential community of students and teachers offered us something unique about the concept later known as *diversity*. In such a setting, there were many opportunities to confront, accept, resolve, and sometimes intensify the differences among us, so that the possibility of developing human values—as well as an inescapable commitment to academic values—could be greatly enhanced. Of course, our challenges were far from great in the early 1950s. All of us were White males of a certain age and (with few exceptions) we came from a common American culture, primarily rooted in New England. We also took for granted (without using the term) the dominance of Western civilization. Whether the challenges were small or large, however, this journey in learning had a profound effect, and left me with the vision of an inarticulated but nevertheless powerful ideal—the concept of a residential academic community—that was never to be attenuated.

I also learned something important about moral imagination and its energizing effects. When the verdict in *Brown vs. The Board of Education* was announced—that all public schools should be integrated, and that "separate" schools for Blacks were not "equal"—Wooster's headmaster, John Verdery, immediately decided to begin integrating his school, even though there was no compulsion to do so. The Supreme Court's ruling did not apply to private schools, but on this issue, Verdery could see no difference between the public and private spheres. When he announced his decision at the Annual Meeting of the Headmaster's Association, he was told by one headmaster that his own school was already prepared to admit any qualified Black students who applied. To which John answered: No one will apply; you must reach out and find the students—and then persuade them to come. And offer scholarships to all those in need.

From that moment on, my own commitment to what was later called *diversity* was born. I was no longer a Wooster student at the time of the Supreme Court's decision in 1954, but John Verdery's action had a powerful and lasting effect that never left me.

Finally, Wooster taught me, obliquely but vividly, about many aspects of life itself—how one might delight in it, as well as how one might begin to cope with its exigencies. A number of years after I graduated, I was asked to give a talk at the school (in 1982). I tried to describe to an audience of alumni and parents why Wooster had meant so much to me, including especially what I had learned from my teachers. Donald Schwartz, I said,

> was willing to talk with equal animation about the Brooklyn Dodgers or the boulevards of Paris or the major battles of the Civil War or the poetry of William Butler Yeats. I began to see … that almost any event or person or object could be genuinely interesting if only one was alert and sensitive enough to view it from the right angle of vision, and approach it sympathetically and imaginatively.

Then Joseph Grover—a Princetonian and World War II military officer— taught us history and literature. He was the very model of intelligence and style. He epitomized the sense of order and lucidity that was often conspicuously lacking in our own adolescent selves. He managed to communicate the value of scholarship and disciplined study without being either portentous or pedantic. Most of all he carried everything off with a wonderful mixture of sympathy and irony—a manner that was a triumphant combination of empathic bearing and Princetonian aplomb. We barbarians were completely bedazzled.

Grover was offered any number of headmasterships but remained with John Verdery (who was also offered many such opportunities) throughout his entire career. So there was yet another lesson to be learned: the great value of commitment to an institution, to a person who embodied humane purposes, and to genuine simplicity. Not loyalty, which despite its potential positive aspects, is susceptible to moral blindness; but commitment—something different, self-conscious, perspicacious, and capable of continuous magnification.

THE FIFTIES AND CONFORMITY

When I was still some distance from college, a Wooster teacher suggested that I should read F. Scott Fitzgerald's *This Side of Paradise*. Fitzgerald's romantic prose—and his image of Princetonian camaraderie amongst neo-Gothic spires and gargoyles—were my first encounter with collegiate education in any form at all. It also happened that the headmaster of Wooster (and the deputy headmaster) were Princeton graduates with a distinct leaning toward their own university. When I began to think about college applications, I visited Harvard (in my junior year) on what turned out to be a bleak March day of wind, clouds, and rain, together with a cordial but mainly professional interview. Later in the year, I was shepherded to Princeton by John Verdery. It was May and the seductive campus—with its magnolias and other flowering trees—was in full bloom. The lawns were littered with students pretending to study. The interview was friendly. The spires and gargoyles really did exist. When it came time for me to decide where to spend my next four years, I chose Princeton. The gargoyles and magnolias stole the show.

Princeton in the 1950s was in most ways not so very different from the institution that Woodrow Wilson had robustly transformed by the time he left its presidency in 1910. His immediate successor, John Hibben, was so relaxed that he was ultimately eased into retirement. Harold Dodds followed him and he set a steady course through the Depression and World War II. He was president during my own undergraduate years, and he led an unobtrusive expansion of the university. He was perceived as a form of "care-taker" and he presided over a time when there were few if any student issues of consequence, and no turmoil.

This state of affairs defined virtually all of American higher education in the 1950s, even though dramatic and indeed revolutionary changes were beginning, almost invisibly, to take place beneath the surface of collegiate (and national) life. My generation quickly became known as a "silent" one. We were viewed as young "conformists"—"organization men" destined to join emerging American corporations and wear gray flannel suits, even when we didn't. Many failed to fit the stereotype, but we were admittedly a studious, well-mannered, rule-abiding brood.

The 1950s literature on the subject of "conformity" is interesting because it captures, in oversimplified form, much of the tenor of the time. It is also important because it raises an inevitable question: How did the quiescence of 1956 (when I graduated) turn so suddenly—a brief decade later—into the ferment of the mid-1960s? The Vietnam War was of course a major factor, but did not by any means account for all that occurred.

David Riesman's *The Lonely Crowd* (1950) was one of the defining books of its time. Riesman saw postwar America as a society composed increasingly of people who formed their values and took their cues from their peers rather than from a set of strong inner convictions (or powerful traditional views). They were lonely "other-directed" men and women set adrift in a land that was rapidly becoming more and more prosperous, with new social and organizational structures that prompted many Americans to seek financial security and "success" above all else. Burgeoning new corporations suddenly began to dominate the nation's economic landscape. As a result, managerial jobs multiplied and college graduates soon discovered opportunities that were enticing but not necessarily inspiring.

Riesman noted, for instance, that *Fortune* magazine surveys of recent college graduates showed "a safe and secure job may be preferred to a risky one involving high stakes." [4] Individuals were more inclined to "fit in," to be "well adjusted" to their milieu, to be tolerant (rather than forcefully outspoken), and to seek to be popular. "Approval itself," said Riesman, "irrespective of content, becomes the only unequivocal good in this situation: one makes good when one is approved of ... [making] good becomes almost equivalent to making friends, or at any rate the right kind of friends." [5]

Were there ways to escape this predicament? Riesman offered two ideas to help counteract the disheartening situation he described. He advocated new forms of "autonomy" and "utopia" as paths to a better future.

Autonomy could be achieved by a heightened degree of individual self-consciousness—an increasing awareness that enabled one to understand and then rise above the nature of postwar American society. Autonomy depended "not on the ease with which one may deny or disguise one's emotions but, on the contrary, on the success of one's effort to recognize and respect one's feelings, one's own potentialities, one's own limitations." Riesman, however, was far from optimistic about the ability of most people to become "autonomous." Nor was he very hopeful about the possibility of creating a new utopia:

> I think we need to insist today on bringing to consciousness the kind of environment that Marx dismissed as "utopian," ... [Such] thinking where it is rational in aim and method and not simply escapism, is not easy. It is easier to concentrate on programs for choosing among lesser evils. ... Both rich and poor avoid any goals, personal as well as social, that seem out of step with peer-group aspirations. The politically [ambitious] ... seldom commits himself to aims beyond those that common sense proposes to him.[6]

Riesman's hope for a "utopian" vision on the part of some people—especially radical students—was realized sooner than he suspected, but in a form that he regarded ambiguously at best. In 1950, however, he asked whether "Americans would wake up one day to the fact that they overconform?" His answer:

> Since character structure is, if anything, even more tenacious than social structure, such an awakening seems exceedingly unlikely—and we know that many thinkers before us have seen the false dawns of freedom while their compatriots stubbornly continued to close their eyes to the alternatives that were in principle available.[7]

Riesman's book had a major influence on other thinkers and writers, including William H. Whyte. Whyte's *The Organization Man* appeared in 1956 and he documented the extent to which the United States had already become a nation of large organizations whose employees had developed a new social ethic, who often lived in recently created cookie-cutter suburban communities (such as Park Forest), and who somehow managed to reconcile their belief in a traditional Protestant ethic (which relied on hard work and individual commitment) with the very different demands of new-style corporations that championed a belief in the value of "groups" working cooperatively together for the good of all.

For Whyte, the calling-card of the new social ethic was "conformity"—a body of thought that

> makes morally legitimate the pressures of society against the individual. Its major propositions are three: a belief in the group as the

source of creativity; a belief in "belongingness" as the ultimate need of the individual; and a belief in the application of science to achieve that belongingness. ... [The] gist can be paraphrased thus: Man exists as a unit of society. Of himself, he is isolated, meaningless; only as he collaborates with others does he become worthwhile, for by sublimating himself in the group, he helps produce a whole that is greater than the sum of its parts.[8]

As part of his argument, Whyte traced the 1950s rise of technical–vocational studies (in preparation for "organization" jobs); he tracked the increased use of "psychological testing" to screen out all but the "right kind" of employees and managers; he related the stories of individuals who moved to the suburbs and then changed important aspects of their lives in order to conform; and he described the "messages" of some of the era's best-selling books (such as *The Caine Mutiny*). He found, for example, that the number of business-administration "majors" in college increased steadily for seven straight years, so that by 1954 it was the largest group of "concentrators" in the nation, except for those in the field of education. Meanwhile, the number of job-seekers who were asked to take personality tests also increased, and the entire field of public rela-tions—or *social engineering* as it was often called—developed with similar speed. In addition, if one consulted the *Journal of College Placement*, one would find headlines such as:

A Gateway to Lifetime Security
Careers Unlimited
Why College Graduates Should Consider Union Carbide
A Wise Choice Today Puts You Ahead of Your Future
Dow Chemical Offers the Graduate a Bright Future[9]

When he talked with students, Whyte heard one recurring theme: Adventure was all very well, but it was smarter to make a compromise in order to create a depression-proof sanctuary. "I don't think AT&T is very exciting ... but that's the company I'd like to join. If a depression comes there will always be an AT&T."

Not all "organization men" moved to the suburbs, but many did—and once there, group pressures often made themselves felt. Advertisers of the new communities (such as Park Forest) heralded:

You *Belong*
The moment you come to our town you know:

You're welcome
You're part of a big group
You can live in a friendly small town
instead of a lonely big city.
You can have friends who want you
and you can enjoy being with them.
Come out. Find out about the spirit of Park Forest. ...
a cup of coffee—symbol of PARK FOREST![10]

One might—or might not—"belong." Levittown, for example, had a policy against the admission of Jews, and there is no indication that Blacks would ever have been welcomed.

Some of the most interesting passages in Whyte's book show how a great many readers responded to the central moral dilemma in one of the era's best-selling novels, Herman Wouk's *The Caine Mutiny* (1954), which won a Pulitzer Prize. The novel traced the fate of a World War II ship and its captain—Queeg—as well as one of his lieutenants, Maryk. Wouk seemed to leave no doubt that Queeg was (in Whyte's terms) "a neurotic, a coward, and what is most important, incompetent." The ship at one point ran into a fierce typhoon, threatening the boat's destruction and the death of all aboard. Maryk saw that the only possible way of saving the situation was to sail directly into the wind. Queeg refused to listen to him. Maryk relieved Queeg of his command and took charge. The ship and all hands were saved.

Maryk was court-martialed for "mutiny" but was eventually acquitted. Queeg's career was finished. Later, at a celebration party where the entire crew was assembled, Maryk's defense attorney, Barney Greenwald, made a sudden speech in defense of Captain Queeg and all others who remained steadily and dutifully at their posts throughout the war. Greenwald said that he was "a Jew and that his grandmother was boiled down for soap in Germany." He then applauded the Captain Queegs of the world, who kept their ships going in spite of everything. At that point, a junior officer unexpectedly declared, "I see that we were in the wrong. ... The idea is, once you get an incompetent ass of a skipper ... there's nothing to do but serve him as though he were the wisest and the best, cover his mistakes, keep the ship going, and bear up."[11]

Whyte later decided to try an experiment with a group of secondary school students, asking them to write an essay about the novel's central moral issues, stating whether they thought the final resolution accorded "with life as you know it." Fifteen of the sixteen students agreed with Greenwald (and Queeg), not Maryk. Here is a sample of their views:

In everything we do there are certain rules and regulations [i.e. obedi-
ence to the Captain] we have to abide by. ...

I cannot agree with the author in that I believe that one should obey
orders no matter what the circumstances.

[Everywhere] there are rules and laws set up by many people for the
ultimate benefit of all. Yet there are people who think as the young
rookie that their actions should be directed by what they think is
right, not by what everyone else had determined ... [The] one who
breaks society's laws will be punished by fine, jail, or even death.

Men have always been subjected to the whims of those in authority,
and so it will be in the future. This plan must exist or anarchy will
be the result.[12]

In short, Queeg's ship and all aboard should simply have gone down
in the high seas to ensure that society's "rules" prevailed.

Given Whyte's general analysis in *The Organization Man*, what—
if anything—does he offer as a possible way to counter the threat of
overwhelming conformity bred by society's new "ethic"? He hopes that
a new form of "individualism" can emerge, and he believes that this can
be achieved only through an education in the liberal arts consisting of
"rigorously fundamental schooling" for people of all social and economic
classes. He wants "the great bulk of people" (not only a special elite) "to
have the best that is within them demanded early":

Is it "democratic" to hold that the humanities can have no meaning
for them? They do not have to be taught to shake hands with other
people, society will attend to this lesson. They have to be taught how
to reach. All of them.[13]

The final lesson is to do battle:

[The] options are there, and with wisdom and foresight ... [man] can
turn the future away from the dehumanized collective that so haunts
our thoughts. He may not. But he can.
    He must *fight* the Organization. Not stupidly, or selfishly, for
the defects of individual self-regard are no more to be venerated than
the defects of cooperation. But fight he must.[14]

Alas, Whyte's exhortation was as vain as Riesman's hope for new forms of "autonomy" and "utopia." Rigorous formal schooling, involving education in the humanities for people of all social and economic classes, turned out to be precisely what the coming decades—from the 1970s onward—would fail to achieve. And although one had the theoretical freedom to "fight," few appeared to do so, and few seemed to succeed.

THE UNIVERSITY AS SANCTUARY?

I arrived at Princeton in September of 1952. I had certainly not yet read Riesman, and Whyte's book had not yet been published. Nor had there been quite enough time for the media to provide a definitive label for our generation. So I continued to think of myself very much as I did at Wooster: as someone beginning to find a way, with an uncertain future and with no clear idea of a specific vocation or career.

My parents drove me from Danbury to Princeton, and we soon discovered that undergraduate life was more primitive and less democratic than we had suspected—as well as less resplendent than today's arrangements. For instance, dormitory rooms were rented (or "priced") according to their relative luxuriance and location. I had little money except for my scholarship, so I chose the least expensive establishment I could find: 26 South Edwards, a tiny one-room sanctuary in an unrenovated less-than-Gothic Victorian dwelling. Not far from Edwards, I could glimpse the commodious student domain in the upper reaches of Blair Tower—a highly symbolic architectural vision with turrets, apparent emblazoned windows, and a grand archway overlooking and dominating part of the lower campus. When we first entered my South Edwards room, my parents and I found it completely empty—not even a bed. So we raced about Princeton buying a supply of second-hand furniture. Even Wooster had beds!

First and second-year students then ate in large anonymous halls called *Commons,* where it was difficult to meet people one knew. And there were, in those distant days, no informal gathering places: no cafés, no student center, no lounges, no "fitness" facilities or similar amenities. Yet none of this made us feel unduly deprived. It was the system, and we accepted it as divinely ordained.

There were also admission quotas—not announced, but clearly present. In our class of 750 first-year students, I can remember only one "negro," who was nearly white in skin color. There were some but not very many Jewish students. Even the number of high school students was limited. The majority of my classmates were from well-known wealthy boarding schools such as Andover, Exeter, Deerfield, St. Paul's, Hotchkiss, Groton, Lawrenceville, and others. They came in troops of [about] fifteen or twenty or more per school, and usually roomed with one another.

Was it all class conscious, wealthy, and complacent? Not quite. Was it provincial? Quite—but most of us did not realize it. We rarely ventured to New York (occasionally meeting friends beneath the obligatory large clock at the well-known Biltmore Hotel— since vanished). We had telephones but no television sets. We mainly listened (on our "record-players") to "LPs" of the Modern Jazz Quartet, Ella Fitzgerald, Broadway musicals, Louis Armstrong, and Benny Goodman. Of course, there were a good number of far more sophisticated classmates—who listened to more sophisticated music—among us. There was also, for instance, a self-denominated group called *The Bulls and Bears*. It was some time before I discovered that the term concerned the stock market. Neither Danbury (nor the *Danbury News-Times*) nor even Wooster had prepared one for such rarified fare, or many other aspects of Princeton. It was, after all, the early 1950s, and certain news did not travel either very far or fast unless one lived in certain circles—and read *The Wall Street Journal*.

Toward the end of my freshman year, I was invited by Professor E. D. H. Johnson ("Dudley"), the Director of the Special Program in the Humanities (SPH), to join a relatively small number of students who began their area of concentration in sophomore year and—by finishing their "major" in two years—would have their senior year entirely free to write an ambitious "thesis." Since I was already on a pathway toward studies in the humanities, I joined the program and immediately became part of a group of fifteen to twenty classmates who were all committed to precisely the fields of study that most engaged me. Among other things, the program also gave me the chance to meet and work with several faculty who were strongly committed to SPH, and this proved to make an enormous difference, not only immediately but in the years to come. One way or another, I was eventually guided (and was also naturally inclined) to take courses that introduced me to a number of the then-standard "great books"—from Plato and Aristotle to Augustine, Aquinas, and Pascal; and then to Descartes, Locke, Hume, Voltaire, Rousseau, Kant, Hegel, Nietzsche, and others. The courses were not by any means required of all undergraduates and were not referred to as constituting a *canon*, but they were personally invaluable. Literature from Chaucer to Virginia Woolf and T. S. Eliot constituted another part of the design. In short, I emerged with a superficial and obviously limited but nevertheless useful idea of what constituted Western "knowledge worth knowing."

These works were not viewed as the embodiment of timeless truths, but were approached as an informal type of intellectual history with a modest amount of context to buttress them. In the 1950s, Great books courses were still common, and my own experience reinforced the view that there was in fact a tradition to be honored—even if the tradition consisted of books whose fundamental concepts were often completely at odds with one another. During the next two to three decades, this tradition would of course come under sustained attack—and then largely disappear—for a variety of reasons. But during my own Princeton years it remained, not precisely sacrosanct, but certainly celebrated.

If SPH was in fact special in its attention to students, so was Princeton as a whole. When Woodrow Wilson was appointed president of Princeton in 1902, he began his tenure by revolutionizing the college's entire approach to teaching. He decided to recruit about forty young faculty called *preceptors,* so that nearly all academic courses could then have the benefit of a small weekly discussion group of six to eight students, led by a preceptor. This single step increased the size of the faculty by 50 percent, and made it possible for every student to begin to know several faculty members over the course of four years. Faculty members generally worked closely with us, reading and commenting on our assigned papers and talking informally with us often, not only during office hours.

During this time I realized that poetry, rather than fiction, was what engaged me most powerfully. In this respect, I was led mainly by my own interests, but it is also important to remember that major poets could—in the 1950s and somewhat later—still be regarded as heroes of a kind. T. S. Eliot was only in his 60s and *The Wasteland* had been published just three decades earlier: It was still a "new" and revolutionary work. Eliot was internationally famous, and was received nearly everywhere as a distinguished literary envoy. In fact, his latest play, *The Cocktail Party,* had recently opened (in 1950 with Alec Guinness) and it instantly became a Broadway hit. Robert Frost was a globe-trotting reader of his own verse, to large audiences everywhere. I heard him first at Princeton, and later in England. He was a masterful, finely cadenced reader, and crowds packed auditoriums wherever he appeared. Somewhat later, the Ford Motor Company commissioned the poet Marianne Moore to create new names for their forthcoming automobiles. None of the names were chosen ("Tur-cotingo," "Silver Sword"). Instead, Ford christened its latest model "Edsel" (after a leading family member); the car was anything but a success, and it sank swiftly into oblivion. Dylan Thomas was another mesmerizer, and Robert Lowell was one of the last of this line. When I was running a summer speaker's program at Harvard in the latter 1960s, I invited Lowell to read from his poetry. I received in return a no-nonsense postcard from his wife, Elizabeth Hardwick. It said simply, "Robert Lowell does not read publicly for less than $500." I wrote back immediately with a check for the required amount, and he then accepted. When I advertised the event, I found that I would have to move it from its original lecture hall to the largest auditorium I could find. Even then, literally hundreds of people were turned away. So it was not unusual, sixty or seventy years ago, for students to be interested in poets and poetry, and for some poets to be celebrated public figures. As a result, I felt anything but eccentric in following my own strong bent.

My Princeton years were impressive in a very different way from my time at Wooster. I had the benefit of being taught by accomplished scholars, and the diminutive Special Program in the Humanities brought me into close associations with faculty and students who shared my interests and worked together in a spirit of camaraderie. I began to feel that universities might be congenial places—especially because Princeton's modest scale and sense of unity made me feel very much at home. My friends took their lives seriously but also enjoyably, and their commitment to learning encouraged me to think that my own interests were not unusual or esoteric. Finally, I remained captivated by the beauty of Princeton's campus, and its image as a place that symbolized something close to the ideal of a university. In the mid-1950s, it was not unusual to feel that universities were, in effect, sanctuaries that were worlds unto themselves, rather than institutions indissolubly and vividly linked to the larger prag-matic society beyond their gates. Princeton might consider itself "in the nation's service," but to be there during my own time was to feel fortunate, unfettered, and free to learn: a very different conception from what many students were to assume only a decade later.

STUDENT VOICES: UNCONFORMIST?

By 1954 or 1955, I had met a number of Princeton classmates who found themselves faced with career choices that seemed to be leading toward "conformist" futures which some of them wished to avoid but found difficult to resist. Others were equally determined to find a way out of what the media seemed to have prescribed for us. By this time, we had been thoroughly branded as an inglorious submissive flock, bereft of all political venturesomness or any vestige of even microscopic militancy.

A Princeton faculty member named Otto Butz decided to test the reigning conformist hypothesis. He invited a number of students from the Princeton class of 1957 to write candid anonymous essays about their values, their views of American society, and their career or vocational aspirations. Eleven of the essays were subsequently published as a book called *The Unsilent Generation* (Rinehart, 1958). Not surprising, they revealed a range of views, but many of them did in fact focus explicitly on the issues of conformity and financial security. For example:

> When I come right down to it, I think I have two conflicting goals in life—achievement and security. I'm ambitious in that I want respect for the work that I do. I want to rise in status as far as my abilities will carry me. But I'm a coward when it comes to taking a chance. I don't want to gamble. What I want is a stable order of things in which I can work without exposing myself to ruin.[15]

Where might one find such an "order"? In "graduate studies and a Ph.D., and from there probably to another 'secure order' in a company hierarchy." In other words, a PhD leading not to scholarship but to corporate leadership and presumably a handsome salary.

Not all the students, by any means, agreed. One senior was certain that he would

> never sit behind a desk in a way that would glorify a total commitment to a job which now seems to be a precondition for success. ... Success for me would mean a job that I could leave after eight hours and that would provide for self-fulfillment within a framework of inconspicuous luxury.[16]

What job or career might lead to both "self-fulfillment" and "inconspicuous luxury" simultaneously—in exchange for an apparent maximum of eight slender hours of work per day? The young man was far from certain. Indeed, he felt that he was "foundering among sincere irrational antipathies." But the idea of security per se held no attraction for him, because it would demand a life committed to "popularly approved values, and ...

socially approved goals. And this is the problem: if one does not conform to the values and subscribe to the goals, one will have no security." [17]

Having defined his dilemma, he sees his "continuing problem" as an effort to "find my identity." He has had "job interviews, but I do not want to sell soap." In the end, he is left with little more than daydreams and fantasies:

> One day I think I might want to study business administration at graduate school; another day I want to go to Paris and study existentialism or to Heidelberg or Oxford. ... Sometimes I feel like going to Florida or Acapulco to work as a waterski instructor or a deck hand on a tourist fishing boat. But this I do want: to live in freedom, unrestricted by exterior compulsion. I want my contribution to be a living testimonial that individual freedom is compatible with the welfare and progress of society.[18]

How can one live "unrestricted" by any "exterior compulsion" at all? And do so in a way that is compatible with society's "welfare and progress"? If the "welfare and progress" are in fact genuine, why not embrace them? If not, why invoke them? The answers are far from clear, and the student's fantasies in the end give way (in his last sentence) to a rhetorical assertiveness that sounds vaguely heroic but does little if anything to resolve the actual issues at hand.

Two final seniors were no less aware of the dangers of conformity, but they sought to find ways of living rewarding lives without surrendering unconditionally to what seemed to be America's prevailing values or escaping into the realm of pure daydream. "One of the most serious charges," writes one of these two students, "levelled at my generation and Americans generally is that we are terrible conformists, that we have lost our grip on our individuality."[19] Indeed,

> With our present ... deep and widespread economic grievances and with our everexpanding and highly scientific political as well as economic advertising, we can find all too many examples of this damaging kind of conformity in our society.[20]

Nevertheless, conformity turns out to be more complex than it may first appear. On the one hand, "we must be alert to and resist this phenomenon wherever we find it," but, conversely, our concern should be tempered by such common-sense considerations as the following. Is not a high measure of voluntary and even unconscious conformity a precondition for the very existence of a society? Is this not particularly so in a free society which hopes to live as much as possible without imposed authoritarian order and regimentation?[21]

Conformity is seriously "damaging"—it must be resisted "wherever we find it"—but it also turns out to be essential for a society that requires coherence as well as freedom from "externally imposed" authority. This paradox might well have been very troubling, but our student quickly found a way of solving the potential difficulty it presented: "among the fairly sizeable educated groups in the country, the individual is aware of his conformity. ... We may conform, but we know it. "[22] In other words, self-awareness can apparently save one from the fact that one will, after all, "conform" (rather than "resist"). The point, however, is not elaborated, and it remains conveniently obscure.

The last of Butz's essays was written by someone who agreed that

Conformist is the name most often given to us. Statistics are cited to prove that we are marrying earlier than our predecessors, that we're less adventurous than our forebears, that we are more willing to accept secure jobs and settle down in the cool suburbs than we ought to be.

Our student recognizes the truth of all this, but then goes on to offer a novel way forward. He suggests that because so many people in his generation accept the statistics as accurate, he and others "are becoming increasingly sensitive to their consequences." As a result, "many of us are going to escape the predictions set for our futures." Indeed, they are "taking measures to protect themselves from [conformity]."[23]

Those measures involve avoiding illusions—utopian or otherwise. For example, many of the "saving" credos once entertained by the students' parents are now viewed as thoroughly failed adventures:

We envy the dizziness of speculation [in the 1920s]. ... We envy—without daring to imitate—our fathers' freedom to join Communist cell groups, to cultivate Dadaist fads, to commit themselves to any of the fragmented creeds that were bound to fail. With us, the dizziness is necessarily gone. A Federal Reserve System of the Imagination is with us to protect us from our parents' glorious flop.[24]

With no apparent overriding creed to follow, the writer finds that "the redeeming characteristic of my generation is a certain rigor of intellect that, if it is without any outlets now, may someday become a truly regenerative force."[25] Except for the rather vague commitment to "rigor of intellect," there is so far no hint of what one's actual work might involve. Only later is there a clarification:

> The university is traditionally the place where the worth of the mind has always been honored as an end in itself; and the responsible graduate has often been able to absorb enough of his teachers' mental rigor to wish to imitate them.[26]

I found out later that this essay was written by a friend, Arthur Gold, and it struck a resonant chord. Arthur was already committed to a life of teaching and research, and I was of course some distance from making any decision at all. But his essay had an unquestionable effect on me, and it also reflected a more general feeling shared by myself (and many of my classmates): Princeton was a form of cloister or "sanctuary" and it helped to foster our understanding of ourselves and of many fields of knowledge. To live and work in such a haven was tempting, but not yet (in my case) irresistible.

Glancing backward, the irony of that early moment (in view of later incidents) is all too clear. In the fifties, colleges and universities were often viewed as communities that offered to a good number of students a potentially satisfying career of learning: a career that could be rich in the rewards of teaching, scholarship, collegiality, and a common cause in the pursuit of values that were more than simply worthwhile. Academic life would not be highly remunerative, but the possession of significant wealth mattered less to a number of undergraduates. One would be prosperous enough to live moderately, while enjoying the fruits of all that a college or university vocation could confer upon one.

Within a decade of course, this mode of thinking was dramatically altered. Higher education was soon viewed by many students (and others) as part of the Vietnam "war machine," which was undermining the nation's fundamental humane values. Some individuals would nevertheless enter the academic profession, but massive and unprecedented changes were taking place. Matters would never again be quite the same as in the fifties, despite some later moments of respite.

If I and others found it difficult to choose a profession or calling during our college years, it was obviously not because jobs or careers were difficult to identify and pursue. In this sense, our generation was a fortunate one. We came of age at a moment when our American world was plentiful, and we did not feel it was necessary to choose between a practical career-oriented education and a broad venture in the liberal arts and sciences. If a desire for financial security—or a desire to conform— preyed on the minds of many students, few if any of them felt that their choices were limited by a sense of scarcity rather than by their own hopes. We would probably not have agreed with all aspects of the vision of a 1970 *Daedalus* article concerning the 1950s, but we might well have endorsed the writer's description of a university's central purpose:

> Turning back to the fifties, I will assert we were right on one absolutely vital point: we knew what the university was for: learning. The university is for learning—not for politics, not for growing up, not even for virtue, except as those things cut in and out of learning, and except also as they are necessary elements of all good human activity. The university is for learning as an airplane is for flying. This is its elemental and defining purpose: no other institution has this mission, and no other mission justifies the university.[27]

When I left Princeton in 1956, I was—in terms of a possible occupation or vocation—still undecided. But I was rescued from my indecisiveness, not by anything conclusive, but by the sheer opportunity to continue studying at yet another university. I had won a Rhodes Scholarship and I sailed from New York to England intending to study Oxford's singular conception of *modern history*. Its curriculum began with the revels of Roman Britain, two millennia earlier, and seemed to end with what the English regarded as a recent climactic event—the Reform Bill of 1832!

OXFORD: EDUCATIONAL COUNTERPOINT

The train from Southampton arrived late, so our automobile ride to Oxford's New College (founded in 1379) took place in complete darkness down a winding narrow lane that led to the porter's lodge. It was an adventurous arrival for someone who had never before been abroad. The car spilled out the few Americans who were to be members of the College, and we scattered through the dark (helped by the porter) to find our rooms. This was the autumn of 1956, and my fortress-like residence hall, built of heavy stone, seemed designed to keep cold weather inside, and any trace of warmth outside. My "sitting room" proved to be very large, and (blessedly) had a small gas stove burning in the fireplace. But the next-door bedroom was quite another matter—bereft of heat, with a wash basin but no hot water. Retiring for the night was an exercise in indecision. But I finally sprinted to my bed, fell asleep, and stayed so until the next morning when I was awakened by the sound of my large window curtains being drawn apart by a friendly man who also brought hot water for shaving. "Good morning, sir," he said. "Good morning—and may I ask who you are?" "I am your 'scout,' sir, and will be happy to attend you. My name is Charles Dickens." And so it was.

If American higher education in the 1950s was typified mainly by the qualities described in the previous pages, what was Oxford like in the same era? Briefly, it was still overwhelmingly an undergraduate institution. Indeed, it offered nothing that corresponded to the American version of graduate studies—that is, two years of coursework followed by a doctoral dissertation leading to a PhD. As a result, most Americans studied for a second BA in a subject that was relatively new to them. Although there were two or three interdisciplinary fields from which one could choose, virtually the only other alternatives were single topics (such as history, or English literature). There was, in other words, no concept of general education at Oxford, and there were no requirements (or "electives") outside one's chosen field. English secondary-school students were usually compelled to make early choices between the sciences and nonscientific subjects, enabling or forcing "concentration" well before they graduated. As a result, they were ready for advanced work by the time they entered university. Why was this the case? First, English college-preparatory school was not only more specialized but usually more extended (by a year) than its American high-school counterpart. In addition, it was highly selective and generally more demanding. Finally, much of English "culture"—what one learned at home and from the tenor of one's society as a whole—had greater depth and breadth than most of America's; as a result, Oxford students had simply learned more—as part of their everyday lives—than most Americans were fortunate enough to do.

The contrast in educational philosophies and systems could not have been more stark. In the United States, newspaper articles would in due course begin to deplore the fact that it was possible to graduate from most colleges without having studied Shakespeare, or the classics, or biology, or history. At Oxford, no one would have expected (or imagined) that such a range of topics should be required at university. It was assumed that one was ready to specialize, with no additional formal exposure to areas outside one's chosen subject. In fact, one could even begin to study medicine or law as an undergraduate. For Americans at Oxford, this approach was actually an advantage: we had already experienced one or another version of a broad undergraduate education; concentration in a single field was exactly what we wanted in the hope of beginning to achieve some real mastery.

Oxford soon meant many things: not only my academic work, but an encounter with the large new worlds of England and Europe, and a simultaneous sense of being in a small collegiate sanctuary of bright fellow students, including the company of other Americans as well as English compatriots. The time of my arrival was also a special one. England was still recovering from World War II—some signs of bruised buildings and streets were still visible, but its spirit, including the spirit of Oxford, was mainly hopeful. Modest scarcities (and even some rationing) persisted, yet there was a sense that the very great weight of recent wartime experience was lifting. The world—one felt—had been given a new lease on life. Indeed, there was even (in spite of all that had happened) a touch of revived innocence in the air, mainly because Oxford was still so modest in size, overwhelmingly residential, and very much a confined precinct that existed before new systems of universities had—worldwide—been created (and expanded); before the number of academics working in every conceivable field of learning had grown to such vast proportions; and before the professionalization of methodology had arrived, serving to help swell the avalanche of academic books and articles that soon began cascading annually into print. In short, it was a time when the power of consequential minds and presences could be felt—when there was a very great deal of output for a moderate amount of input. The yield was high and the number of interlocutors was still small enough to constitute an actual community engaged in creative study and continuous conversation (as well as skilled and sometimes scathing argumentation).

Some consequential minds were making their words and voices heard just as I was arriving. W. H. Auden was the new professor of poetry, and had only recently delivered his inaugural lecture, "Making, Knowing and Judging." Soon, Isaiah Berlin gave his own inaugural lecture as a distinguished professor: "Two Concepts of Liberty." Then there was Trevor-Roper's lecture as Regius Professor of History. George Kennan was in Oxford and was also giving the Reith Lectures on the BBC—

indeed, everywhere one turned, there was intellectual fare that mattered, and that was simply available for the asking.

Meanwhile, my own work on the French Revolution offered me an encounter with one particular historical cycle: national revolutionary ideals leading to the overthrow of an autocratic regime—leading then to a more egalitarian or "democratic" temporary victory soon marred by political struggles and violence—leading finally to a new autocratic or despotic regime. This was a pattern that I knew from my knowledge of early twentieth-century Russia, and that I would remember in later years as world events (sometimes in South America, in Africa, or the Near and Middle East) seemed to repeat themselves in ways that began to seem all too predictable.

Much as I learned from the French Revolution, however, I found that by midyear I was intellectually unsatisfied. History, I had discovered, was too elusive for me. Clearly, any serious field of study demands ceaseless exploration, interpretation, and reinterpretation. But in literature, there was—for me—always a central, identifiable, and significant object to return to: the actual poem, play, or work of fiction. And it was this tangible human and aesthetic creation that was, after all, the original reason—the constant point of departure—for any further searching that I might want to undertake. After exploring, one could always come back to "the thing itself." So I changed my field of study by the end of my first year, and went back to epics, odes, sonnets, and free verse.

Once I returned to literature, I discovered that I had also resolved—almost unconsciously—the question of what to do in the future. I would go to graduate school and become a university teacher and scholar. Literature had become, nearly unwittingly, my vocation, and universities had become my home. Oxford was certainly not Princeton, and Princeton was certainly not the Wooster School: but all of them were residential academic communities of a kind that now seemed to be my natural habitat. They had the capacity to be constantly rejuvenating from an intellectual point of view, and communal from a human point of view. They had teachers who were interested not only in their subjects but in their students. They were to be my universe, and in effect my home. In 1959, I applied to Harvard for doctoral studies, and in due course I would set off for Cambridge, Massachusetts.

Oxford and Europe had altered me in ways beyond my imagining. I made new friendships that were to last many decades. I had seen and studied aspects of Europe's past two millennia. I had decided on a vocation.

I was also travelling home with an undergraduate woman—Angelica Zander—whom I would soon marry. I had spent three years at a university that seemed nearly mythic, and that later drew me back to visit, year after year. More than once I reread a passage from Max Beerbohm's novel *Zuleika Dobson*—a tale that enchanted me with its romantic, parodic, comedic, and affectionate vision, not simply of Oxford, but of an idyllic university, which, in its sometime contentious variousness, was no less an alluring, glimmering unity:

> There lay Oxford far beneath me, like a map in grey and black and silver. All that I had known only as great single things I now saw outspread, and tiny, tiny symbols, as it were, of themselves, greatly symbolizing their oneness. There they lay, those multitudinous and disparate quadrangles, all their rivalries merged into a great catholic pattern. ... Oxford was venerable and magical after all, and enduring.

ACADEMIA'S LADDER: THE EARLY 1960s

We arrived in Cambridge in September 1960. Harvard was another world altogether. Wooster, Princeton, and New College were modest or even very small in scale. But my first Harvard event took place in a large lecture hall with rows of seats slanting down toward the podium and new PhD candidates filling nearly all the available places. How many were in English and American literature, I could not begin to tell. But later, when I had met several of them, I thought there must be two or three dozen—and there were of course similar numbers for each preceding entering class who were now beyond their first year of study. Altogether, perhaps a hundred and fifty of us or more.

Part of the reason for the multitude of doctoral students surrounding me, was that I was obviously at a larger single institution than any I had ever before attended. Even more important, however, was the fact that I had arrived at an historic moment in American higher education and simply failed to realize it. I had been abroad in England for three years, and then in the army (as a former ROTC student) during the previous academic year. So after four years, I was completely out of touch with the huge expansion that had been taking place in American colleges and universities. By 1960, that growth was well underway, and I suddenly found myself in the midst of it.

What did this mean in practical terms? There was, to begin with, no occasion when new arrivals in the English department were brought together to meet one another. Nor were we ever introduced to our departmental faculty. Senior faculty offices were scattered all about the campus: some were in remote parts of Widener Library book stacks, so even faculty members might rarely see one another. There was no ample common-room or other place where department members could gather and talk. In short, if there were to be an anchor in life at Harvard, it would not be the Department of English and American Literature. There were simply too many students and faculty, and we were haphazardly dispersed here and there in odd sanctuaries of the campus as well as off campus.

Because of my studies at Oxford, I was only required to do a single year of coursework at Harvard, before beginning my doctoral dissertation. I chose my courses partly because of the name and reputation of the faculty member.

My most lucky encounter was with professor Reuben "Ben" Brower. He very happily and unexpectedly invited me to take his seminar on late seventeenth- and eighteenth-century poetry. Not a period that beckoned to me irresistibly, with the writers Rochester, Dryden, Johnson, Pope, Thompson, Gray, and heaven only knew who else. But Brower was open, conversable, friendly, and forthcoming in a winning way, so I signed up immediately. It was one of those decisions that made far more than a mere difference to my Harvard future. I soon found myself in the company not only of Dryden's heroic couplets, but of a dozen lively doctoral fellows who had also heard about Brower's combination of ability and approachability. Ben was not at all charismatic. He was not impressive in a self-conscious way. He was only natural, congenial, intelligent, and altogether himself.

Beyond Harvard Yard and its freshman dormitories, Harvard College consists of several residential student "Houses," occupied by sophomores, juniors, and seniors. Each of these minicolleges has a dining hall, a library, a lounge or two, and some space for extracurricular activities. Most of the houses are grand neo-Georgian establishments, created nearly a century ago with funds provided by a Yale alumnus, because Yale improbably failed to accept the gift. Harvard's president, A. Lawrence Lowell, was only too happy to receive the money, and he promptly began to build the imposing bell-towered structures that stretch baronially along the banks of the Cambridge River Charles.

Ben Brower was the Master of Adams House, which was actually not on the river but was well known for attracting students interested in the humanities and arts. He invited me (in 1964) to join his House as a tutor, and I immediately accepted. Adams then had about 300 students, and it quickly became my Harvard home base. I was given an office (once a dormitory room); a daily noon-time meal in the student dining hall; and membership in the Senior Common Room, which included a weekly lunch with the Master, the other tutors, and a small group of senior faculty who were nonresident members of the House. So once again, I was part of a small residential academic community where I soon felt very much at home.

A tutor's duties in the mid-1960s were not negligible, but they were fortunately stimulating. I taught a number of very bright Adams House juniors and seniors who had elected to take an "honors" course in English and American literature. This involved hour-long weekly meetings with each of about six to eight undergraduates who were working on writers as various as Emily Dickinson, Melville, Jane Austen, Henry James, George Eliot, Shakespeare, Conrad, Virginia Woolf, and Milton. The authorial cast shifted each term or year in tune with the changing interests and needs of the students. In addition, the seniors were writing ambitious theses that needed supervision.

Ideally, tutors would be blessed with the talents of a literary Leonardo, but our band of ingénues generally felt more like entrammeled Laocoöns, bound tightly by their texts and tutees. The challenge of sustaining weekly conversations on *Moby Dick, Riders to the Sea, The Waves, The Tempest*, and *Typhoon* demanded a species of wizardry that few if any of us possessed.

Although one of my own approaches to literature involved close reading in what Ben Brower called *slow motion*, it soon became clear that I and my students would have to be content with a transcontinental express that barely offered a blurred vision of poems, plays, and novels as they swept by in swift succession. Then, in 1964, I was asked to offer a graduate seminar in Renaissance English lyric poetry, and Ben Brower invited me to teach a "section" or class (with occasional lectures) in his first-year general education course called *Humanities 6: The Interpretation of Literature*. As a result, I was soon teaching twelve to fourteen hours a week, while also grading term papers for two senior faculty who had large undergraduate lecture courses.

What else was expected of an aspiring faculty member at the time? Above all, the writing and publication of a well-received book, with a second one well along the way. In the late 1950s and early 1960s, this standard was becoming the norm for humanists seeking a tenured position at a major university. These expectations were accepted without much question, just as most of us assumed that the chance of gaining tenure at Harvard was less than zero. But there were—we knew—fields of light elsewhere, and we were mainly content to enjoy and profit from our Cambridge days while they lasted.

Before writing a book, one obviously had to produce a substantial PhD dissertation. As advisers, I asked Douglas Bush, whose approach to literature was historical, and who was a kindly if also laconic (and overworked) figure of considerable renown, and Harry Levin, also renowned but utterly dissimilar from Bush in every way. They were an odd couple, but they were in their different ways intriguing, and they agreed to take me on. I had decided to work on the sixteenth-century poetry of Sir Philip Sidney, and I began my research in the fall of 1961. I started writing in the middle of 1963, and finished in mid-1964.

The process was a strain, partly because I knew that my career rested, not simply on completing the thesis, but on publishing it in some form. I went through a long period of staring—day after day—at blank sheets of paper, waiting for some spark that might inspire me to say something new about Sidney's verse. Slowly I began to realize that a major issue relating to striking shifts in Sidney's poetic style had never been satisfactorily explained. I found what seemed to be a compelling reason for the change, and began writing until about 400 pages were finished. At first, neither of my advisers said much about the thesis and I simply handed in one chapter after another. Then Bush—always deeply immersed in his work, but also very attentive as well as monosyllabic— one day said to me, "It looks as if you have hit pay-dirt." That was more than enough to make not just my day but my week, and well beyond. Finally, the dissertation was officially submitted, and officially accepted. Meanwhile, I was applying for jobs at universities across the country, without knowing at all what the finale might be. While this was a highly uncertain and at times nerve-stretching process, it was also—in one crucial way—free of undue strain. American higher education was, in the late 1950s and 1960s, expanding at a rate never before witnessed. As we know, new institutions were being created rapidly, and most existing colleges and universities were expanding. As a result, jobs were plentiful—

more than ever before (or since). So one might or might not secure the position one hoped for, but there was nevertheless a high probability that one would secure *some* reasonable position somewhere.

Then, one late afternoon that spring, sitting at my ill-lit carrel in Widener Library, I sensed the presence of someone hovering behind me. It was Jere Whiting, professor of medieval literature, with whom I had had virtually no contact throughout my graduate-school days, but who seemed to be a benevolent if remote figure with philological inclinations. Inevitably, I wondered what this near-twilight visitation might mean. Without any preliminary remarks, Professor Whiting asked whether I would be interested in becoming a member of the Harvard English department. Startled, and very much at a loss, I simply said yes. There was no noticeable further conversation, and Whiting vanished as vaporously as he had arrived.

That was all. I had never been asked for a resumé. I had published no articles, nor made any official submission of my work to the department, nor made a presentation to a faculty search committee. In fact, as far as I knew, there had been no formal search at all. There was no interview. All of this would today be hopelessly delinquent since it appeared to involve no competition at all for a coveted position. But the 1960s were curious and mysterious in terms of academic procedures and one tended to accept whatever came (or failed to come) one's way. There was, however, no further word beyond what Professor Whiting had said before dematerializing. Days passed, and nothing happened. Then, nearly a month later, I received an official letter from the Secretary of the University confirming my appointment. Another era had begun.

Chapter 3

The Sixties:
Disruption and Its Causes

DOW AND DISTURBANCE

Harvard Yard is the center of Harvard College, and it includes—in addition to most of the first-year student residence halls—Widener Library, Memorial Church, University Hall (the college's main administrative building), Massachusetts Hall (the president's office), and a few classroom buildings.

The student side of the Yard is understated in its simplicity. Its late Georgian and Victorian dormitories manage to dwell harmoniously together despite their potentially jarring differences in style. They form an obvious but loosely arranged rectangular court. Virtually all are made of brick (with an occasional intrusion of stone), and all are nicely unadorned: There is no trace of ivy in sight, and little or no shrubbery at the base of the buildings. Criss-crossing paths and the softening touch of many trees form the center of the Yard, and the total effect is completely different from that of the large mansion-like Houses with their river settings (where undergraduates live after their initial year). Here, there is a sense of modesty and order that seems to reflect the early beginnings of the College, characterized by its Puritan but also humanist post-Renaissance origins. Part of John Harvard's original seventeenth-century gift to the new institution was his considerable library: books and learning were planted firmly, nearly four centuries ago, in a place that was subject to the vicissitudes of war, disease, cold winters, and scant crops.

Outside the gates of the Yard, the campus slips into relative disarray. Some modern buildings are inter-leaved with nondescript scarcely designed older structures. The sense of symmetry and order breaks down. The College begins to be indistinguishable from the University, and the University begins to follow a preordained pattern that is not its own, but that of its neighboring Cambridge streets. The professional schools of Law, Education, and Design (as well as the Radcliffe quadrangle) are clustered here and there rather incoherently, and some of them are nearly overshadowed by the awkward but formidable, handsome neo-Gothic Memorial Hall—a visible tribute to the Harvard graduates who fought and died for the Union cause in the Civil War. In fact, memories of war and other disruptions are never far from the eye or mind in Cambridge. The Revolution's Battle of Bunker Hill had been fought not many miles away and General Washington's troops used the college as its encampment site for a time. In fact, Harvard College moved away for a year in order to give way to the General's forces, while Washington established his own headquarters in Wadsworth House, a building on the periphery of the Yard. Honorary degrees were virtually nonexistent in those days, but Harvard awarded one to Washington before he left Massachusetts in order to battle the British further south, in New York.

On a sun-lit autumn day in 1967, I found myself walking near Mallinckrodt Hall (a Harvard chemistry building some distance from the Yard) when I heard chants and the blare of a megaphone coming from the walkway just outside the building. I saw a crowd of perhaps seventy or eighty students talking and occasionally shouting slogans. There was some pushing and shoving, although the general mood seemed spirited and at moments even good-natured, as if a victory party were underway. Outside the front door, a group of students blocked the entrance. I soon learned that a recruiter from the Dow Chemical company had come to interview undergraduates for possible employment. But he was quickly "imprisoned" by the protesters, who were against Dow's manufacture of napalm, a lethal incendiary then being used in the Vietnam War (not far from the height of its violence and daily destructiveness). Antiwar sentiment was very strong on campuses nearly everywhere, but until now it had (except for one earlier spontaneous incident) been expressed peacefully at Harvard, without any deliberate obstruction.

Two or three of the several leaders turned out to be students whom I recognized. They were from my graduate course, and I knew them purely as talented young literary scholars. I also discovered the protest had been organized by members of the Students for a Democratic Society (SDS), an organization that had already been responsible for serious disruptions elsewhere. I had always assumed that Harvard—civil, ordered, humane—was beyond the reach of potentially harmful or violent demonstrations. But now, as a recently minted assistant professor, I was suddenly face to face with a situation that was unpredictable and potentially capable of spinning out of control.

The SDS was committed—paradoxically—to potentially obstructive tactics as well as a "democratic" organizational ideology: That is, everyone in the group was theoretically equal, and a primary goal was to operate according to group consensus. Although there were obvious SDS leaders, they tended to understate their role and insist on the importance of the entire membership and the democratic nature of its decision-making. As a result, the megaphone in the demonstration was used by a number of students and, completely to my surprise, I unexpectedly asked for a turn. Quite instinctively, I told the students that their actions were completely out of bounds. The Dow recruiter had (like dozens of other recruiters) been granted access by the university to interview students. The demonstrators were not only obstructing him but they were also depriving some students—who wanted interviews—of their rights as members of the university.

I had never before seen a university disruption and had never given serious thought to the issues at hand. But I felt that this event threatened fundamental values—and the institution itself—in a way that I had never expected. The "imprisonment" was to my mind completely at odds with what the university represented. At one point, Fred Glimp—dean of the College—appeared and warned the students that they were in violation of university regulations and could well face disciplinary charges.

After using the megaphone, I continued to talk with the students, spending two or more hours in debate. Gradually the SDS leaders began to realize that if the Dow recruiter had no means of exit, neither had they. They might stand guard indefinitely, but what would that accomplish? Moreover, the day was already beginning to wane. Soon, there would be a new morning of classes and perhaps university disciplinary charges. We continued to talk. Finally, around 6 p.m., the students decided to vote on whether to stay, or whether to disband and release the recruiter. They voted to disband. I was relieved, but also uncertain. Was this the end of what might be a single aberration, or was there much more to follow?

I lingered a few minutes and then walked past the professional-school buildings, past Memorial Hall, and through the quiet of Harvard Yard. There was a poster on one of the Yard's billboards that said "Make love, not war." My Adams House office was on a nearby side street. When I returned to my desk, I took up the manuscript of the book (on Sir Philip Sidney's love poetry) that I was just finishing. Sidney himself had died at a very young age in a sixteenth-century war abroad. His war was utterly different from Vietnam, but nevertheless deadly. As I reviewed the last chapter, it did not occur to me that the day's events would eventually change the course of my entire career.

The Dow Chemical protest was widely publicized on campus and beyond. It had been the first deliberately planned obstructive event at Harvard, and I had been somehow identified as the faculty member who had intervened to help bring it to an end. This was a total surprise because I had not discussed it with anyone except Angelica. I was unexpectedly the subject of newspaper articles from the Danbury *News-Times* to a piece in *The New Republic*. I was asked to write something for the magazine *Dissent,* edited by Irving Howe and Michael Walzer, and I was then invited to contribute (with a number of others) to a series of recorded (later published) dialogues on universities, sponsored by *Daedalus* (the scholarly journal of the American Academy of Arts and Sciences). I accepted this invitation essentially because I suddenly realized the extent of my naiveté, and the degree to which student protests—and the Vietnam War—were becoming a matter of acute concern on many campuses across the nation. I felt more than merely ignorant and decided that I should find out as much as possible.

In the *Daedalus* "dialogues" I was in the unexpected position of discussing the student "revolution" with Ed Levi, president of the University of Chicago; Prof. Daniel Bell; Carl Kaysen, director of the Institute for Advanced Study (in Princeton); Prof. David Riesman; Hanna Gray (later president of the University of Chicago); and others whom I had only heard about, or whose books I had read. I interjected my own views from time to time, but I mainly listened.

The most significant personal result of these events was a telephone call from John Coburn, dean of the Episcopal Theological Seminary (located in Cambridge not far from Harvard Yard). He was the son of

Aaron Coburn—founder of the Wooster School—and I knew him slightly from my Wooster days. He was a close friend of Wooster's headmaster, John Verdery, and was also on the Princeton University board of trustees. He knew that Princeton's president, Robert Goheen, was looking for a new dean of Students—someone who would be able and willing to help manage the likely challenges that seemed to be facing universities in the immediate future. Might I be interested in the position? I had no difficulty saying no: My book manuscript was in the process of being accepted for publication by the Harvard University Press, and I had also just won a Guggenheim Fellowship to study Italian lyric poetry as a backdrop for a second volume on sixteenth-century English lyrics. Angelica and I were planning to be in Rome during the following year, and we were also very happy with our current Harvard life. Coburn said that he understood my unwillingness to pursue the Princeton possibility, but he urged me to continue to think about it.

The Coburn conversation left an inevitable impression on me, but it began to fade quickly. Angelica and I carried on with our lives. Soon afterward, I had a second call from John, asking if I would be willing to meet with President Goheen in Princeton, giving him a chance to discuss the deanship with me—with no obligation involved. I had assumed that I would go no further down the Princeton road, but I now found it more difficult to simply sweep the entire matter from my mind. If President Goheen were asking me to come for a meeting, he must be more serious about pursuing the matter than I had originally assumed. I had taken the first phone call from John Coburn as a preliminary inquiry, but no more than that. Now, the matter seemed more consequential. Finally, I took the long train ride from Boston to New York and then to Princeton, where I had not been since I graduated. I had never before met with anyone in the Princeton administration, and I had never been inside Nassau Hall, where the president's office is located.

Nassau Hall is an eighteenth-century handsome building clad in a stone—imported from nearby quarries—that has some warmth and subtle coloring. When it was built, it was the largest single college building in the United States, and it housed nearly all the activities that were then needed for the education of Princeton's few (indeed, very few) undergraduates. The building had been badly scarred by British cannon fire during the Battle of Princeton—a turning point in the Revolutionary War— that took place shortly after Washington's famous winter crossing of the Delaware River, followed by his major victory at Trenton. Princeton's leaders and graduates had been active supporters of the Revolution, and the Continental Congress made Princeton its home for several months in 1783, because Philadelphia was for a time too dangerous a place to meet. When Princeton held its commencement exercises that year, on the graduation platform were seven signers of the Declaration of Independence, eleven future signers of the United States Constitution, several members of the Continental Congress, the French ambassador, and George Washington himself.

So Princeton was a storied place, and I felt some of the resonance of its history as I walked down the central corridor of Nassau Hall (its eighteenth-century stone floors still intact) to the president's office. I was impressed by the room's lack of obvious elegance: no sign of presidential imperialism here, and no ornamentation to speak of. There was an ordinary desk, a sofa, two or three chairs, and a 1946 photograph of President Truman and General Eisenhower attending Princeton's bicentennial celebration. The most striking object was a portrait of Woodrow Wilson smoking a cigarette: the painting was focused on his face, which looked straight out of the frame. The portrait was said to be by the American painter Robert Henri and had the air of a candid-camera photo. Wilson was often portrayed full length, wearing his academic regalia. But Goheen clearly responded to the informality of this off-guard human revelation of an active, impatient, impolitic, but powerfully effective Wilson who—in spite of his very great failings—played a pivotal role as Princeton's president, rousing the institution from its turn-of-the-century torpor, and turning it into one of the nation's leading colleges.

Robert Goheen was a person without pretense. He had served with distinction as an officer in the Second World War, became an assistant professor in Princeton's classics department, and soon afterward—at 37—was chosen to be Princeton's next president (just following my graduation in 1956). There was nothing self-consciously presidential about him: He was serious without being solemn, and he radiated—above all—a form of integrity that communicated itself as quintessential candor and honesty, together with a deep commitment to Princeton, not only as an institution but as an embodiment of the values of a liberal arts education.

I was unprepared for this impressive combination. Bob said how much he appreciated my visit, and quickly added that he hoped I would seriously consider the deanship. He felt that universities were facing a crisis unlike anything he had ever known or imagined. Princeton needed a dean who could confront student protests, form strong relationships with the faculty (because their firm support would be essential), and also create links to as many student groups as possible. He understood that I would naturally prefer to continue teaching and writing (as well as going to Italy). But this was no ordinary time and I could, he pointed out, serve as dean for just a few years and then return to my full-time academic work, with decades of literature still ahead of me.

To my surprise, I found myself listening to him more receptively than I had expected. The memory of the Dow Chemical event was still vivid, and such events were indeed beginning to spread from campus to campus. How tranquil would I be if Harvard, Princeton, and other universities became engulfed in protests? How damaged would they be, and how would I feel if my own institution was overwhelmed?

I left Goheen's office much more uncertain than I had been on arrival, and I began to wonder whether a move to Princeton made sense. For Angelica and me to give up our present lives and the imminent year abroad—and for me to set aside, even temporarily, my academic life to take on an administrative role for which I was completely unprepared: all of this seemed, on the face of it, absurd. But I was impressed by Princeton's president and was by now increasingly aware of the potential threats to universities. For the first time, I was somewhat tempted by the idea of joining Goheen—and that set in motion a long, tortuous process of deliberation for Angelica and me. Throughout the time following my visit to Princeton, I was only too aware of the fact that we really had no rational way of making a decision. The two options, staying at Harvard, or leaving, were so utterly different that there was no way to compare them.

In the end, it was Goheen's compelling character, my new awareness of the serious state of universities, and the vivid memory of the Dow Chemical disruption that tipped the scales. Whatever instinct led me to take the megaphone and intervene at Mallinckrodt Hall on that autumn day, persuaded me to follow a similar intuition now. I had been sufficiently startled by the Harvard situation that I stepped into a completely different role at that earlier moment, and I now began to think that such a role might be a plausible one for a limited period of time in the immediate future. Because I was convinced that I would return to my academic career before long, I also began to think that if I were to join Goheen, I would have to become a tenured member of Princeton's English department. Otherwise, I might well find myself stranded without either an administrative position or a faculty position in a very few years' time.

Moreover, any tenure offer would have to be the department's own decision, without presidential pressure. The possibility of tenure was in one sense far-fetched and would have seemed unthinkable except for the fact that I had graduated from Princeton summa cum laude, and most of my former teachers were still in the Princeton English department. I had finished Oxford very well and had won a Guggenheim. Most important, my new book would soon be published by Harvard, and I was planning another volume on Renaissance verse. On January 20, 1968, I wrote to a friend:

> A quick letter, mainly to let you know of the cataclysmic change that has just come over our life: I just accepted last night a job as Associate Professor of English and Dean of Students at Princeton University. ... It all happened ultimately because of Bob Goheen's having consulted John Coburn about the need to find someone, and John suggested me. ... Goheen was in a hurry. The English department voted yesterday to have me, and Goheen anticipates that Princeton will be changing a great deal in the near future.

COLUMBIA AND CATACLYSMIC CHANGE

I began the late winter and early spring of 1968 in high spirits. My Harvard tutorial students were as bright and interesting as any I had ever taught, and Angelica and I had begun to look forward to our new Princeton life in the coming autumn. The *New York Times,* however, soon began writing articles about student protests at Columbia. As the weeks passed, the situation there seemed increasingly ominous. News about Berkeley had for years been disturbing, but Berkeley was an exceptionally large public "multiversity" with several thousands of students. It was also a continent away, and one of its main issues—free speech—concerned controversies that then bore little relation to Harvard, Princeton, or similar private institutions.

Columbia, unlike Berkeley, was modest in size and just a ride down the highway to New York. Any serious Columbia events were bound to strike home with unusual force, although it never occurred to me that the university would soon experience one of the most spectacular cataclysms in the history of American higher education.

By February and March, I began to pay closer attention to what was happening there, although it was difficult to learn details. A core of about one hundred SDS students, led by an undergraduate named Mark Rudd, steadily incited student opposition to the university's purported support for the war in Vietnam. They also became the advance guard opposed to the construction of a new Columbia gymnasium not far from its neighboring African American community in Harlem.

The intensity of feeling at Columbia grew quickly throughout the spring. In late April, a series of explosive events took place. A student rally was called by the SDS, to be held in the university's most visible "public square" in front of Low Library (where President Grayson Kirk had an office). The SDS issued a series of nonnegotiable demands related to previous protests as well as to some current ones: Gym construction was to be halted, university ties to a government research facility (the Institute for Defense Analyses, or IDA) were to be discontinued, and disciplinary penalties that had earlier been issued against various protesters were to be dropped. Not surprising, there was no immediate university response, and it was then far from clear what the SDS leaders would do to maintain their rally's momentum. Indeed, it seemed that nothing at all might come of the entire affair. Then someone called for a march to the site of the proposed gym, and about three hundred students followed— one of whom was arrested. People then returned to campus, and Mark Rudd—faced with a possible humiliating defeat—called for action (including taking a "hostage"). This suddenly led to the invasion of Hamilton Hall, the main administrative building of Columbia College. Several hundred students entered Hamilton and refused to let one of the College deans leave. Soon afterward, Tom Hayden (of the national SDS) arrived on campus to support the demonstrators.

The takeover of Hamilton Hall was catalytic. It was as if a dam had broken, followed by a flood. By the next morning, a number of students called for the "liberation" of Low Library's administrative offices—including President Kirk's—and about 250 demonstrators forged ahead to do so. By the following day, another building had fallen. By the end of the week, five Columbia buildings were under the control of about 700 to 1,000 students (as well as some faculty and outsiders). In just a few days, one of America's greatest universities was totally paralyzed, and all efforts to negotiate a settlement had so far failed.

On Monday, April 29, President Kirk took a fateful step. He decided that the only way to clear the occupied buildings and restore order was to call the police. He hoped that the students would leave voluntarily in the face of a large show of force, but he could scarcely have been more mistaken. Many students resisted, and the police response was only too predictable. When the struggle was over, more than one hundred students (and some faculty) were hospitalized, and nearly seven hundred were arrested. The SDS called for a university strike. Columbia was crippled.

I witnessed as much of this as possible from afar, on television and in the press, but it was only later that I learned more about the details of what had actually occurred. Archibald Cox, a distinguished Harvard Law School professor, led a special Commission to report on the events and their causes. He published his findings in *Crisis at Columbia* (Random House, 1968). In addition, there were dozens of other reports and commentaries, including an account by *The Spectator*, Columbia's student newspaper: *Up Against the Ivy Wall* (Athenaeum, 1969) which offered a running commentary of the past year's events. A revealing article by Daniel Bell, then a Columbia faculty member, was called "Columbia and the New Left," and it appeared in the autumn 1968 issue of *The Public Interest*.

I read Cox's report as soon as it appeared. It showed, to my surprise, how many years the Columbia situation had been building toward its climax and made me realize how totally oblivious I had been—how buried I had been reading Renaissance literature as well as teaching and doing research. I discovered that in May 1965, a full three years earlier, student protestors attempted to block the annual presentation of awards to students enrolled in Columbia's Naval Reserve Officers' Training Corps (NROTC). The university's own security force could not handle the situation and outside police were called. As a result, NROTC ceremonies were cancelled in each of the next two years and were then totally discontinued in 1968.

And there were other early Columbia disruptions. In 1966, a CIA recruiter left campus in the face of SDS-organized student demonstrators. In 1967, an SDS group stopped CIA attempts to interview Columbia students. In April 1967, US Marine recruiters were blocked, and in February 1968 there was a similar action against Dow Chemical recruiters. Both of these last events were also spearheaded by the SDS. Meanwhile, the proposed construction of a new Columbia gymnasium had begun to draw more and more criticism during the mid-1960s, although the opposition grew slowly. The gym had been planned as early as 1958 and was at first viewed as a harmless—even welcome—addition to the university and the local community. It was to be built on public park land in the zone between Columbia and West Harlem. Community leaders did not object, partly because the terrain was not very inviting (about two acres of rocky hillside), and partly because the community would have its own assigned recreational space inside the gym, as well as its own entrance.

But the planning and approval process was astonishingly slow, and when a large public hearing was held in July of 1961, opinion about the gym was already split. By then, some of the facts about the building's design were well known and were viewed unfavorably by many people. Columbia would command 87.5 percent of the space, and its entrance to the gym would inevitably be on the upper side of the hill, whereas the community would have just 12.5 percent of the space, and its members would enter, symbolically, from "below." The process nevertheless moved forward. In 1965 John Lindsay was running for mayor of New York City, however, and Thomas Hoving would soon become Parks Commissioner. Both came out publicly against the gymnasium, saying (among other things) that any use of public park land should be decided largely by the local community, not by a single private institution.

From then on, opposition steadily grew. By 1967, CORE (the Congress for Racial Equality) and the West Harlem Morningside Park Committee joined the opposition. Columbia was soon faced with accusations of racism. Not everyone (including the student newspaper) agreed, and President Kirk continued to press ahead, offering to add a swimming pool to the enterprise. But it was too little, too late, and too insensitive to the views of the local community. As he did on several other important occasions, Kirk failed to understand the human and political realities that confronted him. On February 20, 1968, six Columbia students (and six other people from outside the university) tried to block the bulldozing of the land where the gym was to be constructed. This initial action was also organized by the SDS, together with a local citizenship council. Then, on February 29, about 150 protestors attempted to stop the gym's construction—and twelve students were arrested. The battle was joined.

Quite apart from the gym, there was another major (and durable) SDS issue at Columbia: the accusation that some Columbia faculty were actively involved in research that was aiding the Vietnam War effort. The charge was originally quite general, but it soon developed a clear focus: purported university collaboration with the IDA. The Institute had been created in 1955 by the Joint Chiefs of Staff. It was intended to forge links between government researchers and faculty members at a number of major universities. There was nothing secret about the organization, and in 1955 there was obviously no Vietnam War in progress. Many of the individuals associated with IDA had served—only a decade or more earlier—in the Second World War. They wanted the United States to remain strong in the face of its new adversary, the Soviet Union. President Goheen of Princeton was a member of the IDA board: he had been a decorated officer with a distinguished military career during the war. Grayson Kirk and several other university presidents were also IDA board members.

By the mid-1960s, however, IDA was viewed very differently: not as a vestige of WWII, or even of the Korean War, but as a "collaborator" with the Vietnam "war machine." The faculty at Princeton, for example, voted in 1968 to cut all ties with the institution, and Goheen then moved ahead to do so. IDA had already been the object of one Princeton student demonstration, and Princeton's IDA facility was highly visible, located on land that was leased from the university and was immediately adjacent to its Engineering School.

At Columbia, however, little was known about IDA, despite the fact that it circulated annual public reports. At an informal Columbia faculty gathering, a dean was asked (in March 1967) about the university's affiliation with IDA and the dean confessed that he knew very little. The SDS immediately reported—inaccurately—that the IDA relationship had been kept secret, and the students demanded that the university should cut all ties to the organization.

At the time, only three Columbia faculty members are known to have had a continuing relationship with IDA, and a few others worked occasionally as consultants. Nevertheless, the issue began to take on a life of its own. President Kirk failed to respond to the SDS demand that Columbia should dissociate itself from the institution. In fact, Kirk did not give serious attention to the issue for nearly a year—a significant blunder. When he and the trustees finally did propose to disaffiliate (in the spring of 1968), Kirk also announced that a distinguished member of the university would continue to serve on the IDA board. This condition created immediate outrage. Instead of helping to resolve the situation, the president's proposal made the matter even more combustible. From then on, IDA continued to remain a prominent campus issue, and one that the SDS relied upon more than once to help enlist broad student support against the university.

There is no simple way to summarize all the events that led to the Columbia "revolution," or to trace their full implications. But because the total spectacle was so consequential, I felt it was necessary for me—in the spring and summer of 1968—to understand all I could about the entire trauma. Violent episodes and police "busts" (such as those at Berkeley and the University of Wisconsin) were rare and had previously been mainly the result of massive demonstrations at immense institutions. At Wisconsin's Madison campus, for example, the police and National Guard were called as soon as student disruptions began to take place: tear gas was used, bayonets were drawn against students, a Jeep with a mounted machine gun suddenly appeared on one occasion, constant injuries and arrests took place, and a mathematics teacher was killed when his building was partly destroyed. At Berkeley, about eight hundred students took over Sproul Hall (where the main administrative offices were located) as early as 1965, and police were soon summoned to clear the building.

But Columbia was different. The initial protests (in 1965) involved only a small number of students, and more than two additional years passed before a sizeable group of moderate and liberal (as opposed to radical) students were moved to participate in actions that involved not simply picketing and rallies, but actual disruptions. In fact, as late as the third week of April 1968, even after the very first Columbia building takeovers had taken place, a survey of 5,500 Columbia students (not including those inside the buildings) revealed the following responses, as published in *Up Against the Ivy Wall*:

- I favor amnesty for all students involved in the demonstrations of the last three days [an SDS demand]:
  Yes: 2,054
  No: 3,466
- End gym construction [an SDS demand]:
  Yes: 4,093
  No: 1,433
- End university ties with IDA [an SDS demand]:
  Yes: 3,572
  No: 1,855
- I favor dropping disciplinary probation charges against the six students involved in the prior IDA demonstration [an SDS demand]:
  Yes: 2,167
  No: 3,263
- I support a student strike in favor of these demands [an SDS demand]:

Yes: 2,365
No: 3,095
• I agree with the demonstration tactics used by SDS and SAS [the Black student organization]:
Yes: 1,325
No: 4,124

Given the evidence of the April poll, how did it happen that student (and other) opinion swung so powerfully negative within a few days afterward? The police "bust" was the obvious turning point. It seemed to indicate that the administration did not care about the fate of hundreds of its students. Kirk was viewed as "brutal," and he quickly lost most of the support he had retained to that point. Within a few more months, he had resigned.

Columbia's actions might well have served as a warning to other administrations about what *not* to do in difficult situations, but the warning was unfortunately not always heeded. Meanwhile, the building takeovers and the "bust" emboldened the SDS (and some other student groups). They showed—for the first time—what might be possible, not at multiversities, but at smaller institutions. And it was only after Columbia that any other similar institution suffered disruptions that were even remotely like Columbia's. The takeover of Harvard's University Hall—and its subsequent "bust"—took place a full year later. Princeton's first takeover of Nassau Hall was also a year in coming. Cornell's sensational events occurred in the spring of 1969. And the University of Chicago's prolonged sit-in also did not take place until 1969. In other words, Columbia altered the political landscape of many American leading private universities. It set the stage for much that was to come and, at a personal level, it changed dramatically my own sense of what the deanship at Princeton might now entail: something more far-reaching and even potentially violent than I imagined when I had accepted the job only a few months earlier.

Some of Columbia's "lessons"—as we have seen—were obvious, but others were more subtle. There was no question, for instance, that the impact of the war (and especially the threat of the draft) was having a greater effect on more and more students with each successive year. If the April 1968 poll of Columbia students showed a clear majority against several core SDS demands, one nevertheless had to recognize that 2,000 out of 5,500 students actually favored amnesty for those involved in the building takeovers, and 2,365 were in favor of a strike even before the "bust." These were obviously very substantial numbers, and they showed how many students were already sympathetic to the antiwar—and anti-university—campaign. Moreover, Columbia administrators were persuaded that events concerning the war were moving in a fateful direction. David Truman, vice-president and provost, stated to the Cox Commission:

> Some of us have felt for a very long time that if it were inescapable that the current war in Vietnam had to continue on, it was debatable whether university communities could survive, because the tension is not only among students but in faculties, and the whole fabric of the institution is strained.

Not all administrations at all institutions were by any means so pessimistic about the ability of their communities to survive, but the war was undoubtedly a major force driving student protests against most American institutions of higher education, and one could expect the situation to become more and more difficult as long as the conflict—and the draft—continued. Indeed, without the threat of the draft, it is far from clear that the student antiwar movement would have taken hold to any significant degree at most colleges and universities. It was no coincidence that the concept of an all-volunteer army was introduced after the Vietnam War and before the advent of subsequent wars—in Iraq and Afghanistan.

Granted the antiwar fervor among students, we might nevertheless wonder why the university, rather than the federal government and the defense department, was the primary target of the protestors. In fact, the rationale for this was articulated as early as 1962 in the SDS Port Huron Statement, a document that accused universities of not being the "neutral" places of learning that they claimed to be, but of being intrinsic parts of America's "corrupt" society, including the society's war on Vietnam. Port Huron is discussed in greater detail at a later point, but the Cox Commission offered a brief synopsis of the SDS position:

> The university became the focus of both criticism and frustration wherever it could be linked with the defense establishment: in furnishing class ranking to draft boards [highly ranked students were less likely to be drafted], in permitting recruitment for the armed forces, in making facilities available for the armed forces or war-related industries, and in government research. Militant young men and women, frustrated by their inability to shape a vastly complex society upon an issue that seems both moral and simple, turned to make their weight felt on nearer and more vulnerable institutions.[1]

Making a case against the university—instead of the government—actually took considerable time at most Ivy League universities. Students tended to admire their institutions and felt fortunate to attend them. Their faculty (and often their administrations) tended to be against the war. The relative power of the case against their institutions, therefore, often depended on quite specific factors, such as the structure and coherence of an institution and especially the responses of its administration to student protesters and their tactics (and demands). For example, the Cox Commission concluded that Columbia lacked a great deal of coherence as a university, and this clearly helped to seal its fate. The faculty played little or no substantial part in the actual governance of the institution, and therefore tended to be aloof from administrative and student affairs. It was also balkanized. There was not one unified Faculty of Arts and Sciences, but three separate competing entities: one was called Philosophy, one Political Science, and the last was Pure Science. In addition, there was a special Faculty of Columbia College. In short, at the very heart of the university, there was no single body of academics capable of speaking in a united and authorized way on major policy issues. Nor was there an Academic Senate that might possibly have played a helpful role.

As the Cox Commission wrote, this strange structure "created a wide and unbridged gulf between faculty and Administration (i.e., the president, vice-presidents, and deans). That the faculty and Administration should be conceived to have disparate interests—that there should be need for a *tripartite* committee on discipline" only magnified the lack of institutional unity and operational capacity.[2] When the crisis of 1968 arrived, there was literally no authoritative faculty group that could be consulted for its views on major issues such as IDA, or the gym, or campus recruiting, or student discipline. As a result, a self-created ad hoc faculty group emerged during the April crisis, but it had no official power and its membership had no legitimacy. It was well intentioned, but all its efforts to mediate among the main conflicting groups proved ineffectual. Given Columbia's structure (or nonstructure), the university was fatally vulnerable.

In addition, President Kirk was generally not inclined to consult broadly. He tended to act authoritatively, partly because of his own temperament and manner, and partly because of Columbia's tradition (formed largely by its earlier autocratic president Nicholas Murray Butler). One example: after the disruption of the NROTC ceremonies in 1965, Kirk sensibly appointed a committee of students, faculty, and administrators to make recommendations concerning the handling of such incidents. The committee was allowed—implausibly—to deliberate for nearly two years. It finally submitted a thoughtful confidential report to the president (in August 1967).

It covered a range of issues, including the difficult problem of indoor student demonstrations (which had at times been chaotic and even potentially dangerous). The report actually allowed for the continuation of such demonstrations, but it did so within new guidelines. A month later, President Kirk issued (without any warning) a statement that declared "Picketing or indoor demonstrations may not be conducted within any University building." There had been no consultation between Kirk and his committee, and there was no explanation of this sudden unilateral decision by the president. Meanwhile, Kirk did not make the committee's report public. He finally did so seven months later, after the committee itself threatened to release the document. Given such behavior, one can imagine the impact on faculty and student confidence in the president's credibility. A week after the document's release, the takeover of Columbia buildings began.

Unfortunately, Kirk acted similarly on a number of important occasions. Each time, he undermined the support of many campus "moderates," and helped radicalize others. As Daniel Bell wrote in his article "Columbia and the New Left":

> Neither Kirk nor Truman had any "feel" for the volatility of social movements or for the politics of ideology. Consequently, when Kirk decided to call the police in April 1968, he effectively enabled the SDS ... to prove the truth of an old revolutionary adage that no demonstration is successful unless it compels a repression. For the strategical intention ... is to provoke brutality on the part of the opponent, and thus win the moral and psychological case. The lesson of Berkeley four years ago, and of Wisconsin earlier in the academic year (when the police were called to clear an occupied building and went wild) is that such repressive force is self-defeating. The Columbia administration may have known about Berkeley and Wisconsin, but they did not show it.[3]

If Kirk had paid more attention to Berkeley, for example, what might he have learned?

As early as February 1965, the assistant editor of the *New York Times* editorial page, A. H. Raskin, interviewed Mario Savio, the leader of Berkeley's Free Speech Movement (FSM). Raskin reported that the Berkeley

> activists obviously have developed a vested interest in finding things to fight about. They seem to operate on the theory that, in a system they believe is basically corrupt, the worst things get, the better it will be to generate mass resistance.
>
> This is not a novel theory in radical movements, but it is not one that makes for stability. When the police dragged Savio and the 800 others [occupying Berkeley's Sproul Hall], he exulted, "This is wonderful—wonderful. We'll bring the university to our terms."
>
> The reckless prodigality with which the FSM uses the weapon of civil disobedience raises problems no university can deal with adequately. Mass discipline [of students] carries the danger [of creating student martyrs] and a spread of symbiotic disorder to other campuses.

By 1968, Columbia's SDS—under Mark Rudd—had learned what Savio already knew, and what Bell (as well as Raskin) had described. The Columbia anti-IDA demonstration (in March 1968) was initiated by an SDS subgroup called the *Action Faction*. The group's premise was simple:

> A physical confrontation—a sit-in, a blockade, the takeover of a building—is set up to discomfit the adversary who holds the power, in this case the university administration. He can respond by giving into the substantive demands of the radicals or by crushing them with coercion of his own. If he is unusually perceptive, he may be able to trace a third course, resorting to neither capitulation nor repression. ... But in the coming days, such political sophistication was to prove beyond the resources of the men who ran Columbia.
>
> The tactical elegance of confrontation politics lay in the fact that the radicals had a good chance of winning whether the administration gave in to their substantive demands or overcame them by repression. The use of coercive force ... could be a powerful force to "radicalize" liberal or moderate students.[4]

In addition to its other tactics, the Columbia SDS had become more adept at delivering public insults while taunting President Kirk and his administration with provocative actions. For example, at a chapel service (on April 9, 1968) intended to memorialize Martin Luther King, Jr.

(following his assassination), Mark Rudd took over the speaker's podium and called the event an "obscenity," given the university's purported racist record. Kirk and Truman were accused of "committing a moral outrage against Dr. King's memory." Rudd then walked out of the chapel, followed by about forty students.

Less than two weeks later, on April 23, Rudd wrote an open published letter to President Kirk:

> Dear Grayson,
>
> You are quite right in feeling that the [present] situation is "potentially dangerous". For if we win, we will take control of your world, your University, and attempt to mold a world in which we and other people can live as human beings. Your power is directly threatened since we have to destroy this power before we can take over. ...
>
> You call for order and respect for authority; we call for justice, freedom and socialism. There is only one thing left to say. It may sound nihilistic to you, since it is the opening shot in a war of liberation. I'll use the words of LeRoi Jones, whom I'm sure you don't like a whole lot: "Up against the wall, motherfucker, this is a stick-up."[5]

Rudd's letter, with all its bravado, was both knowledgeable and naïve. It was designed to provoke—as it did indeed manage to do. But it was also hopelessly naïve in appearing to believe that, if Kirk were toppled and Columbia crippled, the larger society would actually allow an undergraduate and the SDS to take over the university in the name of "justice, freedom and socialism."

Interestingly, Rudd had written (several months earlier) a "position paper" that was consistent in certain ways with the analyses of Savio, Bell, and Raskin. He outlined a series of "Proposals for Demonstrations" during the 1967–68 year. It is in fact a quite crude document in its lack of serious analysis and its casual use of clichés about the war. He began by stating pretentiously that "we have presented our demands to Kirk" and to "the war-makers in Washington." The next step, therefore, was to persuade the mass of university students that "the liberal structure" in which they live actually ensures that "our lives are unfree in this society (and at Columbia)." Indeed, the university acts against students "corrupting and distorting education in a bewildering variety of forms (paternalism, complicity with the war, career orientation, pedantry, bureaucracy)."

Following this odd mixture of undeciphered generalizations, Rudd outlined a list of actions ("Harassment of recruiters, ROTC. ... Publication of all Federal projects with a list of their personnel") which he declared would ultimately lead (in April) to "A sit in at Low Library which ... turns into a general strike. University capitulates."

Only a few of Rudd's specific proposed actions took place as scheduled, but the April culmination (which was not really well planned, and was often improvisational) clearly did lead to the chaos that ultimately engulfed the university. If Rudd's program was intellectually amateurish, it nevertheless showed the extent to which SDS theory and practice had by 1967–68 become a conscious process. The group had learned how to exploit the university's vulnerabilities and how to handle Kirk's failings. And it had learned how to move many moderate and liberal students toward radical action.

When I reached Princeton during the summer of 1968, Columbia was one of my textbooks, and it was not only something that I myself looked to for guidance. It also served—as suggested—the leadership of the SDS. Tom Hayden soon wrote an article (June 15, 1968 issue) for *Ramparts* magazine, titled "Two, Three, Many Columbias" (echoing Che Guevara's "Two, Three, Many Cubas"). Hayden made clear how much he viewed Columbia as a major turning point:

> Columbia opened a new tactical stage in the resistance movement which began last fall: from overnight occupation of buildings to permanent occupation; from mill-ins to the creation of revolutionary committees; from symbolic disobedience to barricades resistance. Not only are these tactics being duplicated on other campuses, but they are sure to be surpassed by even more militant tactics. In the future it is conceivable that students will threaten destruction of buildings as a last deterrent to police attacks. Many of the tactics learned can also be applied to smaller hit-and-run operations between strikes: raids on the offices of professors doing weapons research could win substantial student support while making the university more blatantly repressive.

Hayden saw the Columbia uprising as a watershed, illustrating how increasingly bold tactics could ultimately gain broad student support, even as they became more deadly. Two years later, when I was at Princeton, a student tried (ineptly) to set fire to Nassau Hall while others successfully fire-bombed the ROTC building. Hayden was not wrong in imagining what might become "conceivable." Higher education and its very capacity to function was now under conscious and sustained attack.

A final event at Columbia is worth noting, because it set an important precedent. Hamilton Hall was the first Columbia building to be occupied in April 1968, and the takeover included White and Black students together. But within a few hours, some Black community leaders as well as members of CORE and SNCC (the Black Student Nonviolent Coordinating Committee) entered Hamilton Hall. The Blacks soon separated themselves, occupying a set of rooms of their own. After several more hours, they demanded that the White students vacate the building. At this point, as Cox reported in *Crisis*, "the white students were shocked. ... Mark Rudd, who announced the black students' decision, was visibly shaken, yet he advocated compliance. ... The 70 black students who stayed began to barricade the entrance. Apparently, some of the outsiders from CORE and SNCC remained with them until later." Meanwhile, in the eyes of the Blacks, "the SDS crowd seemed sloppy and undisciplined. Their own discipline was almost military. ... They feared that the blame for any property damage or untoward incidents would nonetheless be blamed on the black students." The Black students had, for the first time, asserted their independence and their own sense of power. It was very late in the game, however, particularly because the SDS (and Rudd) had for a long time led Columbia students on all the main issues, including the gym, the Martin Luther King, Jr. memorial service, the war, and other matters. The Black students' move to make Hamilton Hall their own had no major consequences, therefore, on the Columbia upheaval, but it was nevertheless symbolically important in terms of their own development as a cohesive force.

When the "bust" occurred, however, the Black students let it be known that they would (for various reasons, including their desire to honor the concept of nonviolence) not resist the police.

As a result, they exited Hamilton Hall peacefully. Archibald Cox's summary of the entire Black student–SAS situation concluded that

> As the black students in Columbia grew in number (36 were admitted as freshmen in 1967) and widened their interests, SAS edged toward greater political involvement. They joined with other student groups in an effort to organize the cafeteria workers at Columbia who were primarily black and Puerto Rican. More than a dozen students formed the nucleus of a pledge class of Omega Psi Phi, a predominantly black national fraternity. Nevertheless, despite the degree of unity

achieved among black students at Columbia and their concomitant sense of blackness, their political power remained negligible. The sporadic efforts to achieve political influence were generally ineffective at the University. We do not delve here into the sources of political weakness but merely note that the disturbances of April 23–30 catapulted SAS into a leadership role it had not theretofore sought or enjoyed. ... SAS [then] proved ready and able to act with a disciplined purposefulness that had no antecedent in its past.[6]

By the time I arrived in Princeton a few months later, I discovered that the Black students had not only formed a unified separate organization but they also had identified an issue they were ready to pursue against the university—and to do so with unusual purposefulness. Moving to Princeton, therefore, became something very different from what I had envisioned several months earlier: Change—change of a momentous kind—had overtaken higher education, and I had placed myself in the very midst of it.

PORT HURON AND HIGHER EDUCATION

The American student political movement of the 1960s began in several places. Some commentators have traced its origins to the New Left in England, whereas others have pointed to the Berkeley Free Speech Movement. What seems clear, however, is that the critique of American liberalism, including the condemnation of the Cold War and the desire to ban the bomb, began as early as the '50s. The effort to bring down Senator Joseph McCarthy and the House Un-American Committee also emerged early, although visible student opposition (in various forms) was negligible. Nevertheless, there were growing signs of political discontent—however much they were still scattered and relatively unexplosive—before the 1960s. Eventually, the protests were not simply against "outside" conditions (such as the war), but against the university and its system of education. The following pages focus on the evolution of student radical politics to Columbia's "fall"—and then beyond.

C. Wright Mills's *The Causes of World War III* (1958), for example, was read by some students who would soon become members of the new (1962) Students for a Democratic Society. John Kenneth Galbraith's best-selling *The Affluent Society* (1958) had already pointed out some of the serious problems of a prosperous nation beleaguered—even then—by signs of inequality. Even earlier, Mills's *The Power Elite* (1956) viewed America as the victim of a quasi-conspiratorial triumvirate consisting of three "elites": the military, corporation CEOs, and political leaders. All three groups were said to reinforce one another: corporations produced materials that the military was said to need, then politicians produced the necessary funds. In turn, military budgets continued to swell. According to Mills, Cold War foreign policy provided the rationale for ever more personnel, planes, ships, and nuclear warheads. Peace fell quietly by the wayside. The Cuban Missile Crisis of 1962 made the threat of an atomic holocaust seem to some people, not so much as a disaster that had been skillfully averted, but as a potential catastrophe that was all too close to being real.

The Power Elite was dismissed by many reviewers as a cartoon version of how the United States was governed, and the book was certainly a highly oversimplified version of purported conspiratorial politics. Moreover, Mills's personal style (Texas "outsider," unacademic garb, motorcyclist) helped to damage his professional reputation (while also attracting some left-wing students to him). His contentions, however, were in part less far-fetched than people allowed. President Eisenhower, in his well-known last speech to the nation (January 17, 1961), warned that "our immense military establishment" seemed permanently linked to "a large arms industry." He hoped that good government (and an informed citizenry) would "guard against the acquisition of influence, whether sought or unsought, by the military-industrial complex. The potential for the disastrous rise of misplaced power exists, and will persist."

C. Wright Mills held out little or no hope that the government (or the people) would act as the kind of protective shield that Eisenhower sought. Others also saw correctly that elected officials and their constituents (especially in states where profitable companies created many jobs by manufacturing weapons and other military material) would easily be swayed by Cold War logic. The "arms race" became an institutionalized part of American foreign policy.

If Eisenhower was worried, the so-called Beats were far more concerned and outspoken, in language very different from the president's. They began to make their presence known by the mid-1950s and were forcefully opposed to the popular view that Communists (especially the Russians) were about to infiltrate and take over every aspect of American life. For the Beats, the atomic bomb became one of the reigning symbols of our capacity to destroy others (as well as the possibility that we ourselves might be destroyed). The media, such as *Time* magazine and main-channel television news, were viewed as Cold War proponents. Everyone was "serious" about the situation. In Allen Ginsberg's 1956 poem "America," he focused on *Time* magazine as a purported propaganda machine for those who stood for—and created—the Cold War status quo, and who were (in Ginsberg's view) not genuinely American. He, on the other hand, suggested that he might be a modern-day Whitman in spirit:

> Are you going to let your
> Emotional life be run by Time magazine?
> I'm obsessed by Time magazine.
> I read it every week. ...
> It's always telling me about responsibility.
> Business people are serious.
> Movie producers are serious.
> Everybody's serious but me.
> It occurs to me that I am America.

Ginsberg, Kerouac, Burroughs, and other Beats of the 1950s led the way in articulating some of the political views of the '60s. But they were mainly dropouts from—not active opponents of—their universities. They showed that some bright, creative people found the academy lacking in life as they themselves defined it. Literature at Columbia (where Ginsberg and Kerouac were enrolled for a while) was said to be typified by professors who were liberal, genteel, "professional," removed from the energy and actuality of everyday existence. Ginsberg's style, language, syntax, and ideas represented a sharp new Whitmanesque break from "mainstream" literature. And the decision to leave university life marked the beginning of new (negative) attitudes toward the academy (just when I was finishing my four Princeton years), although these took time to develop. At first, the students, not the universities, were often exhorted:

> *Class Day, Class Orator, Princeton, 1956*:
> Most of us will eventually be a part of a profession or a business concern and there will exist for us a pleasant continuity between our college and our life work. With our friends and our background we will be a part of an unbroken fellowship which will provide a tradition of harmonious good-cheer and goodwill.

Yes, we are fortunate to be part of this happy confraternity. And to the degree that we follow this, the well proven path, that is the degree to which we fail.

I was listening, and I was ready for a bold new thrust. Would we be offered a brash new way to break through conformity? No. Instead we heard something muted (which to the speaker may have seemed clarion-like): "We will fail unless we stand alone. ... We need to be alone, because aloneness can produce new motivations and new attitudes. We need these new attitudes because many of the old ones don't always work effectively in today's world." And so it went: words that left everyone feeling perfectly comfortable and unruffled. In the end, the graduates thought that they could almost certainly have it both ways: continuity and friends, as well as some new thoroughly "lonely" unspecified ideas and attitudes. Nothing was really amiss, and—most of all—higher education itself was not problematic. "We"—not the university—would have to change, if at all.

Nearly a decade later, Christopher Jencks wrote his essay "The Future of American Education," published in *The Radical Papers* (1965). Much had been altered since 1956, and Jencks described the new situation as constituting a unified educational structure in which students had to do well at every step of the way if they were to compete successfully for entrance to the next level—from high school to college, and then from college to professional school. By the 1960s, millions of students were earning BAs but a BA was clearly not the top rung of the ladder: One had to do well there if one was to gain entrance to a postgraduate professional school. Although the educational and career dividends might be very substantial for those who were successful, Jencks pointed out that

> We seem to be headed for a world in which everyone will spend more time in the classroom. ... At least as presently and prospectively organized, this keeps students largely passive and dependent. As a result, significant human capacities may simply not be encouraged or developed. The student ... is not encouraged to discover and define reality for himself. Rather, he is encouraged to accept the definitions and demands of others and is rewarded according to his ability and willingness to adapt to these demands. Such schools and colleges provide appropriate socialization for the corporate and governmental civil service and for many professions. But a society cannot be wholly run by organization men. Somewhere, it must have men who initiate

new activities, who take the lead in responding to new problems and
to a changing environment. [7]

The system as a whole is seen to be primarily training people to meet
society's needs, and the result is still a "conformist" generation of people
suited to become corporate or similar leaders rather than those with the
imagination and creativity necessary to respond to "new problems and to
a changing environment."

But Jencks (and earlier analysts in the fifties) agreed on one important
point. They would not have blamed the universities for the situation.
Jencks saw the huge rapid expansion of American higher education in
the postwar period as responsible for the "laddered" nature of the new
structure. He did not, however, imagine that any form of assertive rebellion
against colleges and universities would be a sensible or effective answer
to the system. His solution was to create a more differentiated national
pattern in which educational institutions would not compete directly with
one another (and therefore tend to be similar in their outcomes). Instead,
every college and university was encouraged to strike out on its own
independent path, emphasizing unique programs and purposes. In that
way, the existing structure of higher education would be intellectually
diversified: there would be a host of different types of institutions—as
different as St. John's was from Rhode Island School of Design or from
Bard or Antioch or Hampshire or Bennington or the New School. But
Jencks's hope was of course never realized: a very few colleges went
their own differentiated ways, but most did not. And the universities
changed very little indeed (except that many grew larger and more complex). So a new—somewhat unsatisfactory—system was in place, with
no obvious way of redesigning and refashioning it.

Clark Kerr's 1963 view of his multiversity in California was mainly
descriptive and analytic, but it also contained a number of significant
evaluative comments along the way. In *The Uses of the University* (1963),
he offered a snapshot of the enormous size and the multitude of tasks
that helped to define the institution of which he was president. The quoted
statistics are from an era nearly 60 years ago, and the analogous figures
have of course grown enormously since then:

The University of California last year had operating expenditures
from all sources of nearly half a billion dollars, with almost $100
million for construction; or total employment of over 40,000 people,
more than IBM, and a much greater variety of endeavors; operations

in over a hundred locations, counting campus experiment stations, agricultural and urban extension services, and projects abroad involving more than fifty countries; nearly 10,000 courses in its catalogues ..., over 4,000 babies born in its hospitals. It is the world's largest purveyor of white mice. It will soon have the world's largest primate colony. It will soon also have over 100,000 students—30,000 of them at the graduate level; yet much less than one-third of expenses are directly related to teaching.

Kerr also described the extent to which faculty were becoming individual entrepreneurs, often more committed to their academic discipline than to their university; the continuing specialization of knowledge so that fewer and fewer faculty and students were able to talk about their work intelligibly with members of even neighboring disciplines; the consequent diminishment of a sense of university community; the creation of a new "class" of graduate students, many of whom took years to finish their PhDs, and were in effect neither full adults or late adolescents. With no job or visible career opportunities, some of them simply drifted, others turned to politics, and still others began to turn against the university itself.

Given the huge number of its tasks and services, the multiversity (in Kerr's words) should have a "soul ... a single animating principle; the multiversity has several—some of them quite good, although there is much debate on which souls really deserve salvation."[8]

Meanwhile,

the multiversity is a confusing place for the student. He has problems of establishing his identity and sense of security within it. But it offers him a vast range of choices, enough literally to stagger the mind. ... The casualty rate is high.

The walking wounded are many. ...[9]

[The] undergraduate students are restless. Recent changes in the American university have done them little good—lower teaching loads for the faculty, larger classes, the use of substitute teachers for the faculty, the choice of faculty members based on research accomplishments rather than instructional capacity. ... The students find themselves under a blanket of impersonal rules for admissions, for scholarships, for examinations, for degrees.[10]

Unwittingly, Kerr provided radical students (from Berkeley to Columbia) with a good deal of the material they would soon use in their critique of

America's universities—material that was closely related to their explicit political attacks.

In an intelligent analysis of the Berkeley "revolt," Professor Henry May (a historian) concluded that both "the so-called conservative political movement and the radical student movement are protests against bigness, bureaucracy, and official liberalism. Clark Kerr is actually a rather better symbol of the Liberal Establishment than is Lyndon Johnson."[11] The context was crucial: "the American mass university [existed] in a time both of quickening intellectual life and collapsing patterns."

Bradford Cleveland, once a Berkeley graduate student in political science, wrote an early "letter" to the university's undergraduates (1963) and he moved the discourse from relatively objective description to a politically radical critique:

> As an undergraduate you receive a four-year-long series of sharp staccatos: eight semesters, forty courses, one hundred twenty or more units, fifteen hundred to two thousand impersonal lectures. ...
>
> You perform. But when do you think? Dutifully and obediently you follow as a herd of grade-worshipping sheep. ... SKILL AND OBEDIENCE ARE WHAT YOU ACQUIRE. ... Aren't you the least bit aware that such a capacity is not only necessary for life in America's giant public and private corporations ...? No matter how well trimmed you keep your grassy lawn in suburbia after you get your bachelor's degree, your moral and spiritual servitude will not be reduced.[12]

So it was that the concept of the university as an enormous "machine" and an oppressive bureaucracy depriving one of genuine freedom to think and learn, gained prominence among some students. The student was not "free"; he was duped by administrative liberals, and soon found himself part of suburbia's servitude to corporate America, bereft of moral and spiritual values.

A little more than a year later, Mario Savio—leader of Berkeley's Free Speech Movement—led a mass of students in the takeover of Berkeley's Sproul Hall, its main administrative building. In his speech that led to the takeover, Savio said:

> Berkeley consists, in its administration, of "a whole mode of arbitrary exercise of arbitrary power." ... And that's what we have here. We

have an autocracy which runs the university. It's managed! ... [And] I'll tell you something, the faculty are a bunch of employees, and we're the raw materials! But we're a bunch of raw materials that don't mean to be, ... don't mean to end up being bought by some clients of the University, be they the government, be they industry, ... be they anyone!

And that brings me to the second point of civil disobedience. There is a time when the operation of the machine becomes so odious, ... that you can't take part. And you've got to put your bodies upon the gears and upon the wheels, ... and you've got to make it stop.[13]

In other words, the response to universities (and the education they offered) shifted steadily from the mid-'50s to the mid-'60s. In Otto Butz's volume, some students wished to become university faculty to escape suburbia's conformist society. The Beats, meanwhile, dropped out of universities and conventional society altogether. William Whyte's "organization men" were actually told to *acquire* a liberal education and thereby resist conformity. Princeton's orator told his classmates to somehow stand "alone" after graduation. Jencks wanted the colleges and universities to differentiate themselves. Kerr somehow expected undergraduates to swim against the tide and survive. But the radical student admonition was different: to rebel and indeed revolt against the university itself.

By the late 1960s, an antibureaucratic view was firmly established among radicals. At Columbia, Mark Rudd, declared that undergraduates would soon

become conscious of their own interests and needs, and of the way the university acts against them, corrupting and distorting education in a bewildering variety of forms (paternalism, ... career orientation, pedantry, bureaucracy).

Slightly later (in 1968), Rudd wrote to Grayson Kirk deploring the fact that "Your University" trains us "to be lawyers and engineers, and managers for your IBM, your Socony Mobil, your IDA, your Con Edison (or else to be scholars and teachers in more universities like this one)":

We can point, in short, to our own meaningless studies, or identity crises, and our revulsion with being cogs in your corporate machines as a product of and reaction to a basically sick society.[14]

Here, the university is viewed as an extension of a "sick society"—partly because it is "conformist" in its "training," and partly because it mirrors the political problems—the war, racism—of society in general.

Rudd's letter to Kirk came just six years after the founding of the SDS. A group of then-current and former students had gathered in Port Huron, Michigan, in 1962, and drafted the Port Huron Statement, which (after subsequent revisions) became the founding set of SDS principles, including its analysis of America's universities. At that point, the number of engaged participants was small, and many of the early members were drawn to join as much by the sense of being part of a fraternity in which close personal relations, friendships, love, and the sense of a shared purpose were as important as clear political objectives. As Todd Gitlin testified:

> this is what moved me most about the SDS circle: everything these people did was charged with intensity. ... They were at once analytically keen and politically committed, but also, with a thousand gestures of affection, these unabashed moralists cared about one another. ...They seemed to live as if life were all of a piece, love and commitment indivisible.
>
> Organized one by one, face to face, most of the early SDS people were drawn into a circle and kept there by powerful personal bonds—bonds that were more important than political analyses or positions.[15]

Given these bonds and given the tendency to think in terms of "next steps" rather than long-term strategy,

> The movement constantly tended to become its own end, its own "program"; more energy flowed into maintaining the collective bond than in making clear where it wanted to take the world, and how the movement was in this way a living protest against both isolation and fragmentation. There was a longing to "unite the fragmented parts of personal history," as the Port Huron Statement put it—to transcend the multiplicity and confusion of roles that become normal in a rationalized society.[16]

Because of the increasing manipulative behavior of the SDS with each passing year—whether at Berkeley, Wisconsin, Columbia, Harvard, and elsewhere—it may be tempting to overlook the idealism of so many of its members. Many of the SDS students had genuine human and political ideals, and their goals represented a desire to move beyond the "stalemate" politics of the late 1940s and 1950s, in order to create a more peaceful and humane world. Indeed, many SDS students were less antagonistic to the university itself than they were against the Vietnam War, or the general suppression and brutalization of African Americans, or the federal government in Washington. Moreover, the growing antiwar movement—beginning especially in 1967—included very large numbers of students who were liberals or "moderates" (not SDS members). They had no strong animus against their academic institutions, but mainly against the pointlessness of the war, including—very crucially—the threat of the draft. Todd Gitlin's ideal of a close-knit band of "brothers" (and "sisters") was a vision that appealed to many young people, some of whom felt "alienated" or simply lost in the expanded American system of higher education. As one tries to assess the nature of the student revolution of the 1960s, therefore, one has to guard constantly against oversimplification. Students engaged in the general activity of protest varied greatly: the range included Progressive Labor (PL) members bent on straightforward revolution; the SDS, with its mix of radical and liberal members opposed to the war and to university policies; and liberal and moderate non-SDS students against the war but not the university.

If motives and attitudes varied among many of the participants, however, there was very little ambiguity about the Port Huron document itself. It is a fundamental criticism of American values and policies, presented as "An Agenda For a Generation." It stated that the new generation's "comfort was penetrated by events too troubling to dismiss":

> First, the permeating and victimizing fact of human degradation, symbolized by the Southern struggle against racial bigotry compelled most of us from silence to activism. Second, the enclosing fact of the Cold War, symbolized by the presence of the Bomb, brought awareness that we ourselves, and our friends, and millions of abstract "others" … might die at any time. … The declaration "all men are created equal" … rang hollow before the facts of Negro life in the South and the big cities of the North. The proclaimed peaceful intentions of the United States contradicted its economic and military investments in the Cold War status quo.

It is not clear how the writers of the statement regarded the expansionist motives of the Soviet Empire, or the nature of its brutal rule in East

Germany, Hungary, Poland, and elsewhere. But they nevertheless concluded that the Cold War was an American policy initiative, and they also viewed themselves as constricted by the watchwords of the day:

> "Ideologies Are Exhausted, Bipartisanship, No Utopias," ... The decline of utopias and hope is in fact one of the defining features of social life today. ... To be idealistic is to be considered apocalyptic, deluded. To have no serious aspirations, on the contrary, is to be "tough-minded."

The central thrust of the Port Huron Statement—nearly 50 single-spaced, typewritten pages—was to chart a way out of the current stalemate, and to persuade others that idealism, hope, and the search for a new kind of "utopia" were in fact realizable goals. Part of the document concerns the role that many groups (such as labor unions) could play in a new radical movement. It saw the nation's future politics, not as a struggle between the Republican and Democratic parties, but of two newly created parties that represented contrasting (rather than "over-lapping") positions, together with a multitude of participating associations that would make their voices heard in a variety of ways—something resembling a vast cluster of dedicated, "equal" organizations.

Perhaps most relevant here, however, was the document's discussion of universities, including their current culpability as well as the role they might well play in a new revitalized society. A section headed "The University and Social Change" began by remarking that

> First, the university is located in a permanent position of social influence. Its educational function makes it indispensable and automatically a crucial institution in the formation of social attitudes. Second, in an unbelievably complicated world, it is the central institution for organizing, evaluating, and transmitting knowledge. Third, the extent to which academic resources presently are used to buttress immoral social science is revealed first, by the extent to which defense contracts make the universities engineers of the arms race. Too, the use of modern social science as a manipulative tool reveals itself in the "human relations" consultants to the modern corporation, who introduce trivial sops to give laborers feelings of "participation" or "belonging." And the use of motivational research is already infamous as a manipulative aspect of American politics.

Here, despite its invaluable capacity to organize and ultimately transmit knowledge, the university is fundamentally seen as inimical: it intensifies the arms race, helps to dupe workers while buttressing corporations, and contributes to the manipulative power of American economic organizations. So the university is part of the "system" standing in the way of necessary social and political change.

Because universities are committed to freedom of thought and expression, however, they have at least the theoretic ability to allow new ideas, new hopes, and even a new politics to take root. They might enable a "militant left [to] awaken its allies. ... The power of students and faculty united is not only potential; it has shown its actuality in the South, and in the reform movements of the North."

Ultimately, the Port Huron Statement became the blueprint of a plan to attack the university itself. Turning

> possibilities into realities will involve *national efforts at university reform by an alliance of students and faculty. They must wrest control of the educational process from the administrative bureaucracy. ... They must import major public issues into the curriculum. ... They must constantly build a base for their assault upon the loci of power* (author's emphasis).

For students to work with the faculty to wrest control from the university administration, to change the curriculum and introduce "major public issues," and to "assault" the loci of power: These were the crucial parts of the new "agenda for a generation."

The Civil Rights Movement, more than any other, was the SDS model for how to move forward: sit-ins, marches, boycotts, building "takeovers" and similar "direct action" tactics. But there were of course major differences between what enabled direct action to succeed so often in the struggle for civil rights in the South, and the obstacles it faced in universities. First, brutal suppression of African Americans in the South—including lynchings, Jim Crow segregation, and deprivation of voting rights— was not only visibly cruel and inhumane, but manifestly illegal. To take "direct action" against such injustices eventually won favor among a large part of American society.

But university students were not suffering conspicuous brutality or deprivation of rights at the hands of administrators in the early 1960s. It was not obvious (especially in 1962) to many students (quite apart to the faculty or the general public) that great university injustices existed and had to be forcefully resisted. If education was less than ideal, it was believed to be open to reasonable change. Faculty defense-related (unclassified) research was not self-evidently pernicious, and many who undertook it were veterans of World War II—they saw it as patriotic work.

A second difference: the Civil Rights Movement under Martin Luther King, John Lewis, and others was committed not only to nonviolence and peaceful forms of protest, but also a willingness to suffer legal consequences if necessary. The SDS articulated no such creed and also habitually (and immediately) demanded "amnesty" whenever violations of university regulations led to disciplinary action.

Finally, the SDS was naïve about creating a strong alliance with the faculty. A few faculty members might ally themselves (in a limited way) with radical students, but most were ultimately committed to their lifetime profession and its work; many to their institutions; and virtually all to their source of livelihood. As a result, faculty were often criticized by the SDS for being comfortable "liberals" who talked rather than acted.

In short, the case against universities was hardly an obvious one, and it would take major changes in the national and world situation to make the Port Huron assault on higher education even partly plausible.

A new view of what might (or might not) be finally accomplished by the SDS began about 1967–68. In conversations with Todd Gitlin and other SDS members, Tom Hayden—national SDS leader—declared that

> Having tried available channels and discovered them meaningless, having recognized that the establishment does not listen to public opinion—it does not care to listen to the New Left—the New Left has moved toward confrontation. The turning point was … October 1967, when resistance became the official watchword of the antiwar movement.[17]

The result: "turn up the militancy." A "*youth* identity said, in effect: To be young and American is to have been betrayed; to be alive is to be enraged."[18]

Among SDS students, the militant faction grew more and more prominent, partly because the turn to confrontation produced headlines and apparent—if only momentary—victories. There

> Unfolded a long-running action theater: theater of the whole. Its incandescent high points ran from Oakland and the Pentagon through

Columbia University; … San Francisco State, People's Park, Kent State, plus hundreds of local student strikes, sit-ins, confrontations, melées—clashes whose images still loom large. …

One can see the late sixties as a long unraveling, a fresh start, a tragicomic *Kulturkampf*, the overdue demolition of a fraudulent consensus, a failed upheaval, a valiant effort at reforms camouflaged as revolution—and it was all of those.[19]

The movement was "no longer the beloved community." Purposes had changed, attitudes changed, tactics changed. Greater militancy in the SDS became the new watchword just as it also came to define other groups. Colleges and universities were attacked with more intensity and frequency. The Black Panthers emerged, as did the Black Power movement. The violence and mayhem at the 1968 Democratic presidential convention— all this and more culminated in the 1970 explosive events following Nixon's military move into Cambodia, with the consequent killing by the National Guard of four rock-throwing students at Kent State University. The Weathermen were beginning to cohere. In short, 1968 was a critical turning point leading not only to systematic and extreme militancy but ultimately to massive national backlash that continued for decades.

BREED-MORE

My last Harvard term as an assistant professor ended in the late spring of 1968, and we quickly began our move to Princeton, where I would soon take up my duties as dean of Students, and Angelica would begin working as a curator at the Guggenheim Museum in New York. The events of Columbia were fresh in our minds as we arrived in our new home, located in a small Princeton enclave where a group of streets and lanes intersected at what was the outermost western edge of the university. It still retained (in the 1960s and 1970s) the feeling of being a "full stop": Nearby, there was a large empty field where young children and teenagers often played sand-lot games, and there was an almost equally large plot next to it where an outdoor swimming pool (to be used by neighboring university families) was hidden behind vine-laden chain-linked fences. Other unsettled fields lay in yet another direction, except for the intrusion of a small brick-built structure that then housed the Princeton Day School: at the time, a small pleasant inelegant establishment that seemed to accomplish all that it was destined to achieve.

"Broadmead"—signifying a large or broad meadow—was the name long-since conferred on this compound of nearly empty lots and perhaps about a dozen nearby three-story houses (all in a mock-Tudor style) owned by the university. They were created during Woodrow Wilson's era, and were intended for new faculty who, given their youthfulness, seem to have been exceptionally adept at procreation: hence the nick-name "Breed-More." That is where Angelica and I landed in 1968, among neighbors who were near-contemporaries, with offspring who were roughly the same age as our own two (soon to be three) young children.

There were scarcely any automobiles that threatened us, so our sidewalks and streets and fields served as wide-open pastoral passages for both our youngest and oldest local inhabitants. Because Broadmead was only a fifteen- or twenty-minute walk to center campus, none of us drove to work.

My office was uptown, so to speak, close to Nassau Street (Princeton's "Main Street"). The university campus stretched along one side of Nassau Street; shops, restaurants, and residential areas populated the other side. In effect, Nassau Street bisected town and gown, although both communities lived almost entirely in long-accustomed congeniality. I was located on the third floor of a three-story building called—imaginatively— *West College*. East College had vanished long ago (razed in 1897 to make way for Chancellor Green Library) so our own structure was something of an anomaly. The building, however, was an appealing small rectangular affair in early nineteenth-century brick. The stairs were narrow and my office was box-like—appropriately so, given Princeton's relative lack of funds just after the turn of the nineteenth century. It all suited me, especially because outside my main office window I could glimpse Nassau Hall, so I felt nicely linked to the university's earliest days.

My first visit to West College—in August of 1968—was on a bright torrid day, and the building (because it was vacation time) was nearly empty. But my one assistant dean, John Danielson, was there to welcome me, and we had a good if brief conversation. John was the finest person one could hope for: friendly, warm-hearted, especially committed to students interested in public service and similar aspects of undergraduate life. He would be a valuable partner, but it was also clear that he had been appointed in an earlier halcyon era and was not (any more than I) remotely battle-trained. After Columbia, I wondered how the two of us would fare if— perhaps very soon—we found ourselves under siege, faced with a regiment of SDS students along with their exhorted if not totally converted companions. Almost immediately, it struck me that John and I would have to double the size of our two-person staff.

As dean of Students, I was responsible for undergraduate nonacademic life, including protests, demonstrations, discipline and other nontraditional as well as traditional activities. Princeton's discipline system was completely unimperialistic: I chaired a committee consisting of five faculty and five undergraduates, and the committee had responsibility for hearing (and deciding upon) all cases involving violations of any college regulations. Punishments ranged from warnings to probation to suspension to expulsion. So there was (unlike Columbia) a well-articulated disciplinary "mechanism"—with faculty as well as student involvement—in place. The only question was whether it could and would function under the pressure of difficult circumstances, including mass protests.

After my discussion with John, I went home and told Angelica about my first impressions. Afterward, we turned our attention to settling into our new home. I was sitting on the floor of the downstairs room that was to become our library. I was dressed in a T-shirt and running shorts when the doorbell rang. It was Bill Bowen, Princeton's Provost, who had come to meet and welcome us. He had a natural informal manner, and looked as if he were in his mid-30s. He was dressed only slightly less athletically than I, and he said that he wanted to help in any way that he could. He added that he was looking forward to working with me. He and Angelica and I talked in a relaxed way for half an hour. When he left, I already felt that he was someone I would be able to call whenever I needed advice or help. Indeed, I made such calls sooner and—during the next two decades—more frequently than I had dared to suspect.

If it took some time for me and Angelica to meet and begin to know members of the administration and faculty, it took no time at all for my presence among students (and even alumni) to be known. I was being asked—almost daily—my views on everything from "parietals" (women's visiting hours in men's dormitory rooms) to coeducation to student protests and the Vietnam War. Meanwhile, slightly later, a stack of some of my books was somehow photographed and the image soon appeared on the bright-orange cover of the *Princeton Alumni Weekly*. The volumes included Erik Erickson's *Identity, Youth and Crises*; T. B. Bottomore's *Elites and Society* and *Classes in Modern Society*; C. Wright Mills's *The Power Elite*; Richard Blum's *Students and Drugs*; Ishmael Reed's *Yellow Back Radio Broke-Down*; Willard Dalrymple's *Sex Is for Real*; and Vance Packard's *The Sexual Wilderness*. This was interpreted by some alumni (and others) to reveal not what I was reading in order to educate myself, but what I was studying for ideological guidance. I was appalled. Since I still knew relatively little about the "student revolution," I was trying to learn as much (and as quickly) as possible. But I suddenly realized how highly visible I was: There was little I could do or say that might not be quoted or photographed or interpreted for possible clues or covert meanings by the student newspaper or other sources. "Freddie" Fox, an appealing, loveable on-campus alumnus with a sense of humor soon dubbed me—in jest—"The Red Dean." I took it in jest, but it signaled to many people that I must be somewhere well to the left of Lenin.

INVISIBILITY

July 1968 was hot and humid in Princeton. The town and the university both seemed deserted. President Goheen and his family spent their summers on Cape Cod: for much of the 1960s (and certainly earlier) university presidents could be away for a month or two because the academic year came to a complete halt not long after commencement. If one did not leave Princeton altogether, one could take refuge in the library, or at home, or occasionally at a nearby shore town.

Meanwhile, the center of the university, composed of eighteenth- and nineteenth-century buildings, stood its accustomed ground. Some of the structures (like West College) were simple Colonial affairs; others were Greek revival in style, or Victorian Gothic (such as Alexander Hall); nearby there were some fine collegiate Gothic residential and dining halls for undergraduates. The entire cluster—despite some of its stylistic juxtapositions—was nicely and spaciously composed. Then, just behind Nassau Hall, there was a large rectangular sweep of lawn that had, at its center, a half-buried Revolutionary War cannon. From "Cannon Green," the campus stretched down a long slope toward Lake Carnegie, at least half a mile away, along meandering paths, through quadrangles, past well-known haunts and wooded ways that made the Princeton campus so seductive.

But if the visible university was familiar to me, allowing me to feel quickly at home, the invisible institution was still unknown. I had learned about the Discipline Committee, but how was the rest of the university— indeed, the heart of Princeton—structured? How were important decisions made? Did the faculty play a major role? How much did the administration operate on its own? Having discovered so much about Columbia's fatal weaknesses, I now wanted to learn all that I could about my own institution.

I had of course great confidence in President Goheen, and I was very impressed by Bill Bowen. But I knew next to nothing about the university's modus operandi. It remained essentially invisible.

Given the nation's great variety of colleges and universities (and their various missions) it would be very strange if they were all organized and governed in the same way. Nevertheless, I think most people assume that specific types of institutions—such as small liberal arts colleges, or large public universities, or private universities, or community colleges— are similar if not identical in the way that they tend to run their affairs, and that the presidents of each kind of institution have something like the same responsibilities and powers. Would private universities, such as Yale, Penn, Stanford, Harvard, Brown, and Princeton, not be very similar in these matters?

Hardly any assumption could be further from the truth. Depending on the specific private institution, faculty and students can participate either a great deal, or scarcely at all, in significant decision-making. Power can be highly centralized in a president and his or her administration— or more decentralized. Financial resources can lie mainly in the hands of the "center," or they can be broadly (and locally) distributed (by deed of gift) among different schools, institutes, centers, programs, and departments. Traditions concerning unwritten expectations on the part of the faculty, students, administration (and even alumni) differ widely. Endowment funds can be plentiful or scarce—and they can be highly restricted for very specific purposes, or largely unrestricted.

All of these and other matters mean that two or three (or more) apparently similar universities can actually be very different in many fundamental ways, including their ability to function for better or ill. Do they have the capacity to change relatively quickly when necessary—or only extremely slowly? Can they deal effectively with serious—often unexpected—problems? Do they tend to function as comparatively coherent communities, or are there long-standing tension-filled (or even "warring") parts that often jar one another?

And of course structure is only a fraction of the matter. The character, intelligence, and versatility of the institution's leaders count for more than one can say. And tone, temperament, and especially judgment count for at least as much. Margot Asquith once said of a well-known English statesman that "he has a brilliant mind until he makes it up"; afterward, perhaps, would come the deluge. Indeed, brilliance is itself a potentially perilous part of what may be most needed in a leader: a very little can sometime go a very long way, in quite the wrong direction.

In other words, a multitude of seen and unseen (and often unsuspected) particles combine to create—and then differentiate—the elements of each organismic specimen that constitutes an American residential liberal-arts university. To learn about one's own variant of the species, or (changing the metaphor) to pierce its veil to discover what lies behind: All of that was critical, especially for an ingénu administrator such as myself.

If Princeton was largely invisible to me, several auspicious things began to reveal themselves near the beginning of the academic term. Angelica and I met—and were warmly greeted by—many faculty and a number of administrators, most of whom we had not previously known. It soon became clear to us that there was little if any serious division between the faculty and administration at Princeton.

This high degree of mutual trust proved to be life-saving, especially as the 1960s progressed. And the trust exemplified itself in shared institutional decision-making, in which the faculty played a consistent and central role. Students also played a visible, active part. I discovered much of this as time passed, but the critical clue was the clear outward, welcoming nature of the many faculty members whom we soon began to meet, and who gave every impression of caring greatly about the university—and regarding us as genuine colleagues.

Piercing the veil, therefore, was easier than expected. In addition, I talked to some faculty and began to learn about the previous year's protests at Princeton. I discovered that in October 1967 (about the time of the Dow Chemical incident at Harvard) a group of SDS and other students had staged a sit-in, blocking the doors of the IDA building. The head of IDA had called the local police: there was no "bust" but 31 students were arrested—peacefully. President Goheen had warned "This isn't Princeton," meaning that the students were off campus and therefore subject to action by IDA, not by the university. The newspaper reports, however, inevitably picked up the other possible interpretation: "This isn't our quiet, equable, predictably placid Princeton!"

Princeton's single faculty of Arts and Sciences undertook—as already suggested—to address the IDA issue, and the faculty ultimately voted to sever all ties with IDA, including President Goheen's role on the IDA board. Goheen was wise (and brave) enough to accept the recommendation, and then to prevail on the trustees to agree. This was very heartening. Given the terrible violence of the Vietnam conflict, and given the government's misleading statements about our purported progress toward victory, it was time for the university to break off unnecessary associations that did not bear on central institutional values. Its relationship to IDA was peripheral and provided the SDS with a major university target—while offering no consequential value to the university itself.

That decision did not, in my view, imply that there should be a halt to campus recruiting (military or otherwise); or a severing of all ties with ROTC; or acceptance of student disruptive tactics as legitimate forms of protest. But it did mean understanding the depth of opposition (which I shared) to what was happening in Vietnam, both to our own drafted youth and to Vietnamese civilians.

I had for some time been increasingly disturbed by the war, and after the American 1970 incursion in Cambodia, I actually asked Angelica to check her English passport to make certain it was up to date. If the war continued to worsen (Nixon was rumored to be considering the use of atomic weapons), I wanted the family to have a sane safe haven to sail to. The tales of *Dr. Strangelove* and *Catch 22* seemed to be merging and seemed to be coming true. In fact, when the Nixon tapes eventually became public, a section from April 25, 1972, contained the following:

> *Nixon*: I'd rather use the nuclear bomb [instead of flooding a main part of Vietnam]. Have you got that Henry?
>
> *Kissinger*: That, I think, would just be too much.
>
> *Nixon*: The nuclear bomb, does that bother you? ... I just want you to think big, Henry, for Christ sake.

So that was the direction Nixon momentarily thought of taking us, and rumors about it added to the reasons why so many people—young and old alike—were increasingly distraught.

Whatever I felt about the war, I had utterly different feelings about the university. In my view, universities and colleges were among the most precious institutions we possessed, regardless of their flaws. Ever since the rise to celebrity status of the left-wing semi-philosopher Herbert Marcuse (and others), however, the tolerance and freedom (of speech, inquiry, and association) treasured by myself and so many others in the 1950s began to be defined by many radicals as a form of ruse: "You can talk and teach and study all you want, and do so freely, but those who are in power will still make all the critical decisions." Tolerance and freedom suddenly came to be regarded as a form of bondage, and the only way to be truly "free" from such bondage was—it was said—for students (and faculty) to take power into their own hands and begin to create a new kind of educational institution and society. As Mark Rudd had written to Grayson Kirk: "If we win, we will take control of your world's corporation, your University, and attempt to mold a world in which we and other people can live as human beings." Justice, freedom, and socialism were to be the new university—and new national watchwords.

Rudd was (as already suggested) not very analytic. If Kirk and his university had been more astute, the SDS would not have succeeded in its effort to dismantle Columbia so effectively. One of the lessons to be learned at Princeton, therefore, was to make certain that the university's collective intelligence could be mobilized to study and reach informed (and politically sensitive) conclusions about important issues, involving those who had a legitimate stake in the outcome of decisions. This was, of course, much easier said than done. Which decisions required serious, thorough study? Who would study them and then implement decisions? Princeton's handling of IDA and other matters in 1967–68 was a comfort, but it almost certainly pointed to a possible future of successive similar situations to be analyzed by individuals and groups, with unpredictable conclusions and outcomes to be carried out in unspecified ways by unspecified people. Were all the relevant groups—administrators, faculty members, students, staff, trustees—ready and willing to agree on what constituted legitimate processes, or a governance system with varying degrees of representation? Was everyone prepared to invest the required time, energy, and patience in the whole endeavor, working through a panoply of decisions? Were excellent faculty willing to share responsibility for difficult and probably controversial recommendations and decisions?

As the year progressed, student activism increased on campuses across the nation. News of Columbia's late April 1968 uprising spread fast, and the Princeton SDS immediately called for a large rally to be held outside Nassau Hall. *The Daily Princetonian*, in an editorial, called for the rally to be peaceful. Unexpectedly, 1,200 students gathered on May 2 of 1968, and there was obviously no way to predict what would happen. Large "peaceful" rallies had a habit of erupting into something very different—as had occurred without warning at Columbia. So the atmosphere at Princeton was a mixture of high spirits and high tension. But as the students gathered, and before anything was fully underway, Goheen unexpectedly emerged alone from Nassau Hall to meet everyone. Nearly all the students began spontaneously cheering him. He began to talk before being presented with any "demands," and went on to promise a "fresh and searching review of the decision-making process of the university": this seemed to him to be "both possible and desirable."

He then invited several student leaders—including three from both the SDS and the recently formed ABC (Association of Black Collegians) to come to his office to begin discussing next steps. An early step was the creation of a Committee on the Structure of the University, to be chaired by Professor Stanley Kelley of the politics department. Other initiatives soon followed. Professor Richard Falk (an outspoken antiwar faculty member) was to look into the question of draft counselling services. Professor Burton Malkiel, a widely respected economist, would undertake a report on Princeton's investments in companies that were doing business with apartheid South Africa. Professor Marvin Bressler, chair of the sociology department, would lead a major Commission on The Future of the College. And Professor Gardner Patterson was already at work on a report concerning coeducation.

Suddenly the university was awash in committees and forthcoming reports. Goheen sought to address virtually all the significant problems that not only Princeton but a great many universities were facing. Equally, he placed the leadership of all the undertakings, not in the hands of deans but of respected faculty members, with committee memberships that included students as well as faculty and some administrators. It was far from an exercise in window-dressing. People like Kelley, Malkiel, Patterson, and others were strong—as well as experienced and smart— individuals who could be counted on to deliver what they thought best.

All of these actions on Goheen's part required considerable courage and a willingness to take exceptional risks. In effect, he was handing over major university-wide matters to groups led by people of good sense and expertise, but without imposing any preordained conditions. And it would be far from easy to turn down their recommendations, even if they seemed to be impracticable. Bill Bowen played a major role in moving Princeton in this new direction, but in the end Goheen had to make the decisions.

In this and other respects, Goheen was admirable. Indeed, he seemed to me to be unique in the way that he transformed both himself and his university during the course of 15 years, from 1957 to 1972 (when he

left Princeton to become the US ambassador to India). He was the only
president of a major university to successfully ride out the entire period
from the 1950s through to 1972, when the crises had passed and an era
of relative calm had been restored to campuses.

When I arrived in the autumn of 1968, all of the new committees
were in full swing. All made sense, although I was taken aback by the
boldness of the charge to the restructuring committee. Should we really
trust a faculty–student–administration group (including some SDS members) to come forward with ideas that could be turned into something
serviceable? What kind of "structural" decisions would be addressed?
What would be the shape of a bright new governance paradigm? I wondered whether the administration would not often find itself at odds with
at least some erratic parts of an invented mechanism that had obviously
not grown organically but had been devised by an ad hoc committee. We
could not expect a sarabande, but could we at least escape the cacophony
of an ill-conceived fortissimo fugue?

Although the president and his administration (together with the
trustees) would remain the final arbiters of any recommendations, the
premise of the entire venture was that individuals and groups, if given
responsibility, would respond seriously and wisely.

At that point I began to think that the actual practice of governance
might possibly be helpful in the service of a liberal arts education. It
might be difficult for committee members to study a subject, such as
"divestment" or governance, without feeling compelled to adduce all the
relevant evidence; to analyze all the arguments in favor and against a
given proposition; and finally to arrive at conclusions that were persuasive
enough to convince their peers. If nothing else, everyone would be compelled to realize that apparently simple matters were actually complex,
and that slogans might be much less useful when people were forced to
deal with data, "facts," arguments, and a variety of points of view. As it
turned out, I was neither entirely right nor wrong in my hopes: Some
slogans survived only too vociferously, while many participants in the
new quasi-democratic regime did indeed learn a great deal about the
complexity of an educational institution.

Although Goheen was nearly always out in front—meeting problems
head-on—he was not alone. He had created the provost's position in the
mid-1960s, and Bill Bowen became its first full-time occupant—as deputy
president—in 1966. Bill was a strong advocate of coeducation and was
no less in favor of the restructuring initiative. Goheen tended to move

more slowly: partly by temperament, partly by virtue of his generational inheritance (having been the product of prewar Princeton), and partly because it was his responsibility to make certain that the trustees, the faculty, a strong majority of students, and the most engaged alumni were willing to follow his lead. He wanted the university to remain a united "whole," and although he recognized that some serious divisions and splits were inevitable in an era like the 1960s, he also knew it was critical to maintain a strong institutional center as he ventured forward.

Bowen was no less inclined to sustain the center, but he was more in tune with the direction and the speed with which some matters (such as coeducation) were moving. He was also not connected, at age 34, with Princeton's past. He had not been a Princeton undergraduate but came from a Midwestern coeducational college—Denison—so he carried no Ivy League baggage. As an economist interested in labor relations, he was also accustomed to dealing with issues that were in constant flux. He was a friend of Stan Kelley, Burt Malkiel, and other recently tenured faculty, all of whom wanted to press the university forward, lest it become anachronistic as well as "elitist" in exactly the wrong sense of the term.

Indeed, I soon felt that a strong surge in favor of change—including the introduction of interdisciplinary studies and other matters—was coming from the younger faculty, including outstanding people like Sheldon Hackney, Amy Gutman, Michael Doyle, and Dennis Thompson in addition to the Bowen cohort. They were nearly all new to Princeton. They were spirited, energized individuals who were inclined to reshape Princeton in some of the ways that reflected their own experience with other colleges and their very different traditions. Bowen was one such person, as were other non-Ivy Leaguers like Marvin Bressler (CCNY), Stan Kelley (University of Kansas), Dennis Thompson (William and Mary), Sheldon Hackney (Vanderbilt), and Gregory Vlastos—much more senior—from Robert College (Constantinople).

Bowen and Goheen were exceptionally well matched, but it took some courage on Goheen's part to invite as provost a fast-moving, bright, effective person to work with him. He knew that the appointment would challenge him—and that was what he needed. Not many presidents would have been so self-perceptive (as well as receptive and strong) to have taken such a step, especially without feeling threatened.

When I arrived at Princeton in the autumn of 1968, I had lunch with a faculty friend from the English department, and at the end of our meal he left saying that although the administration was obviously extremely important, the faculty also had substantial power at Princeton. This was said in a friendly—not quite admonishing—manner. But a message was nevertheless being conveyed. So in the coming weeks, I set out to explore the hypothesis. There were several ways in which the proposition turned out to be true. I already knew, for instance, about my Discipline Committee, composed of five faculty and five students. But then I learned more about the so-called Committee of Three, which was responsible for all faculty appointments to tenure. In fact, the Committee of Three had eleven members: the president, provost, six elected senior members of the faculty, and the three senior academic deans. The record of every individual recommended for tenure was exhaustively reviewed by the committee: What was the quality of the person's teaching? Research? University, departmental, and other service? Personal integrity? Although the president alone had the final decision-making power, he was clearly bound to take the views of the committee (and especially its faculty members) into the most serious account, and I cannot remember any instance when he acted in opposition to a strong majority view (although he sometime had to resolve matters if the committee were divided). So here again, the faculty was very much in evidence, and rightly so—particularly because the elected committee members were invariably highly respected scholars and teachers of transparent ability.

For me, this part of Princeton's structure was comforting: Columbia's lack of a coherent single faculty with any power had of course been a fatal weakness. In addition, Princeton's president had a Faculty Advisory Committee of about eight senior members (also elected by their peers). Individuals, such as Gregory Vlastos, Lawrence Stone, Lyman Spitzer, Stan Kelley and other elected leaders, tended to comprise the group, and they were called together by the president whenever a major university issue requiring consultation—or an unexpected important problem—happened to arise. The committee had no explicit power, and the president called it at his own discretion. But the obvious mutual understanding was that no crucial administrative decisions that might affect the university in a serious way, would be made without some serious discussion with the Advisory Committee.

Finally, the entire Princeton faculty—or as many who wished to attend—met once a month for a formal session, chaired by the president and attended by the deans as well as the senior nonacademic administrators.

Most faculty meetings were routine and even dull, and most faculty failed to attend. But when there were matters of moment to be debated, the rows of benches were filled to overflowing. The president, and then each dean, would make a formal report on any relevant matter. After each report, the meeting would be open: Any member of the faculty could make a statement or ask a question challenging one or more administrators. So there was a clear process of accountability. On significant issues where the faculty had a clear legitimate role to play (such as curricular matters), there would be a full debate and a formal vote. Although these votes were ultimately recommendations, a president or dean would disregard them at his or her peril, unless there were powerful, persuasive reasons to the contrary.

So the faculty did indeed play a central role in Princeton's governance, but the administration had of course also to work with the power that resided on its other flank—the trustees. Although the trustees were ordinarily reluctant to go against the president's recommendations, there were nevertheless divisive issues (such as coeducation) that required very substantial thought, discussion, skill, and patience with the thirty-person body of alumni that constituted the board. Goheen managed—with his combination of talent and integrity—to hold all the elements in balance. But the challenge was, in the late 1960s, far from what had been the case only a few years earlier.

"CHANGIN'"

One of higher education's intriguing puzzles concerns the speed with which the placidity of the fifties turned into the ferment of the sixties. The shift from political quietude to radical protests is relatively easily explained but even there we are faced with some perplexing questions and a need for information that is not strictly political (or war related) in nature.

In a very different sphere, however, few people—including students themselves—would have (during the late fifties) expected or wanted all-male (or all-female) private selective colleges and universities to suddenly become coeducational. Yet within seven or eight years, that is exactly what began to happen. Why—and how—so dramatic a change occurred is at least as enigmatic as it is explicable, especially because there was no visible campaign of student demonstrations in favor of such a step.

The following pages suggest three indirect causes of both transformations—the political and the coeducational. The causes were fundamentally cultural in nature, and although they affected a great deal of American society, they had an exceptional effect on young people.

The first was the sense of individual and group freedom that grew steadily during America's increasing prosperity following the stringencies of the Great Depression and World War II.

The second symptom concerned the nascent lack of respect for authority (of various forms) that began in the decades following 1945 (and then continued with greater speed and force in the latter decades of the twentieth century).

Finally, and most important, was the creation of a pronounced youth culture that was new and distinct—and whose most obvious visible expression was the immense Woodstock Nation gathering of 1969.

The gain in much greater individual and group freedom was a product of the simple fact that, by the 1950s, more families were prospering economically: they had more leisure time, and somewhat more money to spend. Some of the pursuits seemed (and were) innocuous but nevertheless had consequences: more young people went off to newly created summer camps or joined sports teams that had "away" games. More important, many began to go to films on their own, and to watch television. Perhaps most important, however, was the advent of affordable automobiles. Suddenly, cars were not only symbols of status, but were the source of much greater freedom. Indeed, the symbolism and sense of adventure had been potent for some time, when vehicles were expensive and more rare. George Babbitt (in Sinclair Lewis's famous 1922 novel) owned a regal and irresistible one: "his motor car was poetry and tragedy, love and heroism. The office was his pirate ship, but the car his perilous excursion ashore."

By the 1950s, automobile ownership conferred prestige on more and more people, and also endowed them with the power to travel freely whenever and wherever they wanted—all enhanced by President Eisenhower's creation of a major interstate highway system across the nation. Very soon, teen-age driving and "dating" were common, offering youth not only latitude but also privacy that was otherwise scarce. Automobile back seats were put to imaginative uses and male–female relationships began to be more informal, easy, and intimate. In short, there was a pervasive loosening of the ties that formerly bound everyone, including the ties between family and children. James Dean made *Rebel Without a Cause* and was viewed as a young hero of a new type. His death (just after he made *Rebel* in 1955) was symbolically the result of an automobile crash (at age 24). For many young people, according to Todd Gitlin,

> he became instantly the image of a loner maudit, an incarnation of lost hopes. ... His ghostly appearance in *Rebel Without a Cause* became a vivid symbol of how precarious was youth-who-had-every-thing. The road promising everything, could take everything.
>
> *Rebel Without a Cause* was therefore instant mythology, and it prefigures an astonishing amount of the oppositional mood of the Sixties, especially in what it displays of the dynamic of father and sons. ... What is at issue is what fathers fail to provide: authority to boys, love to girls. Fathers without authority produce sons without purpose.[20]

James Dean's tale suggests the emergence of the second of the three developments mentioned previously: the growing lack of respect for (and belief in) authority. Perhaps the most conspicuous postwar spectacle of notorious "authority" was Senator Joseph McCarthy's power and his relentless hunt for Communist "Reds" in every corner of the government and the larger society—leading finally to his spectacular fall when he and his tactics were eventually exposed in the televised Army hearings. Then, when President Eisenhower was shown (in 1960) to have lied about the famous U-2 "spy-plane" incident (involving Russia), there was a further loss of confidence, particularly because Ike was symbolic of unvarnished honesty and trust. As a result, the stage was being set for more overt willingness to take issue with the political and other established norms of American society.

Finally, there was a profound change in the marked creation of an identifiable youth culture that was distinct in any number of ways from "adult" conventions. This phenomenon actually began to emerge in America as early as the late 1930s and 1940s, with the appearance of Frank Sinatra. Sinatra was himself young, and his audience of "bobby-soxers" swooned—and sometimes went wild—over him. When I was only eleven or twelve years old, I remember my young Aunt Susan (who was just a few years my senior) deciding to go to "the big city" to see and hear Sinatra—nothing could be more tempting and riveting for her. It was not much later when other performers began learning new rhythms: Elvis

Presley started playing and singing a novel kind of music—with a twist—
at a very young age. His first major hits came as early as 1954–55 and
after him there was of course a long line of other performers, including
Bob Dylan, the Beatles, the Rolling Stones, the Grateful Dead, and on
and on. They were all young, they were especially focused on audiences
of near-contemporaries, nearly all exuded various forms of sex appeal,
and all created a kind of bond with their audiences that was very different
from that of earlier musical or other "stars."

Anyone who was aware of the Beatles' major 1965 tour of America—
with an audience, for example, of 56,000 young people at Shea Stadium
in New York City—will immediately understand what defined the term
youth culture. A perhaps unlikely source, Coco Chanel, had remarked
earlier that "Youth is something very new: twenty years ago, no one
mentioned it."

The changes that were only too apparent in popular music were also
beginning to take place in other spheres: on Broadway, on television, in
film, in literature, and in the visual arts. Altogether, there were new
heroes and heroines; new cinematic idols and celebrities; new indulgences
(including marijuana, LSD, and sex); new styles of youthful dress; and
somewhat later, new hippies, yippies, long hair, beards, and "alienation"—
including novels with young heroes in flight from society, whether Holden
Caulfield in *Catcher in the Rye* (1951) or Jack Kerouac's *On the Road*
(1957).

In his interesting, detailed volume called *The Sixties* (1987), Todd
Gitlin described how Bob Dylan, for instance, affected him and his compatriots—including the women members—in the early 1960s:

> The tiny New Left delighted in one of our own generation and mind
> singing earnest ballads. ... Whether he liked it or not, Dylan *sang
> for us*: we didn't have to know he had hung out in Minneapolis's
> dropout nonstudent radical scene in order to intuit he had been doing
> some hard travelling through a familiar landscape. We followed his
> career as if he were singing our song; we got in the habit of asking
> where he was taking us next.[21]

Here, politics (the New Left), rebellion, music, Dylan, dropouts,
travel, freedom and youthful camaraderie all come together: a new culture
and part of a new generation riding toward an unknown but alluring
destination. In one sense, this was quintessentially American, but it is

interesting that student leaders in Europe also took note of it. The star of the French student rebellion, Daniel Cohn-Bendit, said at one point:

> I saw Bob Dylan at the Newport Folk Festival in 1965 and have been a fan of folk music ever since. I was a Stones fan too—though I also listened to the Beatles. ...
>
> I was in the States in 1965–66 and met Mark Rudd. ... But essentially the revolt was spurred by the idea of a counter culture, which was mainly carried via rock music. "Woodstock Nation": that was the myth of a new America, and we were all for it.[22]

Meanwhile, we may have forgotten how early a new attitude toward sexuality began to emerge in the United States. Alfred Kinsey's *Sexual Behavior in the Human Male* was published in 1948 (and his *Human Female* in 1953). The first book produced a mixture of widespread shock combined with widespread interest—about the subject matter itself as well as the findings. The fact that so much information on so taboo a topic could be published and widely distributed was a major event. The actual conclusions were in one sense less important than the fact that sexuality was now openly discussed. Many of its characteristics were said to have been "scientifically" recorded, tabulated, and formulated. Kinsey's volume became the subject of a kind of statistical voyeurism, and some of the sense of shame surrounding the topic began to be mitigated. One could talk about it more openly—after all, the book was a best-seller—and it could also be regarded as science, like chemistry or electricity or (given the findings about homosexuality) relativity.

No less influential, new types of heroes began to emerge on stage and in film, and they spoke directly to a new culture that included many youthful devotees. They were novel in manner, speech, action, and "method." Marlon Brando's film of *A Streetcar Named Desire* appeared as early as 1951 (the Broadway play opened in 1947). Brando electrified audiences: Here was someone who could scarcely have been more different from some of the reigning cinematic idols of the day, including Cary Grant, Gary Cooper, and James Stewart. I was at Wooster, just 14 years old, when I saw *Streetcar* (and its rape scene). I came away feeling I had just viewed something that was—for me at least—stunning: Was this our new milieu? There was certainly no "gender parity" here. Instead, there was a potent image of distorted human relations, of self-delusion, of lust and sadism made visible. Was Brando the new icon—or James Dean in *Rebel*? These heroes were obviously far different from the restrained and classy "adults" of the Grant–Stewart type: They were young—vulnerable or tough—speaking a new kind of language and appealing very much to youthful audiences. Some of their lives, moreover, carried a new message: not the optimistic, victorious, or generally harmonious endings of other films but more empty finales where there may have been much to *do*, but little or nothing to be *achieved*, and no obvious "cause" in sight. Brando appeared again in 1953—in *The Wild One*—on his motorcycle, with his gang and his slightly police-military type cap, signifying an inverted form of authority. If the audience was searching for a plot that might endow action with significant meaning, it would certainly search in vain. At one point, one of the characters in *The Wild One* asks Brando what he was rebelling against, and he replied—famously—"What diya' got?" Rebellion was very much in the air, but—as with James Dean—it was rebellion without any particular cause.

Meanwhile Hugh Heffner launched *Playboy* in 1953, with its vaunted centerfolds and its new vision of life as pleasure with apparently boundless young male tumescence at its heart. All of this was given more lift by Marilyn Monroe, mostly throughout the 50s: *The Seven Year Itch, Some Like It Hot, The Misfits, Bus Stop*, and *Don't Bother to Knock*. Marilyn, ever various, could be sultry and just sufficiently exposed in her dress; eyelids open just enough but not too much; her dress air blown. She was not without pathos, appealingly vulnerable, yet at times also bathetic, until fatally so—with her drug-doomed desire to be everything other than how her films portrayed her. Her hope to be "intellectual" was followed by her improbable marriage to Arthur Miller—but the Milleresque liaison lasted barely the briefest of times. None of it made sense—except that in the chaos of *Streetcar, The Wild One, Rebel*, Kinsey, Heffner, and the skin-deep glamor of ill-fated cinematic celebrity, everything made sense. Some of it had even been satirized earlier by Noel Coward in songs like "Louisa" and "Why Must the Show Go On?":

> Louisa was terribly lonely
> Success brought her naught but despair
> She derived little fun
> From the Oscars she'd won
> And none from her home in Bel Aire.
> She said she was weary of living
> On this bestial, terrestrial plane
> When friends came to visit.
> Their hands she would clutch

Crying, "Tell me why should I suffer so much,
Oh, if only, if only, if only
My life wasn't quite such a strain."
And soon after that she was terribly lonely
All over again.

Yet even these tales leave a great deal out. Elvis Presley (as suggested) with new music called *rock 'n' roll* made his first hits as early as July 1954. A nervous, stiff, and slightly catatonic Ed Sullivan finally agreed to allow the new star to perform on his staid television show, so long as the serpentine Presley was not to be televised below the waist or belt, where his twisting torso had its greatest effect, especially on female constituents.

The Beatles began somewhat later (but still early) in 1960; the Rolling Stones in '62, and then the Grateful Dead. Bob Dylan's first major songs appeared in 1962–63 and we have already seen how his work affected Todd Gitlin and his SDS companions. It would be possible to quote Dylan indefinitely, but perhaps one example can show some of the sources of his appeal—apart from his voice, tone, and appearance:

Come senators, congressmen
Please heed the call
Don't stand in the doorway
Don't block up the hall
For he that gets hurt
Will be he that has stalled
There's a battle outside and it's ragin'
It'll soon shake your windows and rattle your walls
For the times they are a changin'

This was 1963, essentially before Vietnam's major turmoil, although during the growth of the Civil Rights Movement. Not many students were at that point engaged in left-wing politics. Nor were that many preoccupied with the Cold War or even the bomb. America was still a land of plenty, and patriots continued to herald the fact that we were on the side of righteousness, despite Kennedy's Bay of Pigs Cuban disaster. This defeat was, in effect, rescued (in the eyes of most but not all people) by the outcome of the 1962 Cuban Missile Crisis: We emerged victorious from it, and Kennedy also inspired many people—the world over—with his "I am a Berliner" speech as well as with his creation of the Peace Corps, and his projection of a new generation of leaders with new ideals.

Nevertheless, Dylan spoke to many young people who saw the world situation (and America) very differently, and wanted another kind of politics:

> With God on Our side—
> But now we got weapons
> Of the chemical dust
> If fire them we're forced to
> One push of the button
> And a shot the world wide
> And you never ask questions
> When God's on your side. ...
> So now as I'm leavin'
> I'm weary as Hell
> The confusion I'm feelin'
> Ain't no tongue can tell
> The words fill my head
> And fall to the floor
> If God's on our side
> He'll stop the next war.[23]

The unfolding sagas of the '50s and '60s were unusual insofar as the emergent youth culture—first as an undercurrent and then more manifest—responded to the new music and its new performers, the new films and selected television stars. A shared consciousness continued to develop among many (far from all) young people. Among other things, it brought young men and women together in something close to a shared milieu and shared *mores*.

Philip Roth's late novel, *The Dying Animal* (2001), is narrated by a university faculty member who is having an affair with an available woman student. It recapitulates in a number of ways the transition from the 1950s to that of the late 1960s. At one point, the speaker reflects on his own collegiate days and focuses on a major turning point—in terms of youth culture—at a moment around 1964:

> The campuses had been perfectly managed. Parietal regulations. Un-questioned supervision. The authority came from a distant Kafkaesque source—"the administration"—and the language of the administration could have come from St. Augustine.
>
> You tried to find your wily way around all this control, but not until about '64, by and large everyone under surveillance was

law-abiding, members in excellent standing of what Hawthorne called "the limit-loving class."

Conventional behavior persisted, but it was not long before students began to campaign against parietals, and male daily dress began to give way from cotton khaki trousers to jeans and then to torn jeans. Finally,

> There came that long delayed explosion, the disreputable assault on post-war normalcy and the cultural consensus. All that was unmanageable came breaking out, and the irreversible transformation had begun.

What was the nature of the total "breaking out" and transformation?

> There were two strains to the turbulence: there was the libertarianism extending orgiastic permission to the individual, ... but with it, and often wedded to it, there was the communal righteousness about civil rights and against the war, the disobedience whose moral prestige devolved through Thoreau. And the two strains interconnecting made the orgy difficult to discredit.

Once the shackles were off, they were off (for some people) on all fronts— social, moral, sexual, political—because the revolt was not particularized: it was a more general youthful revolution against conventional constraints (or "authority") that then grew progressively over the next several years.

Roth, in *The Dying Animal*, is essentially focused on what was happening sexually in the 1960s, and its effect was consequently on relations between men and women rather than on political developments related to the war. The narrator has a student (Janie) writing her senior thesis on what she considered to be America's massive cultural change. The entire scene—from suburban Levittown to William Golding's 1954 novel *Lord of the Flies*—is telescoped:

> The suburbs. The Pill. The Pill that gave parity to the woman. The Music. The Pelvic Backbeat. The kids out there driving together in the Car. The Prosperity. The Commute. The Divorce. The Grass. Dope. Dr. Spock. All of that led to The Lord of the Flies U, which is what ... girls called our college. Janie's was not a revolutionary call that was blowing things up. Janie wasn't Bernadine Dohrn or Kathy Boudin. Nor were the Betty Friedans speaking to her.

Here is the whole mélange: the implosion of virtually everything, intercon-
necting. Individuals, groups, objects, events, experiences, and other phenomena jotted down with scarcely any syntax, existing in simultaneous
juxtaposition: The Cars and the kids; the daily Commutes; Spock and
Golding; Pelvic Backbeats; Boudin and Friedan; Dope, the Pill, Suburbs,
Divorce, and Prosperity—all colliding in staccato prose producing gram-
matical tumult and the new generation's amalgam.

The three-day 1969 Woodstock festival, occupying dozens of farm-
land acres in upstate New York, gathered about 400,000 young men and
women under the banner of Peace, buoyed by music, friendship, love,
drugs, sociability, and sex. Woodstock was the culmination, in tangible
form, of an efflorescent youth culture that had grown from early seeds
to full bloom during the progress of about a decade. It brought untold
young people together unabashedly and constituted, for a brief interlude,
a society bereft of adults that was committed to its own modes of unregu-
lated free-form experience.

Clearly, Woodstock and the cultural revolution had only an oblique
relation to the war and coeducation, but they helped to create the conditions
that made coeducation—for example—seem more desirable and even
natural. Several other factors, however, had to be aligned before all-male
colleges and universities would be motivated to take the bold step of
admitting women. First—and obviously—these institutions would have to
undergo their own internal cultural shifts—especially a shift in admission
policies. This was in fact already happening, incrementally, during the
1960s. In the 1950s, about two-thirds of the students at Princeton, for
example, came from all-male private prep schools, and the rest from
public high schools. During the next decade, however, the ratios were
gradually reversed. As more and more high school students arrived on
campus, coeducation seemed to them to be an exercise in continuity.
These students were unsurprisingly open to coeducational change—something that was altogether natural to them from their public schooling,
although revolutionary to the generations of Princetonians who had preceded them.

In addition, there was a similar alteration in the nature of the faculty.
During the immense postwar expansion of higher education, more and
more of the students who chose to pursue PhDs and become academics
derived from public colleges and universities that were coeducational
rather than single sex. The number of additional faculty members required
to meet the demand of a far larger system of higher education was enor-

mous, and a great many of the new recruits inevitably came from very different milieux than those of the relatively few prewar academics. Consequently, as the nature of the student body changed, so did the nature of the professoriate. Indeed, after I had been appointed Princeton's dean of Students, but while I was still at Harvard in the spring of 1968, I was called by *The Daily Princetonian* student newspaper and was asked whether I was in favor of coeducation. Without hesitating, I replied yes—even though I had been to an all-male prep-school and all-male Princeton. I had, however, been teaching coeducated classes at Harvard for four years, and I saw no reason to think that single-sex classes would be preferable or even as good. Moving from one modality to the other had simply been an easy and intellectually satisfying shift for me.

In short, all the "cultural" changes that took place, as well as the changes in the nature of both the student body and faculty, helped to prepare for what actually happened in the 1960s. Moreover, there were other significant factors that helped to bring the momentous shift leading to coeducation, and they will be described in the following chapter.

POLLY AND PRINCETON

Students were not the only threat to university composure—or the only source of university contentiousness—in the late 1960s. In 1968, as the possibility of coeducation loomed larger at Princeton; as greater numbers of African Americans were admitted (and inevitably staged demonstrations); as Princeton's ROTC was endangered, and its selective "eating clubs" seemed threatened; and as Nassau Hall eventually fell victim to an SDS sit-in, some prominent Princeton alumni decided that forces in the administration and faculty were pressing their institution far too far toward oblivion in a way that was beginning to overturn the university's treasured (and all-male) traditions.

An alumni organization called *ACTIIN* (*Alumni Committee to Involve Itself Now*) was soon founded. Bill Bowen was one of its major targets and I was pinpointed as an inevitable adversary, along with Stan Kelley and other conspicuous faculty suspected of undermining "the best old place of all."

Given the increasing threat by alumni to withhold financial donation, and ACTIIN's growing desire to expunge elements of the university administration, inordinate tensions simply increased. The possible advent of coeducation became the reigning symbol of dissension—a rallying cry to all those who now viewed Princeton as a precinct in visible peril. Potent alumni had of course brought about the swift curtailment of Woodrow Wilson's presidency slightly more than half a century earlier. Robert Goheen was certainly not viewed with anything resembling Wilson's sense of enmity, but the desire to diminish Bowen and Rudenstine's influence was more than tempting. To try in earnest seemed singularly appealing to an increasing number of invigorated "tigers." More than two bountiful centuries of all-male profusion seemed suddenly at risk.

By 1972, ACTIIN had given way to CAP (Concerned Alumni of Princeton), with its own paid administrator and magazine. Coeducation had by then taken place, but a fierce battle was underway to ensure that the university would sustain the preexisting number of enrolled male students—with no reduction at all. When the number of men was sensibly allowed to fall—so that the number of women could consequently rise— CAPs methods became more extreme. Some major (and very capable) alumni were increasingly distressed by CAP's tactics. Eventually the alumni organization lost its influence and simply imploded. Coeducation began to flourish. This early example of a "culture war" eventually came to a beneficent and welcome conclusion.

* * *

Evelyn College was created in 1887 to advance the education of young women. It was an unusual venture, however, because it chose to locate near Princeton University, and the hope was that Princeton/Evelyn would mirror the relationship between Harvard/Radcliffe. But a mere decade later saw the new institution headed toward closure: Funds were in short supply and Princeton was less than forthcoming. Nearly seventy years would pass before another such attempt would be contemplated.

In the 1960s, some barely noticeable steps were taken by Princeton along the way toward women's education. In 1961, the first woman was admitted to Princeton's Graduate School, and she was (a year later) awarded an MA in Oriental Studies. In 1962, the number jumped to eight women entering the Graduate School, and the first woman to earn a PhD finished in 1964. During the previous year, rather more sensationally, five women undergraduate juniors arrived to do a year's study in the newly created Critical Languages Program: They were enrolled in fields such as Chinese and Arabic—not offered at many small liberal arts colleges. This was a first in mini-coeducation, and the women received more than a passing salutation.

By the mid-1960s, therefore, some visible but scarcely shattering events had occurred to break a few all-male barriers at what many people regarded as the Ivy League's most conservative institution. This was not necessarily viewed as a harbinger of coeducation, but it was difficult to completely ignore these sequential steps of a possible minuet in the making. Matters were not moving swiftly or altogether elegantly, but they did indeed (to some observers) seem to be moving.

Meanwhile, I later learned—in talks with Mary "Polly" Bunting— that confidential discussions had been taking place between Harvard and Radcliffe College, starting as early as 1960. I came to know Polly, who had been president of Radcliffe, when she was asked by Bill Bowen to help Princeton—as an informal advisor—after the university decided to embrace coeducation. It was a bright idea. Polly was not only likeable but highly experienced, wise, bright, and willing to advise when asked but never inclined to interfere. Her Princeton office was on Ivy Lane, on the periphery of campus (near the football stadium) and few people even knew of her presence.

She told me that she had approached (in 1960) Nate Pusey, Harvard's president, with the possibility—at some point—of merging Radcliffe and Harvard. She had pioneered "midcareer" programs at Radcliffe, intended to help women who had given up work in order to marry and rear children (or for other reasons). Radcliffe would offer them a way to start again, as it were, in their thirties or forties or later. But Polly also knew that midcareer education was certainly not Radcliffe's primary purpose—and she also knew that Radcliffe was beginning to have financial problems. Finally, she was perceptive enough to sense the coeducational direction in which higher education seemed to be moving.

Nate Pusey responded positively to Polly's overture: a surprise, since his views were not at all predictable. Despite their mutual receptivity, however, both presidents knew that neither of their colleges (and certainly not their governing boards or alumni/ae) were at all prepared in 1960 to take so radical a step as a merger. As a result, a series of significant but smaller moves were taken. Radcliffe students had been taught separately by Harvard faculty from time immemorial, but the idea of having Radcliffe and Harvard undergraduates take all their courses together made more and more economic (as well as other) sense. It began to happen during the war, and by 1963 Radcliffe women were awarded Harvard BAs as well as Radcliffe degrees.

With women and men attending courses together (which was the case when I was teaching at Harvard), it only required another turn of the wheel for "co-residence" to become a reality. In effect, coeducation could be achieved de facto, although there was no formal institutional merger: the two colleges remained separate corporate entities for nearly three more decades, until 1999. There were, oddly enough, two separate governing bodies and two presidents in place—and a good deal of friction began to emerge, especially in the late 1980s and 1990s. Despite remaining independent, Radcliffe began to campaign for more women to be appointed to Harvard's faculty (as well as to the administration and staff). This was a perfectly reasonable desire, and Harvard itself strove to move ahead on those fronts. But Radcliffe anger (and some Harvard anger) about certain faculty appointments (or nonappointments) scarcely helped matters. Indeed, it actually hastened the effort to find a far better "governance" solution.

Yale was altogether different. Yale's president, Kingman Brewster—rather patrician in bearing: tall, handsome, and accustomed to making strong as well as sometimes sudden decisions and statements—began a series of discussions with Vassar College in 1966. The goal was to create a Radcliffe/Harvard "co-ordinate" arrangement, with Vassar moving to New Haven as an independent, legally separate institution but one that would be closely allied with Yale. Clearly, there was a good deal of irony in the situation, given the fact that the two presidents in Cambridge were trying to dissolve their increasingly awkward "co-ordinate" arrangement. But "co-ordinate" was politically more palatable to trustees and alumni in New Haven and Princeton than full coeducation, which would destroy all that seemed essential to many graduates concerning the long-standing centuries-old all-male traditions at both universities.

Brewster's talks with Vassar failed, but Goheen at Princeton initiated similar discussions with Sarah Lawrence College in 1967. Those negotiations also broke down, so both Yale and Princeton—which were by that time engaged in a rivalry concerning which institution would be first in the co-ordinate/coeducation race—seemed to have come up short. Then Brewster suddenly broke the logjam. He simply decided that Yale should forge ahead and become totally coeducational. In September 1968, with no real warning (and with a decisiveness that took some number of his governing board members off guard), he quietly consulted a few individuals and groups—and then announced his decision.

This obviously left Princeton alone, in an awkward position, especially because its next trustee meeting was several months away. Actually, however, Goheen had (after the collapse of the talks with Sarah Lawrence) asked the Princeton economist Gardner Patterson to study the coeducation issue and then produce a major report, which he sent to the president in July 1968. So despite Princeton's lame-duck situation, it had in fact undertaken a serious analysis of the subject at hand (which Brewster did not). Patterson's report, moreover, proved to be highly influential, given the detailed nature of the case that he made for coeducation.

One question, however, still remained partly obscure. What accounted for the great rush in the latter 1960s to press ahead so quickly to bring women and men undergraduates into a shared educational venture? Changes in culture obviously made a great difference, but there was no overt "movement"—no pickets, teach-ins, rallies, or sit-ins—clamoring for coeducation. It is true that Betty Friedan's influential *The Feminine Mystique* appeared as early as 1963, but its main point had to do with the need for women to have precisely the same freedom as men to pursue work and careers outside the home and family. The book had an enormous impact, and by 1966 Friedan helped to found the National Organization for Women (NOW), insisting that women should be regarded as full members of American society on equal terms with their male counterparts. But although opportunities for excellent women's education were an implicit part of this drive, coeducation per se was by no means a prominent issue. In fact, some women feminists strongly favored single-sex colleges for women, on the grounds that women would be able to develop their skills in leadership, in athletics, in science (as well as other subjects) more fully and freely apart from men. It was no accident that several of the best private women's colleges—including Smith, Wellesley, and Bryn Mawr—continued to remain single sex.

One powerful reason for the race to coeducation on the part of some men's colleges, however, was described to me in detail when I had a meeting—just as I was arriving—with Jack Osander, Princeton's director of Admissions. Osander had been instrumental in moving Princeton toward the admission of a much greater number of high school students, and he now told me that Princeton and Yale were both losing an increasingly large share of their best applicants to coeducational institutions—especially to Harvard, because of its close relationship with Radcliffe. The gap was growing, and some Princeton faculty in particular were more and more concerned (especially since selected faculty were involved in monitoring the admissions process). Students wanted to be in a more "natural" social and educational environment, and it was clear from the responses of students accepted by Princeton (but choosing to attend other colleges) that the presence (or absence) of women was one of the major reasons for their decision. If one wanted to stay competitive, therefore, one would have to move ahead—soon.

There had been a time in the 1950s when Princeton was "outdrawing" Harvard, for example, in admissions, but that moment had passed. All the momentum was now in the opposite direction.

Those who knew the situation were eager to make a decision as quickly as possible—especially those Princeton faculty who understood what was happening and for whom coeducation was swiftly becoming destiny.

Professor Gardner Patterson's report on coeducation was made public—in the *Princeton Alumni Weekly*—in September of 1968, and it made an extremely strong case for coeducation. It viewed the issue as a "momentous" one for Princeton, and said that it would determine the university's ability "to remain in the front rank of American educational institutions" during the decades ahead:

> We believe that for Princeton to remain an all-male institution in the face of an evolving social system will ... [weaken] Princeton's competitive position for students, for faculty, and for financial support. ...[24]
>
> The evidence is clear that an overwhelming majority of the most able persons in the age group 18–22 themselves strongly prefer to share the undergraduate experience with members of the opposite sex. This desire is so great that it casts serious doubt on the ability of all male Princeton to continue to attract students in anything like the numbers and quality characteristic of present and recent classes.[25]

Patterson then proceeded to argue that the common popular view—the desire to be with members of the opposite sex was mainly for male exploitative purposes—was simply wrong. Evidence from excellent coeducational institutions (such as Swarthmore, Stanford, Oberlin, Berkeley, and others) made clear the fact that students of both sexes were excellent intellectually, and that they preferred to study with (and learn from) their opposite numbers. No less strong was the Director of Admissions testimony that "there is a marked difference" between the approximate five hundred "top" students admitted early, and the others accepted to "fill out the class," particularly because so many of the top applicants choose to go elsewhere. In 1968, 425 admits were considered "the best" of all who applied, but only 181 chose to attend Princeton (43%)—a marked drop of nearly 10% from the previous year. Reply cards from the "turn-down" students cited three main reasons:

- Lack of women students
- Inadequate social facilities and the general social atmosphere
- The eating clubs and the "bicker" process

Patterson's report contained a number of tables showing the results of various questionnaires sent to students, faculty, and alumni. Those can be easily summarized: 75 percent of polled Princeton faculty (454 members) said that Princeton would attract more outstanding students if it were coeducational, and only 4 percent answered no. The others either did not think it would make any difference, or else did not respond.

Of 2,032 polled Princeton students, 83 percent said that coeducation would attract more of the "best" students to the university, whereas 7 percent disagreed. The alumni poll was split: Only 27 to 30 percent of older alumni said yes to the first question, but 52 to 60 percent of those among the younger (more recent) classes responded affirmatively. Finally, questionnaires sent to 4,500 secondary school seniors had a striking result: Among the top-ranked seniors, 80 percent said coeducation would increase the attractiveness of Princeton, and 70 percent of the less-than-top-ranked students also answered affirmatively. Finally, 76 percent of male students said that the presence of women would not "distract" or "inhibit" them in classroom discussions.

In short, Patterson's document was a powerful one, and it showed that coeducation was clearly the right choice if Princeton were to remain intellectually competitive among the best universities in the years ahead. It also made the additional point that, because so many more colleges and universities had been created during the postwar period, the few universities that had dominated so much of American higher education as late as 1950 could no longer count on doing so in the future.

Indeed, Clark Kerr had pointed out as early as 1963 (in his Godkin lectures) that there was already in the far West a new "mountain range" of major (coeducational) universities, including the California system and Stanford, whereas the University of Chicago and Northwestern and Michigan and Wisconsin constituted yet another range in the Midwest. The "East" and the "Ivies" no longer had, in effect, a virtual monopoly. Princeton would have to play in this new and very different national league, and it would need all the advantages it could garner. This was yet another powerful change that altered the entire American university landscape in an irreversible way.

LET THEM IN!

Much more hung in the balance of the coeducation decision than I realized. I was clearly worried about Princeton's ability to attract its fair share (and more) of the nation's most outstanding students, but I did not know that Bill Bowen was so deeply invested in the decision that he might consider leaving the provostship if Patterson's recommendation were not approved. Some excellent faculty felt equally strongly and might well become sufficiently discouraged to withdraw from giving their time and energy to helping solve university-wide problems. So I suddenly feared that I might experience the loss of some of the administrative and faculty colleagues I assumed would, with Bob Goheen, lead Princeton forward rather than allow it to founder.

The trustees were next scheduled to meet in January 1969—a few months away. Meanwhile, alumni opinion was being partly shaped by ACTIIN. During the autumn of 1968, alumni letters began pouring in, nearly all strongly opposed to coeducation. Several of these are quoted by Nancy Weiss Malkiel in her excellent book *Keep the Damned Women Out* (2016):

> I'm enraged over this! Let 1,000 Alumni sons or other well qualified guys in FIRST—their livelihood depends on a university education. Women's DON'T!

> What is all this nonsense about admitting women to Princeton? A good old fashioned whore-house would be considerably more efficient, and much, much cheaper.

> If Princeton becomes coeducational I will cease permanently all contributions to Annual Giving.

I don't want any part of a co-ed outfit. ... Until recently my wife and I ... have named Princeton ... as the ultimate beneficiary of our wills; but we have now taken it out entirely.

So to the nutty notions
Which feed the campus squirrels,
Let's add the last, which takes the prize,
And let in all the girls.

I was told that Princeton trustees were being battered with letters, messages, and phone calls, and it was not at all clear how they would be affected by the avalanche. Their formal January meeting would, I felt sure, be a stolid affair: If they voted for coeducation, they could scarcely celebrate in the face of organized alumni hostility, and they could hardly be cheerful if they turned down Patterson's recommendation in the face of such near-universal faculty, student, and administrative support. So I foresaw a grim gathering, and a somber resolution, whatever the outcome.

Trustee meetings were held in the formality of Nassau Hall's faculty room, and I took my assigned seat at the assigned time on the assigned day. It was only the second trustee meeting I had ever attended, and I knew far too few members to know what their views might be, or even which trustees were likely to be most influential. What I learned, however, was that a special trustee committee on coeducation had been appointed to make a recommendation to the full board, and that John Coburn was one of the committee's leading members. I was completely confident about John (and his influence). I also knew two other members slightly— Bill Atwood and Laurance Rockefeller, both of whom I felt were likely to be positively inclined. For the rest, I had no information, although I was worried that alumni sentiment was weighing heavily on the minds of many trustees who were still being contacted by friends and classmates strongly opposed to coeducation.

What I did not know was that the special committee had met the previous day and voted to confirm Patterson's recommendation, so by the time of the actual full board meeting, the matter had been effectively settled. The chair of the trustees was a somewhat solemn-looking heavy-set person named Harold Helm. I had barely met him. He struck me as being rock-like, sturdy, and committed above all to the stability of the university. I thought he was unlikely to go against Bob Goheen and the faculty, but this instinct was completely speculative. Helm gave an introduction at the start of the meeting, and then asked for the special committee's report, which proved to be strongly in favor of coeducation. I leaned back, relieved, in my bench-seat. It was, I thought, all over.

The full trustee discussion then took place and, in the end, only eight of the approximate thirty trustees dissented—although eight negative votes were not a trivial number given the fact that the overwhelming university sentiment, and the special committee's report, were so much in favor of moving ahead. There would be, I was certain, a bruising battle in the months—perhaps years—to come.

After the trustee decision, the real work began. Intense planning was immediately undertaken because we decided to receive our first group of women undergraduates in the fall of 1969 (not 1970)—just eight months away. We had to develop an admission process, find residential spaces for the new arrivals, hire more staff, begin recruiting women students and faculty, deal with serious and potentially harmful alumni reactions, and start raising money for scholarships and the new facilities we would need. Most of all, we had to prepare for an immense cultural transformation of the university in an effort to make the new women students feel not only officially welcome but actually at home (and there would only be room in the first year for only about 170 of them). This was a formidable challenge and, try as we might, it would be essentially impossible to achieve in the way that we hoped for. More than 200 years of history attuned to men, their frames of mind, and modes of behavior would simply not be remotely easy to alter.

At the top of my own list of priorities was the need to find a superb woman assistant dean to help make the transition to our local new world order as smooth as possible. Bill Bowen knew of someone (Halcyone "Halcy" Bohen) who might be interested. So Bill talked to Halcy and she did register some possible interest. She and I, however, would obviously have to see whether we thought we could work effectively together. We soon met, and we both felt that the new venture would be exciting if also challenging. She had graduated from Smith and had an intuitive understanding of what would have to be done in the coming months and years. She would set about learning the names and backgrounds of all the new women students as soon as they were admitted, making herself accessible not simply as a "dean." Once the first group of women arrived, she created a women's counselling service that would be available to talk confidentially with anyone about difficulties they might be experiencing. In other words, Halcy got us off to the best possible start. She was an ideal leader and it is impossible to imagine having had anyone better suited to the task ahead.

Moreover, the situation would turn out to be full of surprises, quite apart from the issues that we were (more or less) able to anticipate. Some problems were, I thought, inconceivable—until they arrived on our doorsteps. As we began recruiting women faculty, for instance, an excellent woman scholar and teacher whom I knew applied for a position in our history department. I thought she would be excellent and the department had a similar view, so we began planning to invite her.

In the midst of her "recruiting visit," however, she turned up in my office looking upset, somewhat bewildered, and indeed angry. She had just met with our dean of the Faculty, a well-intentioned person who had not yet fully understood all the implications of coeducation. When our potential woman faculty member asked about university housing, the dean replied that it was reserved for men. Astonished when I heard this, I picked up the phone and called the provost's office. Bill Bowen was quickly on the line, and I simply said, "Bill, we have to make a major university policy change in the next five to ten minutes." He needed no explanation beyond the brief one I gave him. His office in Nassau Hall was directly across from the dean's. Minutes later, my phone rang. It was Bill: "What kind of housing would the woman prefer?" So she decided to come, and we realized we would have to warn absolutely everyone (including ourselves) not to devour the daisies growing so abundantly about us.

ABC

Princeton had been recruiting and admitting larger—but still very small—numbers of Black students since about 1963. When I arrived in the summer of 1968, I learned that there were just nineteen African American seniors and a literal handful of Black graduate students on campus. The total Black-student population was still fewer than one hundred in a university with about 3,000 "majority" students. One Black administrator, Carl Fields, was an assistant dean of the College, and I knew that I would need an African American assistant dean for my own office. The Black students had worked closely with Fields, and had recently formed their own organization—the Association of Black Collegians (ABC). I took the name "Collegians" to suggest the educational nature of the group, rather than the more explicit political aims of the SDS, composed of students committed to creating a new "Democratic Society."

Not long after my arrival, there was an announcement of an ABC meeting to be held on Cannon Green behind Nassau Hall. The day was sunlit—Princeton at its autumnal best—and about twenty-five or thirty students formed a fairly large, virtually silent circle on the Green. I stationed myself very much on the periphery of the group, nearly out of earshot, and the "rally" was neither loud nor demonstrative. The students spoke in low tones, largely inaudible to me, and I simply stood there, stock-still, for perhaps half an hour until they broke up.

I remained for a few minutes afterward, and one of the group, Jerome Davis, came slowly up to me. He was soon to be chair of the college's Undergraduate Student Government. He said simply that he and the others appreciated the fact that I had watched and listened intently and seriously. I said that I was impressed by the way he and the group had acted. He had a gentle manner and I felt an immediate rapport with him: Certainly this was not the kind of "radical" I had come to expect. We said little more, but the encounter turned out to be one that made a difference to both of us, and it later led to a friendship that lasted for decades to come. At the time, I came away thinking that, whatever the Black students might do in terms of protests and demonstrations, it was likely to be utterly different from the SDS.

In fact, I gradually came to realize that Princeton's Black students were generally interested in gaining a serious education: Critiquing—but not exploding—the university was the goal of most (not all) of them. Several of those who graduated in the late 1960s and early 1970s remained close to the university. Brent Henry became a trustee; Eugene Lowe eventually became dean of Student Affairs; Jerome Davis became assistant to the later president (Lee Bollinger) of Columbia, and he remained a friend not only of myself but of Bill Bowen. Princeton mattered to them— and they in turn mattered greatly to Princeton. In the autumn of 1968, however, everything was fluid and unsettled. Bob Goheen, Bill Bowen, and the rest of us expected African American student disruptions, but had no idea what form they would take.

Meanwhile I set out to hire a "minority" assistant dean: We could not possibly manage without one, and after a few weeks of searching I settled upon Joseph Moore, a native of Princeton who knew the local Black community (which is considerable) very well. He was not a

Princeton graduate, but he had met some of our Black students, and he had the ability to create trusting relationships with them. In addition, he had an uncanny political sense. He turned out to know instinctively which students were likely to be genuine leaders, which were primarily interested in making a bid to gain personal prominence for themselves, and which were uncertain or confused about what course to follow and could not be counted upon in difficult situations.

Joe had to work largely behind the scenes, because even those Black students who were not fundamentally antagonistic to the university and its administration had to maintain their distance. Joe soon forged a link with Carl Fields, so there were now two Black administrators in important positions, and both cared about both the institution and its students. How they might create a path that could help the Blacks to pursue their political objectives in relatively restrained ways was their shared goal. Carl and Joe were particularly adept at achieving it, but there were always serious and even insoluble problems along the way. So even the best of possible pathways was bound to be, not only difficult to discover, but even more difficult to pursue.

APARTHEID

In the autumn of 1968, I said very little during the first two or three weekly "cabinet" meetings. I had met only four of the ten members, so I mainly listened. Our lunches took place in a dim-lit neo-Gothic room with dark wood paneling. Before long, one of our inevitable subjects for discussion was how we would respond to a student takeover of any university building, given the catastrophic results of the takeovers and "bust" at Columbia during the previous spring. I felt strongly that unless such an event actually threatened physical harm to individuals, we should not call the police or use our own security force to evict students. It would be better to warn the occupiers that they were violating university regulations (endorsed by the faculty, not simply passed by the administration), and then wait them out. Sooner or later, they would decide to leave.

No one strongly disagreed, but some cabinet members were obviously uneasy about appearing to do nothing in the face of so serious a situation. Then Bill Bowen decided to call Ed Levi, a legal scholar who was president of the University of Chicago. Levi agreed: We should not call the police, but he advised that if the students did not leave reasonably soon, we should ask for a court order demanding them to de-camp. If the order were not obeyed, the students could be held in contempt of court—a very serious charge to have on one's record (in addition to university disciplinary proceedings).

Levi's advice was immediately accepted. It would lead to clearing any occupied building, avoiding a "bust," and following a path that would be difficult for most of the university community to take strong issue with.

By implication, it also indicated that we would be treating our students reasonably—not brutally but effectively.

* * *

"Uhuru!"

"Racist imperialist pigs!"

So began the rally on February 26, 1969: Six hundred students—led partly by some Black graduate students—congregated to condemn Princeton's endowment holdings in companies doing business with apartheid South Africa. "There is no reason that this building"—Nassau Hall—"should stand here at the expense of any man's life," said a senior (Reginald Penniston '69) who was soon followed by an SDS leader, Peter Kaminsky: "I think that the time for rallies, speeches, for sensitizing people is through. ... I'm sick of it."

We may have forgotten how the student rhetoric of the '60s resonated across campuses, sometime effectively, sometimes absurdly. Being on-stage led speakers to compete oratorically in performances that were intended to be morally pure and no less portentous. The issue might in fact be genuinely significant, but that in itself did not necessarily prevent the triumph of theatricality. In the case of "divestment," Professor Burt Malkiel and his committee on the subject thought through the problem with great seriousness and decided it would be more effective to hold the stock and try to influence companies in ways consistent with the set of established Sullivan Principles (including fair labor practices for Black workers), rather than simply selling the stock. The university faculty and the student government (by just two votes) endorsed Malkiel's report, but that clearly did not settle the matter. Selling the stock would of course mean that someone else—who did not necessarily care about the moral issues—would quickly buy it. The university might then claim to be "pure," but apartheid would remain unaltered.

The February 1967 rally on divestment ended with a threatening ultimatum. The "United Front" (which had called for the assembly) was addressed by its spokesman, William Scott, and he concluded by saying:

> We demand that Robert F. Goheen appears in one week at a public forum to say that he has acquiesced to the demands of the United Front. ... We have attempted to act rationally, morally and responsibly. This university has not acted in a like manner. There is no longer any reason for us to act rationally, responsibly or morally.
> From now on, if there is no response, no holds barred.[26]

The United Front rally left us with a serious question: Should President Goheen decide to make a public address to the university community about the divestment issue? This was not so much a matter of Goheen's willingness to do so, as it was a question of whether he would be shouted down. The SDS and others had learned how to disrupt talks very effectively. And quite apart from a possible disruption, there would of course—should Goheen choose to speak—undoubtedly be national headlines if he were drowned out by members of his own university community. With dozens and dozens of "shouters" spread around the audience of perhaps a thousand people, it would be impossible to stop them, or even to identify more than a modest number against whom to bring disciplinary charges.

So the issue of the president's talk was full of risk. He asked Bill Bowen and me what we thought should be done. We both thought the talk should go ahead. We felt that the radicals would alienate all the moderates and liberals on campus if they disrupted the speech, and they were smart enough to see that they would in the end lose far more than they could gain. Goheen was so respected that we believed he would come through it all—and told him so.

Alexander Hall is an awkward Victorian-Gothic building on the front campus, but despite its odd exterior it is handsome and impressive inside. It seats nearly 1,100 people and was full to capacity on the day of the talk. Goheen was alone on stage and went directly to the microphone. He gave talks in exactly the way that he spoke to people conversationally. There was nothing oratorical about him. Playing dramatic roles was simply not part of his nature. As a result, he could sometimes seem rather dull, although that usually had the effect of making him sound genuine. Even his verbal or literary style was not particularly eloquent, but his lack of ostentation was exactly what made him so often impressive.

The audience listened as he said how much he was deeply opposed to apartheid, and how much the university was committed to opposing it, not by selling stock, but by using it as leverage to help change conditions for Black workers in South Africa. He did not exaggerate: It would be foolish to think we could dramatically affect the system, but we would do whatever was possible, and it would be wrong for us not to try.

At the end, there was a standing ovation. Of course, not everyone stood.

It was a rare day when our home phone rang before seven in the morning, but it did so on an April morning in 1969. The president's assistant asked me to come to Nassau Hall as soon as possible. Within a few minutes I arrived: Bob Goheen and Bill Bowen were there, as well as members of the president's Advisory Council—Lawrence Stone, Gregory Vlastos, Stan Kelley, and others. I immediately learned that Black student members of the ABC had—during the night—entered and taken over New South building, where the financial offices of the university were housed. The SDS had tried to join, but was kept out. It would be an ABC action alone, protesting the university's financial investments in South Africa.

What was happening inside the building was unknown. A rampage? Files being opened? No one knew. What should we do—and how to do it? All the doors were locked and guarded from the inside. Just as we began to discuss the matter, the phone rang. It was for me.

"Good morning, Neil."

It was Jerome Davis, calling from inside New South.

"Hello Jerome. What's happening?"

"Don't worry. Everything is fine here. In fact we are cleaning the place up—it's a mess. We are emptying all the waste-baskets and not touching any files or papers." A pause.

"Can you come down about noon and we will let you in, so that we can discuss plans?"

"I will be there."

I was authorized to make any sensible arrangement that was possible, and I arrived on time. All the ABC leaders whom I knew were there: Jerome, Rod Hamilton, Brent Henry, and others. They said they planned to stay in the building until about 6 pm and would then leave. They wanted to leave unimpeded. I agreed. It was quick but cordial enough. I left to report back to Nassau Hall. At about six o'clock, the front door of New South was opened, and the students walked out in single file, dignified, moving up the campus to a point where they began to disperse. It was a quiet victory march. They had made their symbolic statement.

But at that point, things began to fall apart. For some reason, the university security force had failed to identify virtually any of the students. I knew the few leaders, but most of the others were unknown. This was a massive failure. Nevertheless, I called a meeting of the Discipline Committee for two days later. When I arrived to chair the meeting, however, only four of the five faculty, and one of the five students were there. The lone student, realizing that his colleagues were boycotting the session, also decided to leave. So I had a committee, not of ten members, but of four. Without a quorum, and with no students, we could do nothing. So the entire process was paralyzed—and the Black students let it be known that even if the full committee were able to convene, they would not appear to testify. So an absolutely major violation (a building takeover) had been carried out—with apparently no serious consequences.

In the end, just three students were placed on probation, whereas any number of people insisted that no rules had been broken because the demonstration was short-lived, symbolic, and in a just cause. The reaction among a number of alumni was powerfully negative, and Bill Bowen told me that it was far more adverse than had been prompted by more outrageous SDS actions. I could only interpret this, regretfully, as reflecting the strong strain of racism that continued to exist in the nation. Princeton was said to be admitting all these presumably underqualified Blacks on scholarships, and instead of being grateful, they were reported to be tearing the place apart with impunity. It was far from the last time we were to hear such a refrain in higher education.

IDA REDIVIVUS

Not all SDS obstruction tactics were ultimately serious, although they could nonetheless be highly combative. In late April of 1969, the Princeton SDS made another attempt to close down IDA because its building was on property leased from the university, and the students wanted to break the lease. No stone was to be left unturned. I was in my office when the phone rang. Would I come over as soon as possible because the SDS blockade of IDA's front door was threatening to lead to something very difficult.

The SDS had overlooked the fact that a number of IDA employees were relatively young, very fit, and more athletic than our students had any reason to suspect. When the IDA people arrived for work and found the front door blocked, they were not inclined to back off in the face of a squadron of college kids. Within minutes, fists flew and the Princeton protesters found themselves under assault. I came just in time to witness the beginning of the battle and rushed forward to try to forestall a clash between an IDA heavyweight Dempsey and a hapless lightweight sophomore (or so he seemed).

Moments later, I was on the ground—just in time for a photographer to take a shot of me lying face downward. The IDA worker had mistaken me for a student and hurled a punch that landed. I was unhurt, and quickly rose to my feet, but the pictorial damage had been done. The SDS hastily began a retreat to the safety of the campus, but by the next morning, photos of my prone figure appeared in newspapers across the country with headlines proclaiming, "Down with Deans." And before that, during the previous evening, my unaware parents (in Danbury) were treated to a television image of me with the caption "Princeton Dean Felled." "Felled" was sufficiently vague and ominous to make my situation seem dire. Fearing the worst, my parents tried continuously to telephone us, but the line was totally tied up. Eventually they discovered that I was actually alive. Condolence notes soon began to pour in. But although I had no particular affection for IDA—much less for fistfights—I had to admit that I was not totally dismayed to watch our undergraduates encounter tangible evidence of an actual real world—just beyond our gates—that was replete with brawn. Fortunately, it was not difficult for the students to retreat quickly to the quietude of the campus. It was, however, probably more difficult for them to accept with grace—or any trace of cheer—the score of their most recent exploit: IDA, 1; SDS, 0.

"RADICAL REVOLUTION"

As Tom Hayden predicted, 1968–69 (reaching to 1970) witnessed the most rapid and vehement escalation of militant activism on campuses across the nation. The SDS moved aggressively against a growing number of targets: military and other recruiters, conservative speakers, ROTC,

IDA, and university scientific research—even though "unclassified"—
said to be related to the Vietnam War. Attacks against the war and those
against universities had, in effect, become synonymous, and campus life
was far more than merely disrupted.

As the year lurched forward, one of the most notorious Princeton
incidents took place in early March when Walter Hickel (President Nixon's
Secretary of the Interior) was invited to give a speech on the environment.
Any associate of Nixon was an inevitable target, regardless of the occasion. President Goheen rose to introduce him, but as soon as Hickel
approached the podium, about seventy-five students—led by the SDS,
with many students disguising themselves with red Native war paint—
began chanting. Symbolically, they intended to be seen as indigenous
Native Americans retaking their homeland. The Secretary's words were
drowned out. The demonstrators had stationed themselves in different
parts of the hall's balcony, so it was impossible to reach them easily, and
certainly not to silence or eject them. The shouting continued for nearly
a full hour—throughout the entirety of Hickel's talk, even though Goheen
warned the protestors to stop or else be subject to university discipline.
But they knew they could carry on: Only a few of them at most could
be identified. When the hour was over, there was obviously no way that
the usual question-and-answer period could go forward. Instead, the stage
was set for what promised to be raucous disciplinary hearings.

Ever since the university approved the establishment of a Council
of the University Community (recommended by the Kelley restructuring
committee), the nature of university judicial proceedings had totally
changed. Whenever undergraduate and graduate students were both involved in an event that might lead to disciplinary hearings, the Council's
own Judicial Committee took charge. Even more disconcerting, because
of a recent faculty vote, future proceedings were to be open to all members
of the university. A Council member would chair the affair, while I—
and my colleague Aaron Lemonick (then dean of the Graduate School)—
were cast in the role of "prosecutors." We were all now regarded as
participants in a "trial" with "defendants" and a committee that acted as
both judge and jury. The whole tone, under these circumstances, changed
totally. The defendants were in a position to call and cross-examine
"witnesses" making their case as ingeniously (and lengthily) as they
wished—in hearings that were now "open."

After the Hickel debacle, seventeen students were identified and
charged with disrupting the Secretary's speech. The committee set its first

meeting for 2:15 pm on March 16—very soon after the event. About 300 spectators, mainly students, crowded into the room. "From the moment the opening began," read a report in the *Princeton Alumni Weekly*, "it was apparent that discipline at Princeton would never be the same again."

The "defense attorney" for the "Hickel-hecklers" was a bright 27-year-old philosophy graduate student named Michael Teitelman. He was not only smart, but he had learned some flashy legal courtroom maneuvers and he had some real flair—as well as a relish for dramatic gestures that could rouse an audience to laughter or applause. Once the proceedings began, Teitelman immediately moved that all charges be dismissed against the accused because the case against them was politically motivated. The chair, William Dix—a mild, self-contained, tall, pipe-smoking, academic type was the respected university librarian, and he denied Teitelman's motion. There was some booing.

When witnesses began to be called,

> "The atmosphere"—wrote the *Weekly*—"became increasingly intimi-dating for witnesses. Every person who testified was led through a narrow aisle crowded with students demonstrably sympathetic to the defendants; loud jeers and shouts were directed at the witnesses while testifying; … At one point, during a discussion of the nature of the university, a voice in the audience shouted, "Burn it down!" to widespread laughter.

After the first session, it seemed clear that the hearings would be forced to continue for several days. Teitelman's challenges to witnesses and to the whole proceedings were constant, and so matters moved very slowly though dramatically. It was also clear that Aaron and I were completely outclassed legally and theatrically. Aaron made the point that this was a university hearing, not a trial—but to no obvious avail.

By the time the second day arrived, it was the moment for Aaron Lemonick and me to ask our questions. Everyone was primed to hear what the deans would say. Aaron—large, robust, and ready to be tempestu-ous—was far more at ease than I. I had been pleased enough as chair of my own Discipline Committee, but much less happy as a kind of attorney general. "It appeared," wrote the *Weekly*, "that Rudenstine hoped that, despite obvious strains, the proceedings were essentially sound and the truth would eventually come out." True, but the "obvious strains" were nevertheless only too evident.

About three hundred people also turned up on the second day, and the main witness was Russ Shangle, a university proctor responsible for enforcing student regulations. Princeton's proctors—no uniforms, certainly no weapons (or billy clubs), no apparent professional training— were mainly schooled in detecting violations of parietal rules and other gentlemanly infractions. They were good-hearted old-fashioned fellows who ambled the campus in ties and jackets, chatting informally with bystanders and generally remaining on good terms with their student charges.

They were known by their first names, and the SDS must have seemed like Martians to them. I knew Russ quite well—everyone knew Russ. He was not bright or clever, but was an open, awkward, honest type who said what he thought in his own unvarnished way.

Russ identified ten of the students who were charged, and was then questioned by Teitelman. As the *Weekly* wrote:

> In the eyes of many observers, the defense then made an unfortunate mistake. By asking long and intricate questions, Teitelman forced Shangle into a number of contradictions and grammatical errors that brought forth titters from the group of Princeton educated defendants. In one exchange, Shangle said that he had met Teitelman at an earlier demonstration.
>
> "That was in April, wasn't it?" asked Teitelman.
>
> "Yes, I think so," Shangle replied.
>
> "I am prepared," said Teitelman, with a dramatic gesture that would have put even Perry Mason to shame, "to produce documentation that I was a registered student at Cambridge University in England in April, 1969." The debating trick had humiliated Shangle and raised considerable conviction that the defense was less than admirable in its tactics. Rudenstine, who had maintained cordial relations with Teitelman before and during the hearings, was over-heard telling him that after that day he did not want to talk with him then or ever after.

That ended the second day of hearings. It seemed clear to Aaron and me that the other side had by then outwitted itself. We ourselves had done very little. But as sometimes happened, the SDS did not know when to stop before alienating all but their most ardent supporters. So long as the administration did not now overstep its own well-defined bounds, the chances were reasonable that the students might self-destruct.

On the third day, Herbert Marcuse showed up. This pseudo-philosophic idol of many "New Left" followers caused a stir, but he sat quietly without intruding. Moreover, the atmosphere of the entire event had by now changed. Nearly six hundred people were present, including many faculty with their spouses, and many administrative staff. After the Shangle affair, deflation had obviously struck the defendants, and defeat was palpable. Teitelman moved quickly to a closing statement:

> We stand for the radical revolution in this country. ... We're not going to let them take our heads off. We're going to take the guns and turn them around and blow the heads off the ruling class. ... This is a political trial and that's what we want everyone to understand.

After that, all the defendants walked in strict order from the room, preferring not to bless any verdict that might be levied against them. Rhetoric had led them to bravura and then to verbal and political absurdity.

The hearings actually lasted two more days, and, in the end, all the defendants were convicted. However, three of the seniors were suspended immediately—their degrees withheld. We were suddenly faced with a possible eruption—moderate students as well as radicals were angry, and even some faculty disagreed with the harshness of the penalties. The decisions were appealed, and Bill Bowen was the reviewing officer. Bill discovered a technicality that allowed him to reduce the three suspensions to "probations," enabling the students to graduate. Maelstrom aborted. Balloon deflated. "Weakness!" howled the conservative hard-liners. "Smart" said the rest of us, from the sidelines—especially since the seniors would be leaving forever in a few weeks, and who actually wanted them to stay for a possible additional term?

TUMULT

On Thursday, April 30—slightly more than a month after the Hickel hearings—President Richard Nixon announced that US troops had crossed the border from Vietnam into Cambodia. Within half an hour, several hundred Princeton students pressed into the university's large Gothic-style chapel. There was an immediate call from some quarters for a strike. Very soon, there was a demand that President Goheen should call a major meeting to decide how to respond to Nixon's latest move.

By then, different individuals and groups (including the SDS) had already begun to declare which actions should be undertaken, either at

Princeton, or in Washington, or both. Goheen quickly scheduled a session of the Council of the Princeton University Community (CPUC) for the next evening in Alexander Hall. By the appointed hour, people had already begun to fill the approximate 1,100 seats, and the members of the CPUC (myself included) filled the rows immediately in front of the stage, where the president had already stationed himself. I sat next to Aaron Lemonick.

There had been very few previous CPUC meetings, but the general way of proceeding was for the president to recognize Council members whose hands were raised, so that an individual could make a statement or put forward a motion to be discussed and eventually voted upon. The auditorium atmosphere was alive with talk and tension. The session started about five pm, and a number of Council hands were instantly raised. There was an immediate proposal for a university strike, with end-of-term procedures (such as exams) to be altered in an undefined way. The crowd roared support, and a Council discussion immediately followed. There was, in the end, no vote on the motion itself but—fortunately—the matter was referred to the full faculty for debate and a decision.

Soon, a proposal was made to introduce a two-week break in the next fall term so that university members could go to Washington before the coming election to lobby Congress for legislation that would cut off all funding for the Vietnam War. This was quickly and overwhelmingly approved. ROTC was next. A student moved for the university to break off all ties with the program. I had spent the previous year negotiating a contract with the army to end academic credit for ROTC courses and professorial rank for its instructors—but to keep the program as a student option.

After very little debate, a vote was called. One Council member after another voted to dispatch the entire program and, to my amazement, Aaron also voted yes. Alexander Hall thundered approval. What had happened? Aaron had no patience with the SDS or disruptions or the radical agenda—but he was also a strong academic purist who viewed the university as an institution completely dedicated to the pursuit of serious knowledge. ROTC lay far outside the bounds of his academic vision.

I was next. Stunned by—and influenced by—Aaron, I also voted yes. Another roar of approval, and fortunately another referral to the faculty for debate and decision. At that point, I began to worry that the Council might approve totally unsupportable measures, and this showed itself to be all too true with the next proposal: to break off all ties with the Department of Defense, refusing all research grants (which were of course not "classified"), regardless of their nature or purpose. This was out of all bounds. DOD funded an enormous amount of scientific work unrelated to war, and a great deal of Princeton's entire research capacity in science and engineering depended on funds from DOD (and the National Science Foundation). The bargain struck—following Vannevar Bush's 1945 *Science, the Endless Frontier* recommendations—was about to seem hazardous indeed. In addition, the government was only too skilled at retaliation: If a university took the step of cutting off funds from *one* of its agencies, it could clearly cease funding from *all* of its agencies.

A long debate followed, with the faculty and administration splitting totally from the CPUC students (most of whom did not of course know the possible full implications of their position). In the end, this proposal was fortunately also recommended to the full faculty for debate.

After several hours, the meeting moved toward closure, but there was enough division among members on several issues that there was a sudden move to have a further session beyond the CPUC's. The new session would be university-wide in nature: All Princeton faculty, students, and senior administrators could participate and cast votes on propositions put forward by the three designated groups—the CPUC, the SDS, and the "conservative" block. So the CPUC proposals—just deliberated—would simply be one alternative among others.

The idea was obviously full of jeopardy. If accepted, it would be the first time that the administration would be giving up power from all its duly constituted decision-making bodies, leaving matters to a huge assembly. The president and trustees could of course veto such an assembly's vote, but that would almost certainly cause a complete detonation— a university paroxysm that could lead to potential violence of a kind we had never experienced and had managed to avoid year after year. After much discussion, the idea of the assembly was accepted. To have turned it down might also have produced a detonation.

Two days later, on May 4, 1970, several thousand people gathered at Jadwin Gymnasium, a modern state-of-the-art cavernous building for varsity athletics, with full indoor track-and-field facilities, several basketball courts, squash courts, and many seating sections: all that (and more) under a single roof shaped like a huge tortoise-shell.

All the bleachers were soon filled, with a crowd greater than any I had ever before seen at Princeton (except at football games). In the middle of the stage, at the podium, was Professor Stuart Hampshire: tall, rather elegant, English, above the fray. A philosopher, he was respected by all who knew him, and was unfailingly fair, disinterested, and commanding in an unobtrusive way. He was chosen to chair the proceedings and he brought, simply by his manner and bearing, a certain order to what otherwise might have been a completely tumultuous affair.

There were three proposals to be discussed and voted upon: first, the conclusions of the CPUC meeting; next, an SDS "strike" proposal, including a decision to terminate all relations with (and funding from) the DOD, to cease all military and other analogous recruiting, and to separate entirely from ROTC. There was to be no further review by the faculty. Finally, the third proposal was to leave all such matters in their current state.

Goheen made an opening statement, saying that he had already asked a group of university presidents to request a meeting with President Nixon, expressing the gravity of the war situation, and asking him to begin termination of the conflict. Goheen was followed by Professor Harold Kuhn, a highly respected faculty member who spoke on behalf of the CPUC. He warned that a strike would split the university irrevocably, tearing the institution apart, and accomplishing nothing of positive value. Other speakers rose, one after another, to espouse one position or another, with tensions now running more high at every move. After several more comments, Hampshire began to draw the meeting toward a close, so that the voting could begin.

People designated as "counters" were stationed at various points throughout the crowd and they stood ready to start.

As it happened, the next few minutes of the gathering were recorded, and a voice on the recording can be heard saying:

> OK now, at this time, all those who support proposal number 1—
> the proposal submitted by the Council of the Princeton University
> Community (CPUC) please raise your hands.
>
> It looks as if this proposal number 1 is receiving very great
> support from those in the balcony and upper balcony sections of the
> gymnasium. Among those in the lower stand, it looks as if I would say
> the support is less than half. ... The vote is now being [counted]. ...

At this point, there is a long pause during the counting, and no tally is reported. Then:

> All those who support proposal number 2 please raise your hands.

> Proposal number 2 is a smaller number than for proposal
> number 1. ... The nonofficial number for number 1 is 2,066 and on
> our last count we had [just] over 3,500 persons voting, so ... this
> resolution (number 1) would receive the support as the most popular
> resolution of the university. ... And I have word that this tally is
> now official. [Cheers].

Then there is a pause, with a great deal of noise becoming louder and
louder:

> There is something going on on the other side of the stadium that
> we are not able to see at the moment. [Sounds growing even more
> loud: "Strike! Strike! Strike. ..."]

During the week following the Jadwin assembly, the university
faculty met every day—with four hundred to five hundred members present—in order to consider and vote on the CPUC resolutions (Jadwin
proposal number 1). As the final recommendations took shape, it was
clear that they would be as good as we could have hoped for. The two-
week November recess was approved. Students were allowed to postpone
their end-of-term papers and exams (or else accept a grade based on work
completed to date). The ROTC issue was referred once again to my office
(and the dean of the College). The faculty established a special committee
that soon defeated the motion to cut off all ties (including research funding)
from the Department of Defense. Then, at the end of the week-long set
of lengthy meetings, an extraordinary step was taken. The faculty voted
that, as a duly constituted university body, they were opposed to the
Vietnam War. Taking *group* political positions (as opposed to individual
positions) was something that the faculty had traditionally—and
strongly—opposed. But feeling ran so high that there was no patience
with anything short of sheer unified opposition. Goheen, however, made
it clear that the *university* (as contrasted to the faculty) would take no
such position.

I had been caught up in nearly all of the events and sometimes felt
we were on the verge of coming apart as an institution. In fact, the initial
CPUC meeting, the Jadwin large assembly, and the faculty debates turned
out to be only a prelude to another incident. Within hours of the last
faculty meeting, nearly nine hundred students—led by the SDS—marched
toward IDA yet once again and moved onto the lawn of the adjacent
Engineering Quadrangle. The protest began peacefully enough, as an

apparently symbolic demonstration. But by the following day, about sixty students had decided to sit-in once again at IDA, blocking entry yet another time so that no one could enter. At first, the employees held back. But as the first day led to the next, it became clear that the situation might soon reach crisis proportions. The head of IDA—an unsteady fellow— was impatient, uncertain, nervous, erratic. He began discussing the idea of calling the National Guard—the worst of all possible actions. Mean- while, most of the nine hundred students had formed a kind of encampment near the IDA property line, while the sit-in continued at IDA itself. Some students on the Engineering School lawn began to throw bottles and cans in the direction of the IDA building. I decided to walk—each night—the property line between the school and IDA, in the hope that more students would not try to cross over. I was also hoping desperately for heavy and steady rain, but the days remained obstinately balmy. Meanwhile, patience was quickly running out at IDA. Its main computer—without any staff— had long ceased to function. Goheen and Bowen continued to talk with IDA's director, but he soon went to court to gain a restraining order. When the official arrived, he came with a group of riot police.

Unexpectedly, the sit-in dissolved. Many students also began to withdraw from the Engineering School field. I waited, unsure if there might be an unexpected turnabout. I stayed for what seemed to be hours. Then I walked home.

By this time, it was nearly mid-May. The academic year was slipping toward a close. The students and protests were slipping toward silence.

AFTERMATH

The demonstrations and disruptions of the 1960s and 1970s were unique in the history of American higher education. Disturbances that had taken place earlier—beginning in the eighteenth and nineteenth centuries (or earlier)—could be described as student mischief or disorder of one kind or another, and although some incidents led to the expulsion of some undergraduates (and the resignation of some presidents), they tended to be expressions of carefree or careless—sometimes distasteful, cruel and raucous—outbreaks of late-adolescent anger, frustration, or high spirits. They were far from *political* actions, and they were not intended to transform the educational institutions themselves. The convulsions of the twentieth-century student "revolution" were therefore new and in fact unique. Our institutions of higher education were of course much larger, complex, and even more diverse than earlier colleges and universities; their protests represented a major tectonic shift in higher education as well as in American culture and politics. And they were, of course, not strictly American, but international in nature. In France and Germany especially, there were a number of issues that motivated students and that led to destructive effects on universities, some of which were more grave than those in America.

The Vietnam War and the Civil Rights Movement provided continuing impetus for student protests on (and sometimes off) campus, but the attack on the universities and their values was a significant distinguishing mark of the 1960s—a mark and precedent that ultimately helped to spark several of the assaults of the 2000s. Without the example of the 1960s, the 2000s would have had no obvious precedents to draw upon—no catalogue of actions to emulate: shouting down speakers, calls for divestment, protests against sexual harassment, curricular changes and innovations, African American student protests, and outright challenges to institutional authority. Indeed, once the barrier was broken, as it were— once protests became acceptable and even common, a precedent was set that was effectively part of university life for the duration. Protests might lessen or intensify in the future, but they were unlikely to disappear altogether. The genie was out of the bottle.

Indeed, the student of earlier days—and certainly the undergraduate of 1945–65—had in large measure been transformed. He or she was no longer the studious (and certainly not the conformist) rule-abiding person of earlier eras. Instead, the potential to rebel had been injected, so to speak, into the body politic of those who now came to college, and the possibility of "protest" would never again be altogether out of sight or mind. Not all students would of course be affected, and far from all possible protests would take place. But a new breed of undergraduate had been born and was waiting to demonstrate its rebellious capacity in the years ahead.

Interestingly, most students (even at Berkeley) in the 1960s were actually satisfied with their formal education, but a sufficient number of others were in favor of fundamental change. One SDS leader—not an extremist—wrote in a 1966 article that[27]

> The university's curricular and extracurricular decisions should be
> up to students and faculty alone. ... New political institutions are

needed to localize and distribute as much power as possible; ... [Stirrings] of this new politics [are being revealed] in university reform movements and teach-ins and a scattering of Free Universities ... where student-faculty community emerges.[28]

Meanwhile, the very extreme group called *SLATE* was described by one analyst as

demanding that grades in undergraduate courses and discipline in student dormitories be abolished and that there be a permanent student voice which is effective (that is, independent) in running university affairs.[29]

Slightly later, after the Harvard "bust," the highly respected and senior (émigré) faculty member, Alexander Gerschenkron, confronted President Nathan Pusey. Gerschenkron was against the student takeover of University Hall, which he viewed as a destructive action that deeply threatened the university and its central values:

I know quite well that there are things that are horribly wrong with the United States, but I also know that there are many things that are wonderfully right with the United States. Amongst those things are the great universities, and among them is Harvard. There is no counterpart to it anywhere in the world. And to try to destroy, to disrupt, to attack this University is criminal.[30]

Gerschenkron knew the students were assaulting, not simply the war and its auxiliaries, but the university itself: to "destroy, disrupt, to attack" were what he was persuaded the students had done and it was "criminal."

Finally, one of the most thorough analysts of what was happening in our universities (particularly in California) was Henry May, professor of history at Berkeley. His long (approximately 75 pages) essay, with extensive data, concluded that "militant" students wanted to be granted more "rights" as "citizens" of the university, possessing—therefore—the ability to have an effect on the running of institutional affairs:

[Militants] not only feel the administration, on its own, will not give sufficient consideration to their rights and needs in formulating policy, but that under the present structure they have little influence on that policy.[31]

Indeed, as May says elsewhere,

> the new student of the 1960s, [is] a political animal, who will not
> sit back and be treated as a harmless "post-adolescent." Lest this
> introduce a note of panic in my report, I hasten to add that my
> observations throughout this crisis have been that the extremists are
> very few, and that all the students want is the citizenship that honest
> deliberation concedes is their due.[32]

In fact, this form of "citizenship"—limited but genuine—was afforded
to students at, for example, Princeton, where "restructuring" (and other
vehicles) opened up participatory rights and duties to students well beyond
the opportunities that previously existed. These steps were progressive
and "liberal," in keeping with the university community's interests, and
were well within the reach of any college or university to adopt. They
did not satisfy the SDS, PL (Progressive Labor), or other radical groups,
but they won the overwhelming approval of the university as a whole.

Nevertheless, higher education suffered a great deal of breakage,
and tensions remained astonishingly high for long periods of time, at
significant human and institutional cost. But there was no single devastating incident at Princeton—no "bust" or serious injuries—resembling those
elsewhere.

Perhaps Princeton students were intrinsically more moderate than
those at many institutions, although fire-bombing the Princeton ROTC
building, taking over the IDA building, and an undergraduate attempt to
burn Nassau Hall actually took place—along with takeovers of Nassau
Hall and other actions. I myself am inclined to think that Goheen's willingness—with the active support of Bowen and many respected faculty
members—to institute participatory university changes and to resist calling
the police in the face of provocations—made a crucial difference.

Whatever the reasons may be, the strain and constant investment of
time and energy affected the fabric of the university in a way that raised
the question of how much longer the qualities of Princeton—or any
university community—could be sustained over the long run. How long
would faculty continue to invest so much energy and time in "governance"?
At a moment when the professoriate was becoming more mobile, how
long would faculty remain residential, spending their days and nights in
Princeton (rather than time in nearby New York)? In a talk that he gave
in the spring of 1977, Professor Lawrence Stone—chair of the history

department and a stalwart through the 1967–70 period—ended his address in the following way:

> As for the future, I see [several] ... problems—or questions—facing [Princeton]:
>
> • Will it be possible to maintain indefinitely this combination of qualities: to be as good as, say, Swarthmore at the intellectual and moral education of undergraduates; and at the same time to be as good as, say, Harvard at training researchers and pursuing pure research for the advancement of knowledge?
> • While doing all this, can we also continue to run the university as a participatory democracy—of course, a guided democracy—which demands such a massive infusion of faculty time and energy in university committee work?
> • Is it possible indefinitely to find the ideal faculty members to [help] run such an institution? Do they even exist in the real, fallible, human world? We expect them to be at once inspiring undergraduate lecturers, learned graduate student teachers, creative original researchers, and wise and hard-headed committee members. Will it be possible to sustain such high demands? I have my doubts. ...
> • Can we continue to remain as luxuriously small as we are? This smallness is absolutely essential to the social integration of the academic community, and any further major increase in numbers would destroy Princeton's intimacy, its sense of belonging to an extended family rather than an academic factory. The massive growth of the university bureaucracy in recent years may have been inevitable but it already threatens that sense of cohesion.
> • Can we continue to preserve the principle of academic freedom against the external political pressures which are bound to arise again, as they do every 20 years or so? How will the trustees and administration behave the next time around?
> • How are we to find the money to pay for all this: the lavish research and residential facilities, the expensive first-class faculty, the abnormally high [or low?] faculty–student ratio (which is essential for close student contact), the generous sabbatical leave policy (equally essential if we are to pursue excellence in research), and the large scholarship and student aid program?
>
> I don't know the answer to any of these questions. As a historian, I can only explain to you how we have arrived where we are. As an individual, I will say that I earnestly hope without excessive opti-

mism—that the answer to all these questions is yes, we can, and we will.

MOMENTS OF REPOSE

After May 1970, a sudden calm descended on most campuses when the autumn term of the new academic year began. At Princeton, it was as if the fierce expenditure of energy during the previous spring, with all its intensity and zeal, had simply spent itself.

The Vietnam War was far from over. There was monumental work still to be done in race relations. Congress and President Nixon remained intact (although Nixon had been badly shaken by the consequences of his Cambodia venture). Nevertheless, the student revolution had completely dematerialized. It was as if morning—after a whirlwind and blizzard—had magisterially descended with welcome solicitude and a feeling of quiet repose. I wondered how, in the calm of such a season, a dean of Students was expected to spend his surviving hours and days with no surprising protests to bemuse him.

Of course there was still much to do. Coeducation was beginning, and the first women students were now arriving. A final army ROTC contract had to be renegotiated. But it was nonetheless impossible not to wonder why—and how—all the strife had vanished so swiftly, and what the experience of the last years had actually signified. I walked the campus. Nothing had changed except the fact that all the students seemed to be wandering in a relaxed way to classes or the library or Nassau Street, and there was no reason to believe that their sauntering would cease very soon.

Later, I discovered that in addition to the spring's spent forcefulness, the national SDS had been fragmenting, and serious splits had emerged at their 1970 summer conference. Violence had been growing with the recent emergence of the Weathermen. The strength of other groups (such as the Progressive Labor Party) was also making itself felt. More and more, the different radical tribes were warring with one another, and some became (in their appetite for violence) increasingly detached from reality. "By conservative estimate, between September 1968 and May 1970 there were two hundred and fifty major bombings. ... The prime targets were ROTC buildings, draft boards, induction centers, and other federal offices."

There was, however, no strategy behind all the sound and fury. There was only a growing mania that found in violence and its accompanying rhetoric a form of release that was wildly hyperbolic and destructive in deed as well as word. Moreover, when the government began (as at Kent State University) to use violence in return, students realized they too were subject to mortality. There was now a dangerous opposition growing, and Governor Ronald Reagan (of California) declared—in effect—that if there were going to be a blood bath, it might as well come sooner rather than later, and he would take charge of it.

So the SDS imploded, and the different factions catastrophically warred with one another while the government—including the FBI— became more belligerently adversarial. The center of the "movement" ceased to hold, the campuses collapsed in exhaustion, the students began to go their prerevolutionary or postrevolutionary ways; the backlash began in earnest.

Earlier I suggested some of the cultural as well as political reasons that may have led to the radical turn of the sixties. There was, moreover, another distinguishing characteristic of the era: It romanticized Third-World heroes. These were the years of Che Guevara—daring, handsome Argentinian with his beret and military dress; plus Cuba's Castro, leading the takeover of an island just off our Floridian coast; Mao with his misguided but sensational anti-intellectual move to the agrarian fields; Ho Chi Minh in Vietnam, with the American SDS chant of "Ho-Ho-Ho Chi Minh." In other words, if Jack Kennedy and Camelot had earlier inspired many liberal, idealistic, reformist youth, there were now many "heroes" who exemplified actual revolutions that seemed imitable to many radical youth. As Fritz Stern wrote (in his *American Scholar* article):

> [The] cult of the third world provided heroic alternatives to Western democracy: Ho Chi Minh, Mao, Che Guevara. These heroes embodied the ideas Gurus like Herbert Marcuse were preaching: that the West was (once again) doomed, that salvation had to come from the undeveloped and as yet uncorrupted world of non-whites. This sudden cult of the poor and wretched led to practical ambiguities. Compassion for the blacks in America inspired the ideological exploitation of them—much to the anger of black students who objected to being used by white radicals.[33]

When Princeton was pressed by African American students to provide them with an all-Black social space, Carl Fields (and others of us) argued against the idea. The alternative: a "Third World Center"—symbol of the entire world's oppressed—which was in fact the adopted name and concept. As Stern wrote:

> Western society has witnessed periodic waves of disgust with bour-
> geois culture, the strongest always coming in times of affluence, with
> the "*Société de consummation,*" with what they still call materialism,
> careerism, conformity, and the hundred variations of suburban life,
> with two cars and no meaning, and with moral hypocrisy as an
> additional burden. As an American student leader, a native of the
> rich New York suburb of Scarsdale, exclaimed at a meeting in Paris,
> "No one who has not lived in Scarsdale knows how bad life can
> be." ... [The young] see all those traditional bourgeois values as both
> symptoms and instruments of repression.[34]

If the outcry against the Scarsdale syndrome was in one sense comedic, it could nevertheless command some sympathy. Neither 1950s conformism nor 1960s consumerism seemed to offer much to some young people in search of a cause that was socially or politically or personally inspiring. The real difficulty, however, was that their own proposed solutions were too often ill-conceived; their targets often misplaced or trivial; and their tactics self-defeating. Frequently, neither their parents, elders, or teachers took the time to warn or educate them. After all, there had been student revolutions before—and those of the Weimar era, or Hitler's youth move-ment, or the Leninist–Stalin young Communists—had come to calamitous ends. Even reading Flaubert's *L'Éducation sentimentale* might have helped!

There were indeed some serious conditions that needed remedies—including some in our multiversities and elsewhere—but they were obvi-ously approached, not in a reformist spirit but in ways that, whatever temporary victory they appeared to bring, came ultimately to naught. After the rough take-over of Harvard's University Hall in 1970, with its subsequent "bust," faculty and student responses were inevitably mixed. But when one "moderate" faculty member pleaded to the learned and somewhat old-fashioned stubborn Irish Professor John Kelleher to "Think of it as one of your own children who had been beaten like that" by the police, Kelleher considered replying "if it was one of my children, I could hardly wait to get him home so that I could give him a rousing kick where it wouldn't blind him."[35] It may have been rather late in the game for childhood kicks, but Kelleher no doubt felt that the parents and elders were nearly as delinquent as the adolescents.

When one tries to assess the radical movement of the sixties, it is more than difficult to generalize, given the variety of actions that took place, over several years, on a multitude of campuses across an entire nation. But there is no question that the Port Huron agenda failed to materialize. In spite of persistent efforts, there was no situation, at a major college or university where the SDS and the faculty wrested control from the administration in order to reinvent the curriculum, redirect the institution, and use it as a staging ground for a successful wider rebellion against society's "loci of power." Some universities were incapacitated for a time, but then began to recover. Most weathered the storm, creating liberal reforms but nothing approaching revolutionary change. Many students had longed for a new kind of world, a new camaraderie, a new society—but discovered, as Fritz Stern said, that they found themselves "on committees instead. Participatory boredom was the result."

It is true that few if any of the actual reforms would have come about if it had not been for student pressure, and clearly the students had a significant impact on the conduct of the Vietnam War. But the spectacle of students attacking their colleges and universities—or burning American flags—also produced a great deal of shock and resentment in society, and that reaction led in time to repression, not support. In addition, irrespective of the students, the general public became increasingly disenchanted with the war as it continued, year after year, without clear military gains. As more bodies of the dead were flown home, and as more people considered the prospect of having young men drafted to fight a remote and apparently meaningless war, adult opposition grew steadily. Then the surprise and shock of the potent North Vietnam Tet Offensive unmasked much of the entire escapade, when northern troops suddenly invaded the south with sensational force. The media also went on the offensive and, later, President Johnson began quietly to seek ways to stop the conflict. In other words, many forces against the war were in play, and while the students had a very potent effect, the war itself was also proving to bring about its own demise.

If there were some positive developments that came from the student movement, there were also considerable costs. Fritz Stern mentioned the

> human cost to *all* members of the university. Intellectual life needs a sense of relaxed order. This is true to giving or attending a class, for writing or reading a book. ... [The] life of a disrupted campus is hard and ugly for almost every member of the community. ... I doubt that on balance a single university has been improved through disruption.

Stern realized that many people considered the idealism of the young students, and their successes, sufficient to exonerate or even glorify their acts:

> Of course the young are idealistic: they have no mercenary motives and they are almost never *consciously* concerned with self-serving ends. Of course, the young write on their banners our own ideals of justice, equality and peace, and, of course they impart new energy to the quest for these ideals.

Stern saw all this, but with his historian's eye, and with the vision of a humanist he also saw that the young were prone to give their ideals

> A narrow moralistic definition. Ideals often inspire self-righteousness and the present activists ... excel in self-righteousness. ... But the heaven-strong qualities of idealists, of fanatics—have they not time and again led to the creation of a new hell on earth?

Most costly of all, however, was the inevitable backlash against universities that the student revolt—and the university turmoil—prompted. The move to the political right (initially in California) was already apparent by the late sixties. It continued into the 1970s, eventually resulting in the "culture wars" of the 1970s, 1980s, and beyond. Once the brightness fell from the air, all that seemed less than luminous in our colleges and universities was suddenly ready for the next day's front-page newsprint. As a result of the revolution, adverse stories began to appear: about the bias of the "liberal faculty," the demolition of the "great books" canon, sexual harassment, student (all-male) private "clubs"—and so on. Scandal became newsworthy; the extraordinary research and teaching capacities of our colleges and universities—clearly among the very greatest in the world—no longer stirred interest, quite apart from admiration. Fritz Stern wrote that the "much-discussed backlash has already become a dismal reality." And so it has remained—in our politics, among ordinary "none-lite" citizens, and among the media.

So, yes, in the autumn of 1970, it was possible for a moment to view the campus quietude from an angle of unaccustomed repose. But the serenity was short-lived, even if the insurgency of the sixties had come to a close.

Chapter 4

Student Learning and the Culture Wars

AIMLESS COMMISSION

In 1971, a year after the return of campus calm, Bob Goheen announced that he would resign in 1972. It was not unexpected, and it seemed obvious to most of us that Bill Bowen should succeed him. Although the search took an inordinate amount of time, it finally concluded in its predestined way: Bill was to replace Bob, and all of us were relieved as well as revivified. Princeton would continue to move forward.

Not long after the announcement, Bill called to ask whether I would be willing to become dean of the College. After many talks with Angelica (and others), I said yes. I had come to value and enjoy working with the group of people committed to Princeton. I also learned that Sheldon Hackney—a good friend—would become provost, and Aaron would be dean of the Faculty. These two, plus Bill, would be the best possible triumvirate I could hope to join. Nevertheless, it was a decisive step to take. I had done little but literature from the early to mid-1950s until 1968. To give up my scholarship in the field, with a feeling of likely finality, was more than difficult, although I felt that this new deanship could be inventive and stimulating, as well as greatly energized by the presence of invigorating close companions.

Princeton's dean of the College is responsible for overseeing under-graduate academic matters—primarily the curriculum and related concerns (such as student advising and academic standing). It was the curriculum that intrigued me, especially at a time when new courses and programs, and new undergraduate academic interests, were just beginning to emerge. As it turned out, however, the early 1970s were critical from a very different point of view. They represented the beginning of what came to be called *stagflation*: economic disconcertion for more than a decade, when the stock market was often negative in its returns, and interest rates climbed steadily until they reached double digits. Scarcely any combination could have been more deadly for an institution dependent considerably on its endowment and Annual Giving: no stock market earnings—indeed, frequent minus earnings—plus higher and higher costs for everything. This combination meant either constant program reductions (or "cuts") or increasing deficits, or higher tuition and fees—or, more likely, all three combined.

Stagflation inevitably affected what we were able to do (or not do) institutionally. It also began to affect the choice of student "majors" (and professions) dramatically. It affected—in time—the range of subjects taught by many excellent small liberal arts colleges that were not among the well-known or well-endowed institutions in the nation. Indeed, it eventually drove many of them out of business, a process that is discussed more fully in a later chapter. From about 1972 to 1983, the entire economy of American higher education was impaired and some of the resulting academic and intellectual changes turned out to be long-standing.

In short, I was once again surprised by the agenda of the new job I had taken. I had expected some serenity and even metaphorical spring showers with buds and blossoms to follow. Instead, despite interesting and even stirring moments, there were long periods of drought with desert sands and unaccommodating dunes.

Before contending with stagflation (which took some time to make its full weight felt), there were other consequential issues. First, the visible Commission on the Future of the College, chaired by Marvin Bressler, was already underway, but its precise direction and agenda were as yet unknown. Bob Goheen had set the chariot in motion, but without general directions or even the hint of a road map. What was it to do?

Unlike some similar ventures at other institutions, there was (for instance) no Princeton "core curriculum" to be revived and renovated.

Nor were there important academic elements (such as required foreign language study) that had been allowed to fall into disuse. With nothing obvious to repair or restore, and nothing irresistibly novel—and major—to create, the Commission began to drift, and the ordinarily voluble Marvin fell silent and seemed uncharacteristically bereft. Paul Benacerraf (later, Princeton's provost) volunteered to help, but even Paul—brilliant, interested, knowledgeable—came up empty-handed.

The only substantial idea that was suggested—by a small group of fervent faculty—was that Princeton should seize the moment to introduce a "core curriculum" of required courses of great books, on a model similar to Columbia or Harvard or Chicago. But apart from this miniscule band of humanists, there were no detectable warriors invested in the concept. Anyone who has ever tried to make a major curricular change, affecting the equilibrium of an entire collegiate system, knows that it requires at least two or three years of hard labor, rather like moving a large lumber yard several miles by hand. The laborers would be listless, their brawn less than Lilliputian, and their boredom Brobdignagian. Anyone who is doubtful should read one or more accounts of different university efforts to wrestle with and revise their established "core curricula."

But perhaps Princeton was simply stuffy, self-satisfied, complacent, or just plain lazy? I think not. I myself considered the age of instituting genuine "core" curricula to have passed. Indeed, everything was moving in precisely the opposite direction: One clearly sensed the trend toward broad cultural and international studies, away from Western "hegemony," and while this move was partly modish it was not essentially so. In addition, Princeton already invested—through its preceptorial system, its faculty-guided junior and senior "independent work," its mandatory (for all students) senior theses—more resources in undergraduate teaching than any other major university. To add additional required full core courses, and more than a hundred small-group faculty-led classes, would have meant a huge additional financial investment, and another set of requirements for undergraduates who were already obliged (fortunately!) to undergo a very demanding course of study. All of this would have to be done in the face of virtually intractable faculty politics: which departments would benefit from additional student enrollments because they participated in a required core curriculum, and which would be left out? Not a negligible matter in the inevitable drive for more student enrollments and more faculty positions.

So the "core" concept ultimately deliquesced, and the Commission came up with a scattering of sensible but mainly imperceptible propositions to recommend to the faculty before sliding swiftly into dim obscurity.

WHERE HAVE ALL THE STUDENTS GONE?

My new office—like my previous one—was in West College. I could still see Nassau Hall from my main window. I also felt a sense of the past in a different way: One of my well-known predecessors as dean had been Christian Gauss, the mentor and friend of Edmund Wilson and F. Scott Fitzgerald during the early years of the twentieth century.

My new position was vastly different from my previous one. Now that the Vietnam War was essentially behind us, I shifted from the unpredictability of student group disruptions to the comparative calm of a post in which I chaired the Faculty Committee on the Course of Study. The committee reviewed all new curricular proposals of any consequence, and if approved, I would then recommend them to the full faculty at its monthly meeting.

Princeton's control of the curriculum was unusual. All potential major changes and certainly new programs came before my faculty group for careful review. These had been carefully vetted by their departments before arriving at West College, so virtually everything threaded through the eye of our needle. As it turned out, several significant developments were already taking place, and they had a consequential impact on student life and learning.

First, there was a shift in science, from the era of relativity to the dominion of DNA. This had a strong effect on the pattern of student academic choices. It was increasingly apparent that—after Crick and Watson discovered the structure of DNA—biology and related fields of study would begin to emerge as a major force. For example, if one combined the number of Princeton undergraduates who "majored" in biology, biochemistry, and chemistry, there were a total of sixty-five new students in 1972—and 110 just a few years later. In addition, psychology jumped from twenty-seven students to seventy-one. These swift steep rises could not possibly continue indefinitely, but they showed the way toward a new and very different future.

Other changes were no less striking, particularly in some of the social sciences as well as applied sciences. In the class of 1972, only sixty students elected to major in economics; in the following year, eighty-four; and the next three years alternated between 110 and 123. There were different reasons for this rapid growth, but it was the national economy of the 1970s that attracted an increasing number of undergraduates to subjects which seemed to offer prospects for excellent future jobs and careers. Economics was self-evidently one such subject. Engineering began to show a similar jump for similar reasons. If we combine the number of new majors in chemical engineering, aerospace engineering, and electrical engineering in 1972, they totaled fifty; in 1976, they accounted for ninety. Engineering was a field in which job demand was beginning to be strong, and students quickly noticed what was happening. The era of what would eventually be called *careerism* had begun, and this development proved to be profound in terms of its implications, not only for the humanities but also for the very concept of a broad liberal arts education. Indeed, if we combined the statistics for the fields just mentioned, there was a total of 202 students majoring in them in 1972, and 386 four years later. Since there were then only about 1,200 students per class at Princeton, this swing represented an enormous shift.

Meanwhile, we can trace an opposing change in literature, history, art, music, and most European foreign languages and literature. One statistic, frequently cited, concerns the goals that students regarded as significant when they began college. In 1968 slightly more than 80 percent of freshmen indicated that the search for a meaningful philosophy of life was their primary purpose; by 1972, that number was just over 60 percent; and by 1986, it had fallen to about 40 percent. Meanwhile, the desire to be (ultimately) well-off financially rose from 40 percent in 1968, to 60 percent in 1976, to 78 percent in 1987.[1] These data correlate (very roughly) with the reduction of enrollments in the humanities during the same years (although there was a modest increase in the 1980s).

The extent of the decline of the humanities has been debated but there is simply no question that the number of "majors" in English (and modern European languages and literature) steadily fell, whereas Professor Anthony Grafton reported (*Daedalus*, spring 2006) that "Thirty years ago, some 5 percent of all undergraduates majored in history. Nowadays, around 2 percent do so." Moreover, if we examine the top five "majors" at various leading universities, focusing on the period 1965–2014, we find patterns such as the following one—which traces the history at one major institution:

1965
History
Political science
English
Psychology
Economics

1985
Economics
Human biology
Biological sciences
Electrical engineering
English

2014
Multidisciplinary studies
Computer science
Economics and politics
Engineering
Physical sciences

At another leading university in 2014:

Economics
Political science
Computer science
Public policy
Evolutionary biology

Recently, the leading majors in all higher education were: business (slightly over 20 percent); health care and related fields (9 percent); economics, political science, psychology, and other social science disciplines (8 percent). Each of the many remaining majors represents a small percentage of the whole, and the humanities were toward the bottom of the list. At Harvard, during a recent academic year, the course with the largest undergraduate enrollment was in computer science. Slightly more than twenty students (out of more than 1,600) did the honors course in English and American literature.

If we look nationally, we find that in 1966, 20.7 percent of all undergraduate degrees were in the humanities; 15.5 percent in the social sciences; and 11.6 percent in the natural sciences, for a total of 47.8 percent in the liberal arts and sciences (with the rest in "professional" studies, such as communications, business, nursing, education, health sciences, etc.). Two decades later, the comparable figures were: the humanities, 10.2 percent (-10.5 percent); the social sciences, 12.8 percent (+1.2 percent); the natural sciences, 7.8 percent (-3.8 percent). BA degrees in all the liberal arts and sciences had diminished to a total of 30.8 percent (from 47.8 percent in 1966), with a consonant steep rise of almost 20 percent in professional degrees. In effect, the humanities—and the liberal arts and sciences—were sharing the same fate of being under serious continuous siege.

Was this situation likely to change? No—it has since continued in the same direction. Indeed, several public officials have recently been more than candid about their views. One could quote any number of individuals on the subject, but a recent statement by the governor of Kentucky indicated that he wants his state's educational institutions to offer "what people want"—especially electrical engineering. "All the people in the world that want to study French literature can do so," he said, "they are just not going to be subsidized by the taxpayer." Such statements have become even more common. A recent *New York Times* article, for example, indicated Senator Marco Rubio has called for more welders and fewer philosophers. Former Governor Rick Scott of Florida has questioned the value of anthropologists. And Governor Patrick McCrory of North Carolina has said that higher-education funding should not be "based on butts in the seats, but on how many of those butts can get jobs." These statements have all come from important current or recent public office-holders, and the sentiments reflect the views of a great many other people (including parents and students) when they consider which subjects are likely to be "cost-effective" when attending college.

Given the state of the humanities, it is tempting to try to appraise them once again, and to say why they seem to be so vital to the meaning of a liberal arts education. Given my own interest in literature and the arts, the subject of the humanities is obviously of considerable personal importance to me. In discussing this subject, however, we should recognize that the humanities were never chosen as a distinct and unique set of carefully defined disciplines. Instead, the very term *humanities* came into common usage very late—as recently as the first few decades of the twentieth century, when the social sciences gradually set themselves apart and gave definition to their own forms of inquiry. As a result, those subjects that we ordinarily identify as "humanistic" are really quite diverse. They normally include the study of languages and literature, the history of art and architecture, music, philosophy, religion, and sometimes history (often defined as a social science).

Unlike the sciences (and somewhat differently the social sciences), the humanities are not in search of general propositions that can be finally proven correct—or else incorrect. When new scientific discoveries are made, they normally displace earlier theories that are no longer thought to be valid. In this sense, the sciences are "progressive." Once the real structure of DNA was described, earlier models were simply discarded. The social sciences are more complex, and some of them resemble aspects of the humanities. But they too aspire to be "sciences" that search for ideas in subjects, such as economics, sociology, anthropology, psychology, or politics, intended to advance knowledge in a way that might be proven. Scholars offer new facts and theories about society and social behavior in order to modify or disprove rival conceptions. If the results are rarely if ever definitive, the fundamental goal nevertheless remains.

The humanities are radically different. They often focus on created individual works (or related groups of works—such as symphonies, poems, paintings, and novels—or historical, philosophical, and religious texts that have an intrinsic value of their own. The student can turn again and again to these, seeking to find illumination on each occasion. Shakespeare is a greater dramatist than Marlowe or Ben Jonson, but we still continue to read all three writers for their insights, just as we read much earlier works by Sophocles, Plato, and Thucydides. There is no implacable "progression," although there are obviously "advances" in *scholarship* and *criticism* that alter our conceptions of different texts and fields of knowledge.

Given their nature, what should we expect from the humanities? There are several things, including the capacity—as many have suggested—to help students think "critically." However, the difficulty of stressing this particular characteristic is that the humanities have no monopoly on it. It can be acquired by the careful study of many other subjects such as politics or psychology or evolutionary biology. As a result, I would prefer to focus on different characteristics: in particular, the fact that the humanities include those subjects in which we are most likely to confront significant ideas about—and impressions of—the nature of human experience and existence. Fields, such as history, art, literature, philosophy, and religion, lead us more directly than most subjects to questions concerning mankind's values, actions, and meaning. These subjects virtually insist—if we are at all alert—that we consider different ways of shaping one's existence, different selves that one might (or might not) become, different paths one might follow in life. They cause us to reflect on the lives of other people, or on lives that are dramatized imaginatively in literature or art or in the narratives of religious and philosophical texts. In sum, they help us to envision what kind of a life we might shape for ourselves—what kind of goals, satisfactions, effects, purposes we might choose to pursue.

Kwame Anthony Appiah framed this matter in the following way—in a lecture called "Particularizing the Humanities" (2011):

> But who is going to tell you what satisfactions are worth having? Which effects worth aiming for? What is worth wanting? Who will help you decide whether John Stuart Mill was right to say "It is better to be a human being dissatisfied than a pig satisfied; better to be Socrates dissatisfied than a fool satisfied"? Indeed, who will let you know this question is worth asking?

Appiah distinguished between questions that the sciences might ask, or the social sciences, and asked what the humanities might lead us to consider:

> The answer, I think, is evident. These are the questions you learn to face, learn to live with, learn, in the end, provisionally at least, to answer, with the help of literature and the arts, critically appreciated, through the study of philosophy, and history and cultural anthropology. ... The humanities are [different] ... in providing us with a kind of guidance in the making of our lives.

Part of the reason why the humanities possess this power is that they often bring us closer to the texture and actual flux of human experience than either the sciences or social sciences. They are often palpable, tangible, audible, and dramatic in their ability to capture sensations, impressions, events, characters, and ideas in vivid and compelling ways. When we are reading *Anna Karenina*, or Thucydides, or watching *King Lear*, or listening to Beethoven's late quartets, we know we are about as close to the vital signs of existence as any representation will ever take us. And to this list, we can easily add the work of Yeats, Picasso, T.S. Eliot, Virginia Woolf, Mahler, W. E. B. du Bois, Matisse, Toni Morrison, Balanchine, and many others.

Helen Vendler, the fine teacher and critic of poetry, made a similar point in a Harvard College pamphlet written in 2004:

> I would care most about the development of our students' emotional perceptions and capacity for empathy. This aim is best attained through the study and practice of the arts. I'm not envisaging courses called "The Poor in Literature" or "Sexism in Painting." The arts are not instrumental to concepts, and should not be made so. They exist on their own plane, ... and the study of the arts (if correctly done) presumes a real alerting to the powers of the senses—to feel, to touch, to look, to name—actions terribly neglected when the mind alone is being trained.

Of course, not all the humanities work in a similar way. Not everything is dramatized imaginatively or presented vividly. In philosophy and theology, the approach to fundamental problems is often propositional—through argument and attempted proof, and through the creation of systems that deal with everything from epistemology to ontology, to ethics and moral imperatives, to distributive justice, to faith and belief and their implications for action. Although the methodology is often very different, however, the quest is often similar to that of other humanistic subjects: What kind of "beings" or creatures are we? What do we know, and how do we know it? What values are to be cherished and why? What is our conception of a just society—or a valuable or good life?

In a residential university or college committed to the liberal arts and sciences, it is also the case that one hopes a great deal of "humane" learning will come not only from academic study but from the daily association of undergraduates with fellow students, faculty, and staff. That is perhaps the most important motive for a *residential* institution: to offer its participants the opportunity to learn as much as possible from others who may have similar or dissimilar backgrounds, interests, assumptions, and aspirations. To read about "others" in books is invaluable, but it is not enough. One must meet them and come to know them. John Stuart Mill made precisely this point long ago—in *On Liberty*—when he emphasized that, in order to fully understand the ideas of individuals with whom one may disagree, it is essential

> To hear [the ideas] from persons who actually believe them; who defend them in earnest, and do their very utmost for them, [one] must know them in their most plausible and persuasive form … [and] feel the whole force of [their] difficulty.

Several years later, Harvard's President Eliot insisted that, in a university, there is a continual

> ferment and agitation on all questions of public interest. This collision of views … promotes thought on great themes, … [and] cultivates forbearance and mutual respect.

Eliot was the first Harvard president to recruit "nontraditional" students to the college—and thereby heightened the potential for "ferment" and "agitation," not simply "forbearance" and "mutual respect." When he took office in 1869, the total of all Jewish and Catholic undergraduates at Harvard represented just 1 percent, and there was just one African American student. By the time Eliot retired, Jewish, Catholic, and African American students made up 17 percent of the student body. W.E.B. du Bois and Alain Locke had attended: du Bois was elected a Class Orator at graduation (and later earned a PhD); Locke was the very first African American Rhodes Scholar. Some measure of diversity had indeed arrived.

Finally, in 1951, President James Conant—having witnessed so much of the War—insisted that

> Tolerance, honesty, intellectual integrity, courage, friendliness, are virtues not to be learned out of a printed volume but from the book of experience, and the content of this book for a youth is largely determined by the mode of his association with contemporaries. So, too, are those attitudes so essential for the survival of a modern democracy.

The value of face-to-face education, so to speak, was also noted by Andrew Delbanco in his admirable book, *College: What It Was, Is, and Should Be.* Delbanco is altogether helpful in defining the central purposes of a liberal arts education, and he also makes clear the value of what might be called *residential* learning among students. For example, he quoted, approvingly, Samuel Eliot Morrison's history of Harvard:

> Book learning alone might be got by lectures and reading; but it was only by studying and disputing, eating and drinking, playing and praying as members of the same collegiate community, in close and constant communication with each other and with their tutors, that the priceless gift of character could be imparted to young men.[2]

It is significant that Eliot and Conant stress, not only the importance of a residential setting in stimulating humane learning during one's college years, but also as a preparation for living in a "free" society—a "modern democracy"—where "questions of public interest" are disputed. In other words, undergraduate education can be viewed as a gateway to active citizenship and leadership in later life.

Whether campus life is actually capable of helping students achieve such goals is an open question, particularly during a time, such as the current moment in history, when there is so much divisiveness in our own nation as well as in the world at large—a subject to which I will return later in this volume.

There is a central question concerning the liberal arts and sciences (not only the humanities) that has become increasingly important during the last several decades. It concerns the extent to which a coherent and adequate education in the liberal arts and sciences is possible today. Indeed, such doubts began to be expressed more than a century ago. Quite apart from his unsatisfying experience at Harvard College, Henry Adams later attempted to understand Darwinism and its manifold implications, as well as the powerful new forms of energy—industrial and otherwise— that suddenly seemed to pervade his world. He believed that history had sustained a certain pattern of continuity since at least 1500, but in 1900 "the continuity snapped." As a result

> The child born in 1900 would ... be born into a new world which would not be a unity but a multiple. Adams tried to imagine it, and an education that would fit it. He found himself in a land where no one had ever penetrated before.

Adams felt unable to imagine an education that would "fit" the multiplicity of the new universe that had come into being. Shortly afterward, President Eliot took note of this increasing "multiplicity" as did President Lowell after him. It was Conant, however, who further articulated its possible implications for higher education. He wrote (in 1936) to the governing boards:

> It seems to me a hopeless task to provide a complete and finished liberal education suitable to this century by four years of college work. The only worthwhile liberal education today is one which is a continuing process going on throughout life. It is from this premise, I suggest, that the question of "knowledge of wide surface and little depth" must be judged. I should reject all informational tests applied to recent graduates as indicative of the effectiveness of our general education. Whether a liberal education has been a success or a failure should be measured by the student's breadth of vision fifteen or twenty years after graduation. Has the smattering acquired in college worn thinner with each succeeding year? If so, it has been of little value. Or has it provided a basis for continued intellectual and spiritual growth? In this case it has been the most significant part of the college training.

For Conant, the swift expansion—and specialized nature—of knowledge seemed to make it essentially impossible for an undergraduate to be educated broadly in the liberal arts and sciences: one would have to rely on life-long learning to try to stay abreast. In an effort to help mitigate this situation (and to guard against post-World War II problems), Conant introduced general education requirements into Harvard's curriculum, but this hardly displaced his conviction that the immense sphere of human knowledge was now far too vast for any individual to encompass it—in even the most modest way—during one's college years. Perhaps a lifetime might help one to learn about the most significant matters. Perhaps not.

In the end, we must today make the best of a hard bargain, doing all we can to offer students an "adequate" education. But in an era when faculty and students in a single department often have difficulty understanding part of the work of their nearby colleagues, we cannot pretend that undergraduates can hope to encompass more than the smallest fragment of a fragment of the consequential knowledge that now exists. And programs that are intended to teach, not "subject matter" but distinct methodologies, are in the end not much more satisfactory. There is obviously no *single* methodology to be taught in the biological sciences, or in the interpretation of literature, or in economics or psychology—to name just a few. The main hope (as Conant suggested) is that students will absorb as much as they can in college and, most of all, "learn how to learn," inspired by teachers, friends, mentors, or their own innate curiosity, so that they can carry forward the process throughout their lives. Even that will fall far short of what we believe to be adequate, but it will at least enable one to reach what otherwise would not have been at all possible.

Finally, we will be compelled to recognize that even the most complete education is only a limited defense against all that it must contend with. It may mainly offer what Robert Frost once called "momentary stays against confusion." Even a glance at history, and perhaps especially at the current state of world affairs, is more than enough testimony to the fact that education—in a "post-truth" universe—is not sufficient to stem the continual tide of ignorance and the plain distortion of "facts." Yet for many, education is nevertheless the best of the very few alternatives we possess in our effort to bring a measure of truth, order, and sanity to existence. It will not in itself provide us with ready-made values, or teach us how to live a satisfying and purposeful life. But it can offer us examples against which to measure our own perceptions, feelings, and ideas in an attempt to clarify what we wish to commit ourselves to—what we wish to pursue in shaping a life for ourselves. All of this may not, of course, suffice. But we may find it very difficult to discover an alternative that will stand us in better stead.

MORE TURNS OF THE WHEEL: FROM AFRICAN AMERICAN TO NEED-BLIND

Given my concern about the failure of the Bressler Commission, and the plight of the humanities, it was a relief to turn to ideas that might possibly breathe new life and intellectual excitement into the curriculum.

Sheldon Hackney (of Princeton's history department) skillfully led the creation and passage of an interdisciplinary program in African American studies. At many colleges and universities, this effort was itself highly contentious, and became a major flash point. In addition to African American studies, there was the beginning of a demand—in various parts of the country—for interdisciplinary Latino studies, Asian American studies, Native American studies, Judaica and (somewhat differently), women's' studies.

The rationale was clear: Each group felt it had been "left out" of the university's course of study, whereas each also felt it was a vital part of the nation's and much of the world's—history. The time had come to learn about many of those who had previously been excluded, and several scholars had already embarked upon this journey of discovery.

The drive to create such programs led to different responses at different colleges and universities. Very soon, at least two possible approaches—notably in African American studies—began to emerge. One path led to the creation of academic initiatives that were interdisciplinary in nature and were open to all students and faculty, irrespective of race or ethnicity or gender. This structure allowed many aspects of a particular cultural group to be studied from several points of view, yielding a wide range of insights—and raising at least as many important questions.

A second approach was highly problematic. It assumed—as was the case in certain "theoretical" quarters—that only members of a particular group could genuinely understand and interpret their own history, literature, religion, art, and other aspects of life. The Black theologian Vincent Harding insisted that

> self-definition is an intrinsic part of self-determination. It is *we* [blacks] who must understand our families, our churches, our works of art, the schools our children attend, the economic, political, and spiritual structures which uphold—and oppress—the communities in which we live.

As early as 1966, San Francisco State College introduced a "Black Arts and Culture Series," and some of its courses included "Miseducation of the Negro"; a "Workshop on the Psychology of, by, and for Black People"; and "Sociology of Black Oppression." John Bunzel describes this entire situation at some length in an article in *The Public Interest* (autumn 1968). In addition to taking courses, students would work in local Black communities, would serve as tutors for younger undergraduates, and would cultivate "community involvement and stimulation" that was intended to be a springboard for "an animated communalism aimed at a Black educational renaissance."

Nathan Hare was appointed as the coordinator of the Black studies program at San Francisco State, and he wanted the entire enterprise to train Black "militant" students. His qualifications for faculty members were "teaching effectiveness" and "enthusiasm" (rather than scholarship leading to publication, which he regarded as a traditional bourgeois White obstacle intended to exclude minorities). He then recognized, however, that if Blacks were to "declare void what the white slave masters have written," they must "begin to write their own history." In that case, they will be "forced into copious footnoting and must accept the conventions of the white academic overlords in order to make our history valid and get it published in white journals."

What about the scholarship of White faculty? "It is anachronistic for white men to teach black history to black militant students. The white man is unqualified to teach black history because he does not understand it." From an academic and curricular point of view, the San Francisco State (and similar) experiments were only too obviously political in design. The established traditional curriculum (and its standards) was now viewed, not as natural and "neutral," but as a "White" creation intended to reinforce White values, achievements, and power. In this sense, some of the new initiatives sought to politicize all academic learning.

For example, Margery Sabin's excellent essay (in *What's Happened to the Humanities?* 1997) describes a 1969 talk to the Modern Language Association (MLA) by Frederick Crews, entitled "Do Literary Studies Have an Ideology?" Crews declared that capitalism perverts scholarship for "purposes of exploitation and conquest," and he then went on to plead with his colleagues to "drop the scales from their eyes" and recognize that "capitalist scholarship" fostered "compliance with disguised class governance." He also proceeded to disparage the old justifications for conventional scholarship—objectivity, neutrality, and humanistic value— because (as he said) the best critics were now regarding literary works "not as transcendent icons" that offered a refuge from the world, but as "contingent, imperfect expressions of social and mental forces."

This attempt to redefine the nature of knowledge was a result of new theories that were now increasingly dominant in the very heartland of literary studies, and is discussed in the pages that follow. The movement was well underway when I became dean of the College, although it left Princeton relatively unscathed. The ideas that undergirded the views of Crews simply failed to take root at Princeton and many other institutions.

In the midst of these developments, one of my own main concerns was to increase the number of African American undergraduates at the university. The dean of Admissions reported directly to me, and we decided that our admission criteria for minorities would be the personal qualities and character of an applicant, very high secondary school grades, and a demonstrated record of working hard to succeed in both academic and other pursuits. Thoughtful letters of recommendation from teachers would also count heavily. The SAT scores of many African American applicants were often lower than their peers, but SAT scores had only been one element among several in our effort to predict future student performance, and most analyses of SATs had shown that high scores were generally not a mark of intrinsic intelligence but depended a great deal on the quality and nature of one's schooling. The criteria that we ourselves relied upon turned out to be very dependable. Inevitably, we made mistakes, but as we gained more experience from year to year, our admission decisions became increasingly sound.

Fortunately, "affirmative action" and "diversity" were not yet controversial issues and there were no legal challenges to our ability to move forward. There was also a widespread feeling on campus that this initiative was simply the right thing to do. The Civil Rights Movement of the 1950s and 1960s—including the legislation passed during Lyndon Johnson's presidency—gave increasing impetus to the desire to create a more "just" society. And education was one clear way to help achieve that goal. Within a very few years, the number of first-year African American students rose from about twenty in each entering class to about ninety—a huge increase that began to make genuine diversity a Princeton reality.

We realized, of course, that there were bound to be more tensions, and more racial incidents, as we increased the number of African Americans. But we also knew we could not turn back simply to avoid future problems. It was a moment when a great many of us believed it would be possible to change much of our society in the years to come, and the creation of a vastly enlarged generation of university-educated Blacks was clearly among the most important steps that one could take. So we pressed ahead with confidence, high hopes, and some uncertainty.

In addition to our admissions work, we had—inevitably—to pay very close attention to the adequacy of our financial aid funds. This was a time when our aid policies were in the midst of a series of dramatic transformations that had begun in the1960s, and continued for some time after I left the deanship.

Several major events were happening simultaneously. First, when the university was beginning to reduce substantially the number of students admitted from prep schools—seeking instead more high school students—there was an inevitable need for more student aid, simply because the financial standing of the average Princeton family fell. Prep school families were, not surprising, more well off on average than high school families—and Princeton was finally on the way to becoming more "democratic," and more "national." This change took a few years to complete, but it was visible by the time I became dean, and I simply tried to keep it moving forward. At the same time, the shift would clearly require a continuing need for a good deal more scholarship money, and this involved the pursuit of a need-based need-blind aid policy. The creation of such a policy came into being much later than many people may remember. The process was based on the premise that one would admit the students of each incoming class without any reference at all to their family's financial resources ("need-blind") and then award as much financial aid as each admitted student required ("need-based"). In other words, one simply did not know in advance how much financial aid would be necessary for an incoming class of undergraduates—or how much of an impact the result might have on the university's total budget. When I had entered Princeton in 1952, there was of course no policy of this kind. There were a limited number of scholarships (based on "merit"), but no expectation of anything more.

Harvard was no different. In 1948, for example, President Conant reported (to his governing boards) that the university was very had pressed for the money required to meet its operating budget. The salaries of faculty had to be raised, the cost of scientific equipment and facilities was rising rapidly, tuition had recently grown by more than 30 percent "and could not continue at such a pace." The question, said Conant, "uppermost in the mind of all college presidents today [is] how to meet the increased costs" of higher education. *Plus ça change* indeed!

In his 1950–51 report, Conant elaborated on the situation. As tuition continued to increase, more and more students were applying for financial aid:

> To meet this steadily worsening situation we have, in the last two years, greatly expanded the use of loans and student employment. ... Scholarship stipends have been trimmed. ... Perhaps even more seriously, we have been forced to restrict undesirably the number of candidates to whom we could give scholarship help. We are now making scholarship awards to a significantly smaller proportion of our students than either Yale or Princeton is, and we are losing scores of boys because of our inability to help.

There was obviously no policy of need-blind admissions and need-based financial aid at Harvard (or indeed any leading private university) in the 1950s, and there was no reason to believe that such a conception was conceivable or practicable. Harvard, more than three centuries after its founding, remained an essentially high-cost exclusive institution with rapidly rising expenses, increasing fees, and diminishing scholarship funds.

What changed? By the late 1950s and early 1960s, it became obvious that in order for universities to keep pace with the demands of their expanded and diversified incoming students, as well as with other needs, they would require far more annual income than they had been receiving (and far more than student fees could possibly generate). Several factors soon began to help the situation. First, because of the health of the American economy, stock-market gains in most of the postwar years (until the 1970s) were very favorable. In addition, there was a new drive to achieve higher and higher levels of alumni annual giving, and the move was beginning to be successful—helped greatly by the decision to increase the size of a now more professional fund-raising staff. For example, in 1963, Annual Giving at Princeton yielded about $1.6 million; in 1966, $2.2 million; in 1969, $3.6 million, and in 1971–72, $3.8 million. Moreover, it also became clear that a major task of virtually every new university president would be to undertake an ambitious fund-raising campaign. Finally, professional money-managers were hired to increase the growth of endowments—a job often done well (but not expertly) by trustee committees, which had been the case at Princeton.

Only in the 1960s, therefore, was it possible to imagine a dramatically different way of approaching admissions and student financial aid. The idea of need-blind admissions and need-based aid was conceived, and it began to be introduced tentatively because the new method was far from assured. Very few colleges or universities could possibly afford it, and even those that adopted it were not certain it could be sustained. In fact, the financially disastrous years from the early 1970s to the early 1980s forced many institutions to consider modifying the new policy because of the weakened economy (and President Reagan's threat—in 1980 and beyond—to cut federal education programs). At a certain point, I and the director of Admissions had very reluctantly to tell applicants that although they should apply for the level of financial aid they needed, the university might not be able to award them the full amount. Fortunately, we were able to carry on without changing the system, and when the economy improved (in the 1980s) the policy seemed secure. From then on, the new conception of need-blind admissions and need-based aid began (fortunately) to be regarded as sacrosanct—an absolutely fundamental aspect of unalterable policy. It was soon taken for granted as an integral—long-standing—tradition, yet this was barely more than two decades since it had begun!

TO THE CULTURE WARS

If students began to shift their "majors" in the 1970s and 1980s, and if President Conant of Harvard and others had long since wondered whether a coherent liberal education (or an ordered curriculum) could any longer be created for undergraduates, then the decades following the 1970s made the situation only more complex. More and more courses, in more and more fields of study, came into being, and the existing paradigms—of departmental requirements and long-established course sequences—suddenly began to shatter. There was, in effect, an explosion that simply devastated long-standing conceptions of a contained "Eurocentric" course of study and led to difficult (occasionally fierce) battles over the extent to which "Western civilization" was—or should be—any longer a dominant structure underlying much of our higher educational system.

For example, if we look at Princeton's English department in 1969–70, we find forty-four faculty (of varying ranks, including visitors and part-time members) teaching forty-one courses, virtually all of which are standard "period" courses on the history of English and American literature. There is one course in "Black Literature," nothing in women's studies, and a very few courses on "Public Speaking" or "American Public Expression" (and "Expository Writing"). The remainder focus on Anglo-Saxon, Chaucer, the Renaissance, and so forth—all the way to "The Twentieth Century Novel."

If we look forty years later, we find fewer faculty (42) and many more courses (over 70)—although a good number are not taught every year, and some very rarely. The greatest change however is the expansion in terms of subject matter. Now we find "American Women Writers," "History of Criticism," "Literature and Environment," "Topics in Black Literature," "Women Writers of the African Diaspora," "Studies in the Literature of Dispossession," Chinatown USA," "Contemporary Literary Theory," "Postmodernism and Contemporary Culture," "The Female Literary Tradition," and "Children's Literature."

The standard "period" and major-author courses remain (Chaucer, Shakespeare, Spenser, Milton, etc.) but there is now an entire set of rather different entries: "Reading Literature"—courses on poetry, fiction, drama, the essay; or "Topics in" fiction, poetry, and so on. There are five different "tracks" that departmental "majors" can choose among (including one in Creative Writing and one in Theater), with rather few requirements. So the range of *approaches* and *subjects* has been greatly expanded, and the concept of a single contained literary historical tradition has essentially disappeared. Certainly, the idea of a "canon," or a conception consisting of "great books and writers" in English literature no longer comes close to prevailing. The contrast between 1969 and 2009 could scarcely be greater; and a similar dichotomy reveals itself if we look at other course catalogues at other institutions.

One question worth asking is whether an analogous "explosion"—and a similar explosion affecting the established Western civilization curriculum—had ever taken place before, and whether it in fact reconstituted itself afterward. In fact, the post-1970s detonation had actually happened in at least one previous "modern" era, leaving (for a brief time) no apparent coherence behind, and no required heritage that seemed to be uniquely and fundamentally "ours." For example, the classical world—especially its Latin and Greek languages, and their major historical, philosophical, and literary texts—was mainly enshrined in American colleges and universities by at least the early 1800s (and even earlier), but its cataclysmic fall seemed imminent when President Charles Eliot of Harvard introduced his free elective system. Not only did President McCosh of Princeton disagree, but he foresaw apocalyptic consequences as a result:

> From the close of Freshman year on it is perfectly practicable for a student to pass through Harvard and receive the degree of Bachelor of Arts without taking any course in Latin, Greek, mathematics, chemistry, physics, astronomy, geology, logic, psychology, ethics, political economy, German or even English!
>
> I hold that in a college with variety there should be unity ... . Tell it not in Berlin or Oxford that the once most illustrious university in America no longer requires its graduates to know the most perfect language, the grandest literature, the most elevated thinking of all antiquity.

More than once, the "hegemony" of Western civilization has seemed to disintegrate, only to rise again in an altered but nevertheless familiar form.

In fact, it was not long before Professor Charles Eliot Norton—as suggested earlier—was introducing at Harvard his "new" conception of Western culture and civilization as the major tradition to be studied by future undergraduates. It was also about then (1911) that the famous Loeb translations of Greek and Latin classics began—indeed James Loeb was a student of Norton. If Latin and Greek languages were no longer required, one would read their works in English. Coincidentally, it was also the moment when the young Bernard Berenson—who also studied under Norton—was graduating from Harvard to settle in Florence (becoming in time the greatest connoisseur of Renaissance Italian art). He left his Florentine villa, *I Tatti*, to Harvard for the study of Renaissance art and culture in the entire Mediterranean area. So English and other "modern" Western languages (and literatures) soon replaced Latin and Greek, but the focus was clearly once again on "Western Civ"—whether at *I Tatti* or elsewhere. In this sense, the hegemony of the West remained dominant for at least another half-century after Norton.

Perhaps our most recent "disintegration"—when it is possible to graduate from college without having studied Shakespeare or to have climbed the higher reaches of mathematics or physics; or take any biology, or the classics, or psychology, economics or politics—will be final. But what now exists is still strongly "Western" in its grounding and basic perspective, with a salutary inclusion of international, cultural, "minority," and other studies. Even these, however, are almost inevitably studied from our own Western points of view, although we may do our utmost to complicate the picture by taking account of other perspectives (especially on issues related to race, ethnicity, gender, and international affairs).

One way to view curricula and their shift from a strong "Western Civ" emphasis to something far broader is to recall the drama at Stanford University during the "culture wars" of 1986–88. The question was whether an established required course, comprised entirely of "classics" from Western civilization, should be modified to include books by women, "people of color," and writers from various civilizations.

The faculty discussion of the issue lasted the better part of two years and was greatly influenced by the steady drumbeat of minority student protestors. They had put forward their "demands" (for a more "inclusive" required course) several years earlier, and the situation was becoming progressively more tense as time passed. Inevitably, the conflict began to capture the attention of the press and politicians. The entire saga was a partial replay of the 1960s and 1970s when academic programs for minorities and women were first introduced. But now, with a direct attack on a notable *required* "Western Civ" course, the issue came to be viewed as a symbolic drama of great significance. Was the heart of Western civilization to be sacrificed to what the writer Allan Bloom called "selfish minorities" and others, or would the "West" prevail?

Henry Rosovsky has carefully traced the details of the Stanford affair in a well-wrought essay that appeared in *Universities and Their Leadership* (1998). In essence, after three lengthy reviews there was a scheduled faculty debate to be held on January 21, 1988, and the subject was a proposal that altered the Western Civ requirements considerably by introducing a broader reading list. The first round of discussion ended in a faculty stalemate—a complete deadlock. Just before the debate, William Bennet, President Reagan's Secretary of Education, actually visited Stanford to register his displeasure. Then, on the very day of the debate, *The Wall Street Journal* published an article by a Stanford Classics major, Isaac Burchas, who declared that "The intellectual heritage of the West goes on trial at Stanford University today. Most predict it will lose." And lose it did—ultimately—if we accept Burchas's characterization of the issues at stake. In fact, the January 21 meeting was followed by another two months of discussion that yielded a compromise with which most faculty apparently agreed.

The final proposal stipulated that fifteen of the Western classic texts would be retained while "minority" and women's works (and others) would be used in the rest of the course. Some of those works came to include writers such as Virginia Woolf, Frederick Douglass, Alexis de Tocqueville, and Gabriel Garcia Márquez—scarcely lightweights.

Secretary Bennett charged that the revised course was primarily "a political and not an educational decision"—which in part it was, just as the secretary's battle to retain the original "classics" course was overtly political in the extreme (and just as both versions of the course were educational). "A great university was brought low," Bennett said, "by the very forces which modern universities came into being to oppose—ignorance, irrationality, and intimidation." But—as Princeton's Carl Schorske pointed out in an unpublished talk—the leader of the university's Black students replied: "The West isn't just your vision, but it's ours as well.... We're a part of the whole process." In the midst of this scene, *Newsweek* ran an article titled "Say Goodnight, Socrates: Stanford University and the Decline of the West" (February 1, 1988).

So the battle of the books ended—at least at Stanford. Was the final compromise a reasonable one from an educational point of view? I myself think so. Even if one had kept the course's original focus on Western civilization, it would have been eventually difficult if not impossible to move forward without including some serious discussion of slavery as well as the contributions of Blacks to Western history and civilization, or material related to Latin America, including its formidable body of superb twentieth-century literature; or the works of dozens of women writers. In short, a course dedicated to "Western Civ" would almost certainly have had to become more inclusive over time.

If the "compromise" at Stanford was in some ways reasonable, however, the process was far less so. In particular, there seems to be little question that a sit-in by minority students, as well as other tactics, were intimidating and disruptive in unacceptable ways. One Stanford faculty member wrote privately to a colleague at another university—someone who viewed the Stanford situation as having been rather easily and benignly settled:

> You refer to your file of newspaper clippings. Do they include the pictures of the shouting students organized by the Black Students Union on the site of the Senate meeting? Or the threats of Bill King, its leader, and his confession that at a signal from his members inside the meeting, his group was prepared to invade and disrupt the proceedings? Or the pictures of the students who had taken possession of the administrative office on the day before?

So the process marred the outcome, and there was perhaps another problem: Each faculty member was allowed to choose his or her "minority" or women's texts to substitute for the "classics" that were dropped from the required list. But how much quality might have been consequently sacrificed? There is a strong case to be made in favor of Ellison's *Invisible Man*, or Garcia Márquez's *One Hundred Years of Solitude,* or Virginia Woolf, or W.E. B. de Bois. But Henry Rosovsky mentions other writers who were sometimes included, and who brought important points of view to the course, but whose depth and complexity of thought (or the demands of their prose) were not at a level comparable to that of much more significant—and difficult—works. If so, we have lost a good deal, admitting that there is also some gain. I think that the level of many students' patience for reading difficult and lengthy literature has diminished in the past two decades—perhaps because of "social media" and other computer-related processes. So I am more than wary about any decline in literary standards (meaning *literary* in a broad sense). What we must hope, consequently, is that the books in the Stanford course (and similar ventures) are intellectually complicated, demanding, profound—and perhaps even lengthy. Otherwise, we shall have indeed short-changed our students.

The so-called culture wars of the 1980s and 1990s were epitomized by the Stanford battle, but were of course broad in scope, including attacks on the very concept of making qualitative distinctions among ideas, institutions, or works of art. To make such judgments became "elitist," characteristic of academics and especially of some private selective universities where attempts to change curricula (or "canons") in particular were viewed by conservatives as "liberal" efforts to attack long-standing traditions that were said to define America's values and virtues. Lynne Cheney, chair of the National Endowment for the Humanities from 1986–93, was quoted by one observer as saying that many "academics and artists now see their purpose not as revealing truth or beauty, but as achieving social and political transformation." And among Bennet's many invocations, he insisted that the attack on "the canon" was carried out by those who "seem less interested in creating art or fostering knowledge and more interested in ridiculing, provoking, and antagonizing mainstream American values."[3] So *political correctness* and *academic elitism* became terms of opprobrium, and it was the disruptive political "left" that was viewed as attempting to achieve "social and political transformation" in higher education.

The late Harold Bloom (who was certainly neither a radical nor a Bennet-stripe "conservative") insisted that the canon was of course a construct designed over time in response to particular circumstances, and that—far from embodying eternal fixed values—it consisted largely of writers and books with new ideas who were themselves often disruptive or subversive. How else explain Plato, Augustine, Voltaire, Rousseau, Marx, Nietzsche, and others?

> The silliest way to defend the Western Canon is to insist that it incarnates all of the virtues that make up our supposed range of normative values and democratic principles. This is palpably untrue. ... The West's greatest writers are subversive.[4]

We may not agree entirely with Bloom, but he is clearly more accurate by far than the politically motivated Bennet and Cheney. Today, the culture wars continue, but it is now the "decolonizing" critics who are likely to be anti-elitist as the terms have come to be defined a topic that later has its own chapter.

The previous four chapters have focused largely upon student curricular changes and choices, including the fact that the concept of a shared education in the liberal arts and sciences began to diminish in the 1970s, and then continued to lose ground during the following decades. A great many new courses—and several new departments or programs—were introduced, broadening the curriculum and inevitably shrinking the extent to which many students had something approaching a similar curricular experience. Essentially, the undergraduate curriculum was, like the university itself, expanding and "decentralizing."

In the process, two major developments took place. First, students in the same department (especially in the humanities and some social sciences) were no longer compelled to take the same set of core courses because the options had been enlarged and requirements have been considerably weakened.

Next, at many universities, several new departments or programs were created in "identity" spheres such as African American studies, East Asian studies, women's studies, Judaic studies, and others. These ventures were important and I myself supported their creation at institutions. The courses can illuminate aspects of history and culture whose significance might otherwise be overlooked or underestimated. At the same time, it is clear that many students—from particular ethnic, racial or analogous groups—choose to concentrate in these "heritage" subjects. This can be enlightening but it can also lead to the reinforcement of ethnic or other forms of group solidarity. If one group should find itself at odds with another, the gap between them may then be greater than otherwise would have been the case. "Diversity" might be reinforced, not in terms of an effort to enhance mutual understanding, but in terms of creating stronger differences among groups.

A curriculum has of course many purposes, but one of them should be to enhance opportunities for undergraduates of a diverse student body to meet one another, not only in residential settings or extracurricular activities, but also in some number of shared classroom experiences where they can engage in forms of intellectual exchange that lead to the exploration of commonalities as well as differences.

If the curriculum grows substantially, it inevitably splinters. If requirements are lessened, the splintering increases. If more programs and departments are introduced, they may weaken even further the possibility for some mutuality of academic exchange. Contentiousness is not an inevitable consequence of such developments, but in an institution that is already contentious in a society that is similarly so—the result may alas be to increase divisiveness rather than to foster beneficent forms of understanding and knowledge among the many participants.

BROADSIDES AND MORE CULTURAL COLLISIONS

Virtually all presidents of the United States have viewed higher education as a vital part of America's present and future: a way of nurturing individuals, preparing future leaders, helping to create an informed citizenry, and contributing to the needs of the nation in a variety of ways. These ideas were given early expression in the many pages that Thomas Jefferson devoted to describing his own conception of a university, with its multitude of subjects and "courses" of study. Even earlier, it was symbolized by George Washington's presence at Princeton's graduation exercises in 1783, and later in the creation of the Land-Grant colleges during Lincoln's presidency. Franklin Delano Roosevelt attended Harvard's 300th anniversary, General Eisenhower and President Truman attended Princeton's 200th, and it was Roosevelt who accepted Vannevar Bush's advice (in the 1940s) to rely more and more upon scientific research to help wage World War II and secure the peace that would follow. Then Bush's famous 1945 document, *Science: The Endless Frontier*, made the case for a significant continuing government investment in *university* research, rather than government-run special institutes. Later Dwight Eisenhower served (briefly) as president of Columbia University, and Jack Kennedy's Camelot came close to creating a special jet lane from Cambridge, Massachusetts, to the Oval Office.

Ronald Reagan was the first president in memory to regard higher education as an adversary. The university system was to be punished for its liberal leanings and for the disruptions of the 1960s. The University of California at Berkeley was an early target (when Reagan was governor of California). Soon after his election to the presidency in 1980, he began an effort to slash research and student-aid budgets. As early as February 1981, the National Science Foundation (NSF) was targeted for a 75 percent reduction in funds, and the National Endowment for the Humanities (NEH) for 50 percent. Because the NSF provided support for basic (and applied) research, many universities expected to be especially hard hit. Later in the same month, (in a national televised program) Reagan indicated that he would seek major reductions in the $800 million guaranteed student loan program, the $150 million Basic Education Opportunity Grant program, and the entire Direct Student Loan Program.

Faced with the possibility of these reductions, it was far from clear that one could sustain the full support of some small "under-enrolled" university departments, or a "need-blind" financial aid system. Meanwhile, Reagan's proposed actions were strongly opposed, and did not make it through Congress in either 1981 or 1982. The president nevertheless continued his attempts, but the Congress continued to balk.

If one line of attack on the universities was financial, another was more plainly ideological. Reagan's secretary of education, William Bennett, made headlines in October 1986 when, at the celebration of Harvard's 350th anniversary, he chose to denounce the university's "core" curriculum, which he described as nothing more than an "agglomeration" of shopworn courses. He saw no attempt at Harvard to provide students with a strong "moral education"—that would, for example, prevent on-campus drug use (as if one could devise a campus police system to monitor everyone's behavior). And he criticized the high cost of tuition (and the high attrition rates) at many colleges and universities.

When he spoke at Princeton in May 1987, Bennett attacked high-priced private universities for failing to offer a "quality education" in line with its cost. Fees, he said, were rising faster than the rate of inflation (which was apparently a surprise to the secretary, though otherwise explicable). In his view, endowments should not be "sacrosanct." Perhaps they should be used to reduce rises in tuition? He was apparently unaware of the crucial need to maintain the full value of endowments, as well as the legal and other restrictions governing their use. In short, the secretary made headlines, but made very little sense. Nevertheless, strong public assaults by the nation's Secretary of Education inevitably had an effect, even though Bennett had no serious constructive proposals to put forward.

Some of Bennett's charges (and those of others) were echoed, moreover, in a steady stream of books published during the 1980s, 1990s, and beyond: a very few would include *The Closing of the American Mind* (1987), *Tenured Radicals* (1990), *Illiberal Education: The Politics of Race and Sex on Campus* (1991), *What's Happened to the Humanities?* (1997)— and more than a shelf-full of others. The culture wars were fully underway. Two volumes in particular may deserve some discussion: Allan Bloom's *The Closing of the American Mind*, and Alvin Kernan's *What's Happened to the Humanities?* The two differ considerably in tone, style, and attention to reliable evidence, although they make some similar points. The authors see the universities as having capitulated under the pressures of the 1960s, surrendering a large measure of their authority, and losing a great deal of confidence in the goals and purposes of a liberal arts education. They regard the invasion of subjects, such as African American studies and women's studies, as having undermined the commitment to traditional literary, historical, and other fields of learning, resulting in an increasingly incoherent curriculum that offered students a maximum of freedom and a minimum of guidance. They deplored "grade inflation," and they suggested that "relativism" had replaced a deep search (either by the university or its students) for "virtue" or "the good" (Bloom's terms).

If we turn briefly to Bloom, we find a volume that is a roomy, rambling attempt to describe what has happened to the American "mind" over the course of the last century and more. His book was an astonishing success: 750,000 copies had been sold before I bought my own paperback volume. Bloom found that the American mind had "closed" because it no longer sought actual truth. Instead, it was prepared to accept the fact that different individuals, groups, and societies have their own beliefs or "preferences," and that all of them are perceived by many people as equally valid. Convictions and beliefs that were once instituted by the family (or Church, or even university) had been eroded. Indeed, Bloom saw the collapse of family authority as a major cause of the present crisis:

> The moral education that is today supposed to be the great responsibility of the family cannot exist if it cannot present to the imagination of the young a vision of a moral cosmos [with] ... protagonists and antagonists in the drama of moral choice. ... [Parents] do not have the self-confidence to tell their children much more than that they want them to be happy and fulfill whatever potential they have. ...

Bloom's "moral cosmos" with opposing and presumably warring "protagonists" and "antagonists" sounds rather Miltonic and seems to hark back to an early era of implacable Puritanism rather than to the significant literature, philosophy, and religion of later thinkers. Behind his generalizations (of the kind just quoted) lies a yearning on his part for a past "ideal" society derived from Protestant conceptions of good and evil, and from a quasi-aristocratic conception of order:

> That earlier dominant society gave the country a dominant culture with its traditions, its literature, its tastes, its special claim to know and supervise the language, and its Protestant religions.

It is not altogether clear which era Bloom has in mind here, or which geographical parts of the nation. Surely the gold-rush West, the zone of the Louisiana Purchase, the old "aristocratic" slave-holder South, and the industrial Midwest differed from one another—as well as from New England, which Bloom may be using as his touchstone. In Bloom's mind, instead of an ordered society, we now have a culture of heterogeneous groups—especially "minorities"—that have overturned all that went before (including all that the nation's Founders had devised):

> This reversal of the Founders' intention with respect to minorities is most striking. For the Founders, minorities are in general bad things, mostly identical to factions, selfish groups who have no concern as such for the common good. ... [The Founders] constructed an elaborate [government] machinery to contain factions in such a way that would cancel one another and allow for the pursuit of the common good.

Bloom's obvious prejudice against minorities ("bad things" and "selfish groups") breaks through the surface here, and he seems to use "minorities" in a contemporary (rather loaded) racial way, somehow equating them with the *political* "factions" that James Madison (and other Founders) hoped to contain through constitutional checks and balances. But Madison was of course not at all concerned about the presence or power of "minorities" and he does not use the word in its plural form. For Madison *minority* is employed as the opposite of *majority*, and he never resorts to banal terms such as *bad things* or *selfish groups*. Bloom's claim that there has been a "reversal" of the Founders' "intentions" is simply wrong, and this is true of many of his most sweeping propositions.

For example, if we reread the Federalist Papers numbered 10, 14, and 37, we find explicit discussions of factions. Madison's chief worry, however, is about *majority* factions, not groups who are in the minority. Indeed, "measures are too often decided, not according to the rules of justice and the rights of the minor party, but by superior force of an interested and overbearing majority." As a result, Madison wanted, not a "popular" or fully democratic government, but a "republic" with its representative nature, including checks and balances to control, not selfish "minorities," but overbearing *majorities*. "If a faction consists of less than a majority, relief is supplied by the republican principle, which enables the majority to defeat its sinister views by regular vote." But

> When a majority is included in a faction, the form of popular government ... enables it to sacrifice to its ruling passion or interest both the public good and the rights of other citizens.

To prevent majority misrule in a republic, the government must be large enough to allow for many smaller factions or groups, and therefore one will—Madison concludes—"take in a greater variety of parties and interests; you make it less probable that a majority of the whole will have a common motive to invade the rights of other citizens" [10, 83]. In short, his worry is not about "selfish minorities" but self-interested majorities, and Bloom simply—and fatally—distorts the Founders' views on this entire subject.

Bloom's book, given its massive sales and attendant publicity, obviously struck a highly resonant chord in the nation. It seems clear that many Americans—having been faced with the recent tumult at universities, the changes in "youth culture," the increasing complexities of the modern world, the controversies of the American political scene, and the substantial entry of minorities (especially but not only African Americans) into our national life: Many Americans longed for a narrative that would help to explain their anxieties, appeal to their predispositions, and sketch for them an alternative (if nonexistent) ideal past. Bloom postulated a lost, romanticized age when families instilled in their children clear values in a universe where there were "protagonists and antagonists in the drama of moral choice." In that lost age, there was also a single "dominant society" with its own coherent culture and its own strong traditions. Indeed, it was a male, Protestant, Caucasian, religious society that had a special claim "to know and supervise the language" rather than to have present-day ethnic groups mongrelize it. The fact that most Americans—including women, Jews, Catholics, slaves, immigrants, and the poor—were excluded from any serious role in this "dominant society" was never mentioned.

In short, Bloom was essentially defending all that seemed to be slipping from America's grasp. He could not himself restore that lost world, but he could offer another—if largely illusory—vision to those who feared the apparent anarchy of the present, and who wished for an alternative.

Alvin Kernan's *What's Happened to the Humanities?* is a collection of essays with an introduction by Kernan himself. He summarized his own conclusions as follows:

Free speech movements coarsened the vocabulary of higher education, and student protests, strikes, and sit-ins were only the most
visible of many continuing challenges to [the university's] *in loco
parentis* authority. Democratic egalitarianism found its intellectual
counterpart in pluralism, a multi-cultural curriculum, and the relativistic concept of truth—one person's ideas were as good as another's—
which has been the intellectual "loss leader" on campus for many
years now. ... Affirmative action brought increasing numbers of
minority students into the classrooms, a feminist movement established itself at the center of academic concerns, and all intellectual
activities were declared to be means of seeking power. ... [The]
pattern of social change was summarized by Professor Margery Sabin
in the following way: "radical social protest in the late 1960s; decon-
struction in the 1970s; ethnic, feminist, and Marxist cultural studies
in the 1980s; postmodern sexuality in the 1990s; and rampant careerism from beginning to end!"

A few of the essays in Kernan's volume offer a thoughtful refutation
to some of these views. Francis Oakley—having studied a number of
detailed statistical surveys—pointed out that most of the new courses in
"minority" or "women's" studies were not *substituted* for other more
traditional courses, but were *added* to the existing curriculum (and were
not regularly taught). He noted that in a 1981–82 survey by the American
Historical Society, the "history of both the United States and Europe
dominated" the curricular scene. In literature, a 1985 MLA report demonstrated that the top half-dozen authors named for the American survey
taught on a regular basis were Hawthorne, Melville, Whitman, Dickinson,
Twain, and Emerson. For the British survey, Chaucer, Shakespeare, Milton, Wordsworth, and Donne head the list. Meanwhile, there were "fre-
quencies of less than 1 percent for authors such as James Baldwin,
Langston Hughes, Sylvia Plath, and Alice Walker. Even Toni Morrison
reached no more than 1.8 percent."

Although Oakely's data are useful, they tell only part of the story.
It is quite true that, in required departmental year-long survey courses,
the major literary figures (from Chaucer onward) dominate the curriculum.
But the survey courses barely give one a taste of each major writer, and
are scarcely a substitute for entire individual courses dedicated to Chaucer
or Milton or the Romantics or the Victorian novel. Those traditional
courses remained, but their enrollments began to suffer substantially beginning in the 1970s. A study of offerings by several English departments—
as we have seen—reveals a very large number of "noncore" courses that

are dedicated to an array of new materials in film, media studies, popular culture, women's studies, science fiction, children's literature, African American studies, sex and sexuality, postcolonial literature, theory, and other "modern" topics. And students do very often choose to elect these offerings rather than traditional courses that once were the heart of literary studies. Traditional requirements have also been seriously modified or even dropped at a number of excellent colleges and universities. And twentieth-century and contemporary materials have very largely displaced earlier historical studies.

In actual fact, the new courses just mentioned can be—and almost always are—taught in serious and stimulating ways. They often use some materials that derive from the "standard" core courses. But they rarely study major writers in considerable depth, and it is a fair question to ask "What constitutes a department of English and American literature today, and what do we expect a student to have mastered?"

On the whole, there is no longer any general answer to the question of "mastery," because departments now vary so much in the courses they offer, and the requirements they stipulate. As a result, there is scarcely a common conception of what it means to be an "English major." And this is true not only of students in English but also (often) in music, art history, history, and other subjects. What we have been experiencing for some time is a period of significant upheaval and experimentation when a great deal of change is taking place, but when there is an obvious lack of curricular coherence—and a significant movement away from the once-dominant canon of traditional course material.

If part of this change is due to the introduction of new courses in new fields, much is also due to the fact that enrollments in most humanist departments have simply been declining steadily, often leading to new efforts to "update" the curriculum in ways that may appeal to more undergraduates. For example, I recently took part in a "review" of one English department whose total number of "majors" had recently fallen from over one hundred to just shy of fifty. What was the department doing in response? It was seeking to increase the number of courses in film. Other humanist departments (especially in modern languages) have reached out in similar ways. Indeed, if one insisted in teaching only core subjects, there seems little doubt that the number of majors would drop even further.

This situation is more than simply unfortunate, and one can scarcely blame some departments for seeking new ways to keep the number of "majors" from falling closer and closer to zero. The problem is particularly serious in literature, however, because that is clearly one of the areas in which words must be used imaginatively and precisely, demanding the greatest possible attention to the nuances of meaning. If we cease asking our students to read a great deal of challenging fiction and poetry, we give up—to a considerable extent—asking them to know something altogether significant about words and the realities they can capture or create: that is, something about the range of impressions, emotions, insights, and revelations that human beings experience, but that are *understood* mainly when translated into language that can give them a name and therefore make them "known" to us in ways that enable us to comprehend a greater span of human existence and its infinite variety of distinctions.

In short, Kernan's critique has some validity, but it is also too sweeping. The 1960s "coarsening" of the vocabulary of higher education has—at least in my judgement—greatly receded. Moreover, a certain form of sophisticated relativism is virtually inevitable in a society, such as ours, composed of many cultures, creeds, traditions, and points of view. But that does not mean one must abandon one's own convictions, or believe that all values and ideas are equally valid. It is possible to understand and even be strongly interested in such a variety without becoming merely "relativistic" in a reductionist way.

Indeed, one essential definition of an educated person—in today's world—is that he or she can encounter a multiplicity of ideas and view-points in an intelligent and penetrating way, sifting, and assessing them, while simultaneously forging a coherent life of one's own, with achieved values and convictions to guide one.

It is also true that affirmative action brought increasing numbers of minority students into the classrooms, but surely that is in itself far from deplorable. The implication is that such students are clearly much less capable than others. There is no question that a rapid expansion of a group of students who have been denied excellent early education can lead, during a transition, to mistakes in admissions. But one has to stay with the effort, refining one's admission criteria and expanding one's search process—one cannot simply give up something so vital to individuals as well as to the nation. Meanwhile the "feminist movement" has made major contributions to our knowledge and consciousness. If there were some clear excesses—and there have been—many of them (not all) have been mitigated over time, although the current situation still remains contentious in a number of institutions. Finally, the proposition that "all intellectual activities" are a "means of seeking power" has greatly diminished as a belief—if it ever was a significant one for most college and university students and faculty.

In other words, Kernan was (in my view) a serious traditionalist who had been deeply affected by the successive intellectual, cultural, and curricular "revolutions" that took place. This impact was felt especially strongly in his own field of English literature, and especially at Yale, since it was a leading home of "theory." But he made little allowance for the fact that much (not by any means all) that was disruptive several decades ago had lost—or was losing—a great deal of its initial impact.

The real significance of the two books just discussed (as well as others) lies perhaps less in their specific criticisms than in the fact that they are symptoms of the major backlash against colleges and universities that began around 1970 and has continued (in new forms) to this day. Before the mid 1960s, postwar higher education in the United States had almost invariably been given the benefit of the doubt, even when matters went astray. Since then, the mood has shifted, and we have experienced a long period when skepticism about the value—and certainly some of the policies and conduct—of our educational institutions has grown steadily. The list of "adversarial" books mentioned at the beginning of this chapter has continued to grow, and is by now very large indeed. A number of their criticisms are serious and their substance requires sustained attention. Yet many of them are overblown and often result from a misunderstanding—or misrepresentation—of complex situations or issues that simply deserve far more analysis than they receive before judgment has been passed. For example, if we ask graduating seniors from a great many of our colleges and universities whether they have had rewarding and enriching educational experiences, they are mainly positive in their responses. And if we ask how our best institutions rank internationally, we find that they are at or near the top when measured against their peers on all continents. So we are left with a dilemma: a stream of steady criticism on the one hand, and a set of highly positive achievements on the other. Indeed, the United States has won more than four hundred Nobel Prizes—nearly 100 more than the total of Germany, France, and the United Kingdom combined.

My own view is that we are almost certain to live with this dilemma well into the future. Many of our universities, in particular, have continued to grow in size and complexity during the past few decades, so they now contain—as suggested earlier—a great many quasi-independent institutes, centers, programs, and professional schools that make them more difficult to manage or run—and seem to require more administrators in helping to do so. Consequently, they are likely to make more errors—or at least more controversial decisions. Our best universities have become stronger in research and the successful pursuit of new knowledge, but the many individual institutional "parts" are now less closely related to one another. And they are far more diverse—and therefore more susceptible to tension than before. It is simply a fact that scale and complexity matter significantly, and once there are a considerable number of semi-autonomous enterprises in a single institution, the probability of at least some units—or the institution itself—erring becomes more likely, with the result that there is more criticism of (and more media attention to) colleges and universities, regardless of their fundamental intrinsic quality. The incidents concerning fund-raising by the MIT Media Lab—and Jeffrey Epstein's donations to a Harvard program—are simply two conspicuous recent examples of how single parts of large institutions can go badly astray.

One of my own strong hopes is that our institutions will continue to nurture—and keep at a moderate scale—their undergraduate colleges, where a sense of unity and institutional identity has a better chance of being created and sustained. This will not be easy, given the pressures (from several quarters) urging expansion, or the tendency over time for them to creep a little, bit by bit, in size. I hope these pressures can be resisted, because it will be essential to do so in order to try to preserve the academic values and the sense of a humane community that one strives to achieve, and that should be vigilantly guarded when it exists. Of course, the nation and the world will not always be co-operative: Events from beyond the campus can intervene in such a way as to create fracture *inside* the institution, but even then, the hope of recovery will be greater if the community is such that more students and faculty—and even administrators—know one another and can to some extent begin to trust one another in due course.

Chapter 5

New Departures

PROVOST

After five years as dean of the College, I was asked—in 1977—if I would become Princeton's provost, a position that had chief responsibility for helping to set academic and other priorities from year to year, while simultaneously fashioning an annual budget to support those priorities. As a result, I moved from my early job of confronting student protests, and the more recent task involving curricular affairs, to a region where important educational matters and budgetary matters had somehow to be reconciled through a process that would need to be accepted by all constituencies—the faculty, staff, students, administrative officers, and trustees.

Because I was provost for slightly more than a decade, my experience with institutional contentiousness was limited to a sphere in which competing university priorities and their budgetary implications (including student fee increases) were the main components. Perhaps inevitably, the major disputes were often the extent to which student tuition and other costs would rise from year to year—an issue that became all the more difficult because of two factors.

First, the period from 1977 to 1982 was of course one in which "stagflation" was rampant: annual interest rates rising into double-digits, and stock-market returns on the endowment often negative (together with

173

lower annual giving returns). Stagflation meant, therefore, little or no capacity to fully fund many university needs (such as the cost of the library system or scientific research, or faculty and staff salary increases). Often, the only way to meet—even partially—some of these needs, was to raise student fees by extraordinary amounts from year to year. We had to try to balance the budget, and there simply was scarcely any other source of revenue than tuition, room, and board.

The second difficulty that led to tension was Princeton's system of establishing priorities and an annual budget: the process involved a "Priorities Committee," whose membership involved faculty, students, and staff, chaired by the provost. Throughout the autumn, the committee would hear from—each week—a different officer of a major budgetary unit of the university (for instance, the librarian, or the dean of the Faculty). The officer would describe the state of his or her financial affairs, including what would be needed in terms of future funding to keep the area excellent—or at least to protect it from seriously deteriorating.

Since book and serial prices were rising rapidly, the librarian would need (for instance) considerably *extra* income from year to year. Or, on a different front, with inflation at 8–10 percent (or more) each year, faculty salaries would have to rise substantially, or else ground would be steadily lost. But where was the money to come from if there were no positive endowment returns (or annual gifts of great consequence)? The answer, of course, was—at least in part—from student fees.

There is no need to enter here into the details of the priorities system, except to say that the process of finding a budgetary solution to the needs of the university inevitably required—year after year—compromises of a kind that were obviously tension filled. The most difficult single year involved a moment when, in order to meet moderate budgetary needs, student fees would have to rise more than 12 percent. At that point, the undergraduate members indicated that they might have to resign from the committee. Contentiousness appeared ready to invade the very heartland of the institution.

Faced with this situation, I called for a week's recess, so that a compromise might possibly be reached. As it turned out, the faculty eventually agreed to a lower salary increase. The library and other areas agreed to decreases in their requests for funding, and student fees would then rise only 8–9 percent. After the committee's recess was concluded, the budget was approved.

Perhaps two rather general points are worth mentioning. First, despite the difficulties of the priorities process, it did demonstrate that when different constituencies of the university were confronted with the realities of a significantly difficult situation, they were (more often than not) inclined to think about the health of the institution as a whole. There was nothing quite like reality to compel reasonable compromise, and the different groups on the committee worked (more often than not) to achieve consensus because they had all been engaged in the same difficult process, and all came to understand—and then respect—one another's predicaments. The lack of such a compelling process in other difficult areas of university life—such as invitations to controversial speakers—means, of course, that contentiousness can more easily affect these spheres. Yet imagining such processes might be very far from easy: Indeed, the very creation of Princeton's Priorities Committee (and its makeup) was an exceptionally bold and imaginative move, and few (if any!) other universities have ever emulated it.

Finally, in spite of all the committee's efforts, the cost of student fees at Princeton more than doubled in the period from 1977–82. This of course had long-term effects and it led to other moments (as after 2008) when fees had to make up some of the considerable loss following disastrous endowments performance. The economics of higher education are of course a complex subject, and moments of crisis are themselves far from explaining all (or even most) of constant rises in student fees. But they provide at least one insight into a situation that is more than merely difficult, and rarely understood.

TRANSITION

Bill Bowen was offered the presidency of the New York Andrew W. Mellon Foundation in 1987, and decided to accept it. The Princeton Campaign was over. Fifteen years had passed since he first began to lead Princeton. His move made perfect sense, but left me unsettled. I thought that I would be considered for Princeton's presidency, but I did not want the position and told the head of the search committee before the search was underway. I had already been at Princeton for twenty years, in three different administrative roles. That was long enough by any standard and, quite apart from my own personal feelings, I believed that the university should have the benefit of new leadership.

Then, quite unexpectedly, after two or three conversations with Bill, he asked whether I would consider becoming the executive vice-president of the Mellon Foundation. I would have special responsibility for grant-giving programs in the humanities and arts, while Bill would concentrate on the social sciences. But the split would not be absolute; in effect, we would work closely together, identifying major priorities for the Foundation as a whole, including higher education.

And that is what happened. We announced our resignations at the same time, in the same press conference, and the news came as a surprise to many Princeton faculty. People had assumed that Bill would not stay much longer, but the fact that we would both leave simultaneously was unexpected. Yet I was pleased and relieved. I knew Princeton well and I doubted that I could add anything to its future. I also felt more suited to a position, such as the provostship, which had allowed me to concentrate on the "inside" of the university and its intellectual purposes, rather than the possibility of a presidency and its inevitable focus on many external affairs.

So—with Angelica's strong agreement—I accepted Bill's offer. We would keep our house in Princeton, and find a modest apartment in New York. Princeton would become a retreat or haven for us on weekends. Because New York was obviously the focal point of Angelica's work in twentieth-century art, the arrangement suited both of us.

My four years at the Mellon Foundation passed quickly, and I had barely time to undertake a few initiatives before I found myself moving away. I introduced a new program in literacy, focused on reading compre-hension and on the improvement of student writing—and I funded a program to help narrow the divide between university or college art mu-seums, and their respective art history departments. The age of "theory" had led many art historians to shift away from object-based research—whereas by definition, museums were concerned primarily with "objects." Finding ways to increase collaboration between the two different units seemed critical: Indeed, it proved to be a valuable investment as a start and paid significant dividends in later years after I had left.

Meanwhile, Bill Bowen and I together began to study the most important needs of selected private universities. We met with a few dozen university presidents and provosts, and we finally reached agreement: Financial support for graduate students, which had dwindled substantially in the past decade and more, had become a major priority, and it was unlikely to attract funding from other sources. Helping to educate the next generation of faculty members seemed essential, so we designed a program that would invest $100 million in a few outstanding institutions over the course of the next decade. The only proviso was that the graduate students' lengthy "time to degree" (the years devoted to earning a PhD) should be shortened, especially because some students were now taking as much as seven to ten years to finish. In the end, the program succeeded in underwriting the careers of many excellent future scholars and teachers, but the effort to reduce degree time proved very hard to achieve.

I had not been at the Mellon Foundation for a full three years when I was visited one autumn day by Harvard's well known (previous) dean of the Faculty of Arts and Sciences (FAS), Henry Rosovsky. He came to tell me that Derek Bok had decided to leave the Harvard presidency at the end of the current year. Angelica and I knew this already, since we had remained friends with Derek and Sissela, and we had also heard that a search was well underway. Henry's visit seemed perfectly friendly and casual until he suddenly asked me whether I would have any interest in being considered for the position. I was startled by the question, and even more startled to discover that I did not immediately say no. When I decided not to stand for the Princeton presidency, I actually decided (which had been the case for a long time, through previous inquiries by other institutions) that I did not want to be a university president *at all*, anywhere. I felt that, temperamentally, I would not be greatly interested in representing an institution to its "outside" constituencies, including the government, the press, and various academic organizations such as the American Association of Universities (AAU). As dean or provost, I could focus on the "inside" of the institution, staying close to its academic development and its sense of operating as a unified whole.

Why did I now hesitate? I said to Henry that I simply did not know whether I would be willing to be a candidate. I would have to think about the whole matter, and of course talk with Angelica. Henry seemed pleased. He told me that he had heard I was bound to say no immediately and he assured me that I should take some time to consider it.

Rosovsky's visit disrupted our lives for weeks to come. Angelica and I first had to decide whether I should enter the search process at all, because we knew that if I chose to do so, it might be awkward to withdraw, particularly since the search committee wanted—understandably—to bring the process to a close before too much more time had passed.

What made the idea even plausible? First, we knew Harvard, and we especially knew—from our years there in the 1960s—that it was as intellectually robust and compelling an institution as any that existed. And unlike Princeton, it would be, in effect, new to us: We had been away for more than twenty years. Most important, however, it would offer us the possibility of being, once again, part of a residential academic community—something that had been central to our lives since our marriage in 1960, and part of my own personal life since 1948 at Wooster. I had deeply missed this experience during the few years I was at the Mellon Foundation, and had found no way to remedy the loss.

At the same time, there were all the contrary considerations. My work at Princeton had been centered on the liberal arts: I had never before worked with professional schools—such as law, medicine, and business— and Harvard had *eight* of them, in addition to the very substantial FAS. Then there was the entire scale of the place. It was far larger and more complex than Princeton, with about 18,000 students, and thousands of staff and faculty, including several affiliated teaching hospitals closely related to its medical school. Was this something that I could possibly "run" and lead? In addition, I was fifty-six, soon to be fifty-seven years old, whereas most Harvard presidents (such as Derek) had started when they were about forty or even earlier. In a decade, I would be well into my latter sixties. Would I have enough energy (and good health) to do a presidential decade (which was the most I could contemplate)? We had not yet reached the era, after all, when one's 60s—verging on seventy— were regarded as "young"! Equally important, what would happen to Angelica's professional life? Would there be anything in Cambridge or Boston where she could pursue her work in art history?

These and other questions occupied us for more than two weeks until we decided that I ought to meet with the full search committee. From my point of view, the main questions were simple: What kind of a president was Harvard seeking? What were the committee's expectations, as well as the university's main priorities? I knew that I was suited for— and interested in—certain kinds of administrative work, but less for others. Was there a possible match between their agenda and my own talents and temperament? If not, then I would quickly withdraw. Derek Bok had been a superb leader for Harvard and had left the university in a very strong position. I admired him greatly, and he also had a considerable effect on aspects of American higher education. But I was not like Derek, and I needed to know whether the Corporation was looking for a different kind of leader.

The first meeting—and then soon another—seemed to go well. The "chair" (senior fellow of the seven-person "Corporation," or board of trustees) was Charles Slichter, who was a physicist—very bright, warm, enthusiastic (in good ways), and easy to talk to. Ron Daniel, former head of McKinsey, had recently become Harvard's treasurer and was also on the committee. He was thoughtful and obviously discerning. In addition, there were just a few others, including Judy Hope (daughter-in-law of Bob Hope), Henry Rosovsky, and Bob Stone (later, senior fellow).

These were lively sessions: Would I be interested in trying to reintegrate the university, and make Harvard more a unity? Did I feel ready to embark on a major fund-raising campaign? What did I think of creating a required program in Western civilization? The questions were not at all hostile, but were clearly meant to explore major issues (and we had about two or three hours for each meeting). I had no idea where matters stood, or which other candidates were being interviewed. But it seemed clear that they were taking me seriously—otherwise they would not have spent so much time with me. On my side, I felt an easy rapport with the group, and I thought their agenda might possibly match my own interests and abilities: They wanted, not necessarily someone highly visible outside the university (although there was certainly no objection to that) but someone to bring the "inside" of Harvard much more closely together, in order to create a more unified institution. The desire and ability to undertake a major fund-raising campaign was also crucial.

In early February (of 1991) I wrote the following notes on the search process:

> The Harvard situation is in a strange zone at the moment. My mood and Angelica's has shifted in the last week or so, for some reason the precise challenges of the job, as I perceive them, seem clearer and clearer to me, and also more congenial to my own interests and abilities. Trying to build a real structure, to integrate the university, to find ways to get the parts to function better as aspects of a whole— all of this seems necessary to Harvard's future, and something that I could make at least a good try at doing.

As we approached early spring, Bill Bowen told me that I should think very hard about it all, because he thought it would be my "call"—

that is, that I would be offered the job, and it would then be my decision to make.

Bill Bowen proved to be correct. I was soon offered the Harvard presidency, and had less than a week to decide whether or not to accept. Angelica and I knew that our entire life would change (yet once again) if I decided to say yes. We would be on a seven-day-a-week schedule—but now with an enormous institution to move forward—not to mention the fund-raising campaign, whose goal was ultimately set at $2.1 billion, the largest in the history of higher education. At the same time, I did think that I might possibly be able to bring the different parts of Harvard—and its alumni—closer together, trying to create a more collaborative and "woven" institution.

Angelica and I talked at length with all the children, who did not hesitate: They believed we should go ahead. Then, on the last evening, the two of us had a long dinner at a modest restaurant called "The Isle of Capri," not far from our New York apartment. By the end of dinner, we had decided to accept, and I called the committee late that evening—the last possible evening!—to say yes. We took a taxi to an apartment where a few members of the Corporation were assembled, and we celebrated briefly, because it was already near midnight.

We flew to Harvard the next morning in time for a meeting with the Overseers, followed by a large press conference during which I did my best to answer questions on subjects that I had scarcely begun to hear about. One of the first questions, however, had to do with my salary, since the high level of academic presidential compensation was already becoming a controversial issue. I answered frankly that I did not know what the salary would be, but I hoped that there would be one. We had not discussed the salary issue throughout the search process, nor was there a contract of any kind.

Later, I decided on a figure of $190,000 a year. It was higher than that of Harvard's "university professors," but well below that of many other university presidents. The discrepancy was intentional on my part. From my own perspective, it seemed important to keep administrative salaries within range of the highest faculty salaries, in order to symbolize the fact that there was a single "community" on campus, in financial as well as other terms. By that time, trustees at some universities had already begun to refer to their presidents as *CEOs*, and to pay them increasingly higher salaries. Given the difficult nature of the jobs, this view was realistic and understandable, but I was more focused—given my goals at Harvard—on emphasizing the unity of the institution.

I was, however, still employed by the Mellon Foundation, with about three months more to go before I was to leave for Harvard. Bill Bowen generously gave me two days off each week, so that I could begin to get to know Harvard by meeting the deans, as well as faculty, staff, and students. This was immensely valuable, especially because the key position of the dean of Arts and Sciences was vacant, and I wanted to make that appointment as soon as possible. It was then, too, that I met Henry Louis ("Skip") Gates, who was just arriving at Harvard. We had a brief meeting, but nevertheless decided on the spot that we would build African American studies at Harvard beginning immediately (Skip was to be the new chairman of the department).

I began to make the rounds: lunch with Dan Tosteson, dean of the Medical School; a long meeting with John MacArthur, dean of the Business School—and Bob Putnam (dean of the Kennedy School), who was just leaving his position. Meanwhile, I continued my search for a dean of the FAS, and began to settle on Jeremy Knowles, chair of the chemistry department. Jeremy had once declined to take the FAS deanship, so I knew I had a difficult job of persuasion ahead of me: but we immediately liked one another, and he finally accepted. He was outstanding: an internationally recognized scientist as well as a person of great intellectual breadth and sophistication. A good number of years later, I did a brief summary of what seemed to me to be Jeremy's fundamental qualities: "Deans like Jeremy come only rarely. He had a penetrating mind. He had wit and charm. Above all, he understood the nature of a university and what it meant to search for knowledge, or discover even a single truth. The standard could never be too high. Many other things mattered, of course. But if learning, teaching, and research were not the heart of the matter, why were we here?"

By April of 2001 (still several months before my first academic term would begin in September) it felt as if I were already in full swing:

> Not much time to jot down all that is happening. Busy days: meetings with the Vice-Presidents, five of the Deans. Press conferences. ... A planning process is underway, and a feeling that there is a formidable amount to do in integrating the institution—allowing it to function in a unified way, as an effective organization. Letting people have the chance to work intelligently and energetically together, by provid-

ing the enabling structures, processes, resources and—most of all—
human encouragement. It can't be done completely. But it can be
done perhaps in large measure. ... Now, how to address these major
critical issues—"fragmentation," science and computing, "costs."

As we moved ahead, the question of unifying Harvard internally became
more and more central. At my inauguration in the autumn of 1991, Charlie
Slichter—the Corporation's senior fellow—made a brief statement about
the university and its needs:

> Each member ... has much to contribute and to gain from interactions
> with the rest of Harvard. ... [Harvard's] crucial task ... is nothing
> less than assuring that the whole is greater than the sum of its parts.
> There is perhaps no greater goal, there is perhaps no goal more
> difficult to assure, but in the Harvard of today no other area has more
> potential for enhancing quality. [The need is] for a conductor of a
> symphony role.

DOMICILED: NEW STRUCTURES AND PROGRAMS

Massachusetts Hall—which houses the president's office—is a modest,
almost inconspicuous building that is nearly the smallest structure in all
Harvard Yard. University Hall, headquarters of the dean of the FAS, is
by contrast a much larger stately affair in white limestone; it sits exactly
in the center of the yard, with one façade (where the bronze statue of
John Harvard resides) facing the freshman dormitories, and the other
looking out toward Memorial Church and Widener Library. Massachusetts
Hall, meanwhile, is off to one side, at the Yard's periphery. It is made
of handsome brick nicely toned by age, and its real distinction lies in its
excellent proportions: a low lying rectangle, rather longitudinal, with
fine lines and a gently sloping roof (somewhat interrupted by a row of
dormers).

Inside, there is a long central corridor, at the end of which is the
president's domain: a fairly large office, with President Charles Eliot's
nineteenth-century desk, a few bookcases, and some comfortable furniture
at the far end: a couch and chairs near a fireplace. It is a pleasant room
with ground-floor windows, a good deal of light, and a relaxed atmosphere
that made me (and visitors) feel at home. I liked the modesty of it and—
somehow—the building's relatively diminutive size made it feel all the

more distinctive. The front door was always open, and literally anyone could walk in unannounced to speak to the secretary stationed just inside.

Upstairs there was a cluster of offices with secretaries (there were still secretaries in 1991) and my five nonacademic vice presidents. On the top floor, there were rooms for a number of freshmen—a group that I was very happy to have nearby and visited from time to time. There was no provost, nor indeed any academic person (besides myself) in the entire building. The contrast with Princeton could not have been greater. I had of course nine Harvard deans, but each of them was housed with his or her own faculty and administration, on mini campuses located in a variety of places stretching from Cambridge to downtown Boston, where the Medical School and the School of Public Health were situated. To talk with one of my deans, I had either to telephone or drive—except for the few nearest ones within walking distance.

So Princeton, with its single faculty and its single focus on arts and sciences; with no semi-autonomous professional schools and no distances to span; with the president, provost, deans of the Faculty and Graduate School, plus the chair of the University Research Board all in a single building directly next door to the deans of the College and of Students: Princeton seemed light years away in its sense of cohesiveness and ease of access to the entire administration.

Given Harvard's administrative and geographical structure, it quickly became clear that the president, virtually alone in his building, actually had no direct relationship—or power relationship—with any faculty members (or any students) who were his "own." There was no Faculty Advisory Committee to the president, and certainly nothing that resembled the Council of the Princeton University Community. The president and Corporation constituted, in effect, a kind of holding company, while each major academic unit was responsible for its own functioning, except on those occasions when unusually important new financial—or academic—undertakings, or the appointment to tenure of FAS faculty members, was at stake.

There was no central oversight of the curriculum, for example, and no mechanism for joint planning and decision-making across Harvard. Some universities have faculty senates—which can admittedly be mixed blessings—with representatives from their different parts, to discuss and debate issues that affect the whole institution. Not so at Harvard. The president is of course free to intervene in serious situations that seem to require action, but even there his power is, from a practical point of view, very limited. His greatest powers lie in his ability to innovate (creating new entities if he can find the resources to do so); to foster cooperation and coordination among the deans, so that new joint undertakings can perhaps take place; or to speak out publicly on issues of unusual importance (either to Harvard or to all higher education).

But innovations and coordinated new undertakings require financial resources, and Harvard was—once again—structured in a way that made such actions complicated. Each unit (including every professional school and the central FAS) controlled its own finances: It possessed its own tuition funds, annual gifts, endowments, and research grants. It was essentially a self-sustaining enterprise and did not depend on the central administration for the allocation of resources. Hence the well-known Harvard phrase that "every tub [or ship] is on its own bottom." Every "tub" had its own money, and had to live within its means. In this respect, it resembled an independent college, with the dean playing the role of president, while relying mainly on his or her own faculty and staff for advice and support.

When I arrived at Harvard, for example, I heard almost accidentally that one of the major schools was in the process of building its own chapel. The dean had also chosen his own architect (and had of course raised the necessary funds for the project). I was more than taken aback but obviously could do nothing about it—except to see whether a future process might possibly be different.

Given all this, it was a major challenge for the central administration to support itself financially, particularly because it was rarely if ever the beneficiary of any gifts. Essentially, there was a central "bank" that was funded by an annual tax on all the schools, and also acted as a repository for other funds (such as student tuition and fees) that were initially deposited there before they had to be used by the unit to which they actually belonged. The "taxes" and other money were conservatively invested and produced income that was available to the president and his vice-presidents to support both the expenses of the entire central administration and any new academic or other projects that the president might wish to undertake. For example, shortly after I arrived, I was told that all the freshman dormitories needed immediate renovation. The dean of the FAS did not have enough money to do the full job, so he asked me to divide the cost with him. Given the importance of the project, I really had no choice but to agree, so I used the Center's modest funds, and borrowed the rest from the central bank. The renovations were in fact necessary and made a great difference to the College, but left me with the problem of eventually repaying the bank! So one essential way of trying to shape the university's future, and defining a path for the institution to follow, was in more than short supply: the Center had almost no capacity to distribute funds to the schools for projects, so a possible major source of help and influence was almost entirely absent.

During the Harvard fund-raising campaign that we later mounted, we made a deliberate attempt to raise money for the "Center," and had some success, but not nearly enough. In a report I wrote the Corporation as late as August 1997, I said:

> With respect to the PDF (President's Discretionary Fund), we are certainly in a much better position than before, but the resources remain very limited. This year, the "operating" income available for distribution is actually a negative number (there are some one-time capital funds that can be spent and there is also endowment appreciation that can be drawn upon). But even under the most optimistic scenario, the PDF might have $8–$10 million in flexible annual funds during the early years of the next century, against a total university operating budget of at least $2 billion.
>
> [The] Center has committed something in the range of $150–$175 million in the past five years, to support a wide range of current and "amortized" projects which, in my judgment, really had to be done. As a result of these commitments, there has been a virtual moratorium on any new commitments since 1995. (The list of "rejected" requests since 1992 has, I should add, been quite substantial.) The list of projects supported by the Center is far too long to enumerate in detail, but some examples are: the renovation of the freshman dormitories ($45+ million was the center's contribution); ... the computerized library catalogue (of which $11 million was paid for by the Center); ... a share of the Memorial Hall renovations; support for student aid, faculty positions, and selected renovations in some of the smaller [professional] schools, about $30 million.

Some of these projects were amortized over long periods of time, others were helped by fund-raising, and some benefitted directly from the small amount of discretionary president's funds. The full list was much longer— and much more costly!

When Drew Faust (the first dean of the Radcliffe Institute for Advanced Study) became Harvard's president in 2007–8, she soon discovered that there was not only a PDF dilemma, but also a serious endowment dilemma. She wrote me in early March of 2008:

> Dear Neil—Hope we have the chance at some point to talk about these endowment issues more fully—They are complex and vexing

in many ways. I will send you a copy of our response to Grassley's recent demands for information as I think you would find it interesting.

What I find most challenging about the endowment issues is how we are rich and poor at the same time. Even if the endowment went up to 100B (slowed down on that path yesterday, I fear!), it would still be lodged in 11,000 different accounts, each of which is under the presumptive control of someone—almost never the president and often not even a dean. So how we get hold of the money to finance big projects—like Allston or the Fogg—is not an easy matter, as you know well from the storms that surrounded the introduction of the SIF. If the endowment reaches 100B I don't know offhand what that would mean the endowment of Dumbarton Oaks or Ukrainian Studies would become but it would be eye-popping, yet increases in those budgets would not help us do most of the things so important to the university.

The reference in the last sentence to Dumbarton Oaks and Ukrainian studies concerns two semi-autonomous Harvard units that have their own endowments, which would grow proportionately as the entire Harvard endowment increased. But the added funds would be available only to those specific units, not to the university as a whole (whether the units did or did not have real needs for the extra funds). So too with virtually all the "parts" of Harvard and their endowments.

Although the Harvard endowment and general financial structure was in one sense impracticable, it functioned with a minimum of friction and competitiveness among the university's different professional schools, largely because they (and FAS) were not dependent on the allocation of financial resources from the central administration. If the president chose his deans carefully, and met with each one regularly, then the institution—which had operated this way for much more than a century—could move ahead rather like an armada, although there was very little to ensure that the entire flotilla could remain on the same course. Indeed, setting a course—deciding on a common direction for the university as a whole—was itself a major issue. Was it even possible to imagine such an idea? If so, what form might it take? When the Corporation said that it hoped the next president would be able to bring Harvard closer together and to make it more of a single unified institution, it was obvious that it had something like "a common direction" in mind. But how could we achieve such a result? In fact, as Harvard would inevitably continue to grow and become more complex, one could imagine that the institution would be *less* aligned internally, and less easy to manage, not more so.

How to proceed? Even before taking office at Harvard, I had decided that I would need a provost—and that he or she would need an associate—in order to create a central administration of at least three individuals with substantial academic knowledge and a capacity for university-wide academic planning (as well as acting). The move from one academic officer to three could enable the "Center" to have many more faculty contacts and make decisions in a more informed way (and build more relationships with individuals across the institution). Of course, it was one thing to create the office of provost, and quite another to decide on his or her precise duties. At virtually all universities, the provost plays (as I did at Princeton) a primary role in helping to set university-wide priorities and allocate university financial resources across the entire institution. But because these functions were not centrally located at Harvard, it was not immediately apparent what should be integral to Harvard's provost. Ultimately, I decided that the provost should help facilitate the job of bringing the different parts of the university closer: As we raised money (and used what little we already possessed), the provost would play a key role in providing funds for seed money to stimulate important cross-institutional collaborative programs. In time, these provostial duties expanded greatly, but this initial conception seemed a reasonable place to start—indeed, it seemed to be the *only* place to start.

In addition to the provost, there was the need for a very effective associate, and this eventually became Dennis Thompson, professor of government and head of the university's Center for Ethics and the Professions. I and Angelica had known Dennis and his wife, Carol, since 1968, when we all left Harvard for Princeton, only to return again later. Dennis was not only extraordinarily intelligent but also wise—a superb person with impeccable judgment who remained in his position until 2001. He made an enormous difference throughout his tenure, and we simply could not have functioned without him. I also decided that I would need a small quasi-academic cabinet: that is, a few individuals who were not faculty, but who were knowledgeable about Harvard, and who had faculty as well as administrative friends, to act as a trouble-shooting group as well as a weekly agenda-setting group.

The first person I appointed to this informal cabinet was Michael Roberts, a graduate of both Harvard College and the Law School. Michael had been assigned as an assistant to help me find my way around the university during my first few months. He was excellent, and as soon as the position of secretary to the Governing Boards opened up, I gave it to him. Michael was—by temperament, intelligence, and experience—exactly the right person for the job and he was (somewhat later) succeeded by Marc Goodheart (also a graduate of Harvard College and Law School) who continued to play a similar role—very admirably. Marc became a long-time colleague and friend, and proved to be indispensable to the university during my decade and then long after I had disappeared. He later became a vice-president, and continued to work with a succession of presidents with extraordinary dedication and effectiveness. Thanks to his skill and perceptiveness, the Governing Boards—and the entire university—were superbly served for decades.

As I began to settle in, I began to think that a full Council of all deans should meet very regularly with the president and provost. Derek Bok had periodically met with the deans as a group. I now wanted them to work as closely together as possible, in order to create joint university-wide programs of teaching and research. This would demand a great deal of them and would require frequent sessions, but it seemed to me to be necessary.

I failed to realize that the idea might be problematic. The "big" deans of the major professional schools and of FAS were pleased to meet with me as a group, but some of them clearly wondered why to include the "little deans"—especially those representing education, design, public health, and divinity. This "smaller" group had very little in the way of financial resources, and possibly might not be able to add very much to policy discussions, or ways of organizing the forthcoming fund-raising campaign.

I knew I could prevail to create the full Council, but even if I did, I wondered whether my "collaborative" idea could possibly work. To chair a roundtable with several reluctant chieftains would scarcely advance the cause, and we certainly did not need a dysfunctional administrative (and academic) apparatus at the center of the university. Nevertheless, I decided to go ahead. We would all meet at least once a month for three hours, and—except in rare cases—the only permitted agenda topics would be strictly academic. More precisely, I began by asking whether there were any ways in which the different schools could fruitfully work with one another. It seemed to me that several major problems—whether purely intellectual or societal in nature—needed the skill and knowledge, not simply of different *disciplines*, but of FAS and the different *professions*.

I wondered whether two or three significant topics might become part of a university-wide agenda. If so, which ones?

The Council sessions started slowly. Indeed, on the morning of our first appointed meeting, I said to Angelica that I wondered whether any deans would actually show up! They did, however, and in time, they began to know one another and discover projects on which some of them (without knowing it) were already simultaneously at work. The first significant breakthrough occurred when Dan Tosteson, dean of the Medical School, suggested that we might create a university-wide program on the subject of "brain and behavior"—something that could involve teaching and research from various points of view, touching upon the work of many parts of the university. I was enthusiastic but also concerned: "Brain and behavior" seemed to me to be potentially too limiting, and too likely to become a "behavioristic" program, leaving out important intellectual dimensions. I wrote a letter to Dan, saying that the term *mind* should be added to the title, simply because *mind* was a distinctive and different concept. Dan (and the other deans) agreed to the change, so Mind, Brain and Behavior (MBB) was born, both as a teaching enterprise (it became an undergraduate major) and a research venture. The topic of memory was one of the first to be pursued, and it involved study in the biological sciences, in psychology, in law (related to the validity of eye-witness accounts), in education, and in literature (as in Proust's *Remembrance of Things Past*). Once the ice was broken, other ideas began to follow, and although we decided to strictly limit the number of programs to launch, we were soon in a position to discuss other cooperative ventures that proved to be invaluable.

MBB was actually not the first broad-based program to be created. The excellent initiative "Ethics and the Professions" had been established in the 1980s by President Bok, with Dennis Thompson as its founding director. The program focused on research and teaching in ethics relevant to Harvard's professional schools. My own hope was that we might build on this model, and that the concept might become even more inclusive by creating research projects and discussion topics that would also involve faculty (and students) from many FAS departments, as well as—ultimately—undergraduate students. Dennis Thompson was receptive, and we were soon on our way. So MBB and Ethics established the terms for virtually all the other initiatives we would create in the next few years.

It was, for me, a major breakthrough. There would eventually have to be several different ways to try to bring Harvard together as a more unified institution, but this particular approach was heartening, and seemed likely to produce important collaborative as well as educational results.

TENURE AND ITS RAMIFICATIONS

Academic tenure stipulates life-long employment as an entitlement once it has been awarded to an individual faculty member at a college or university. The effort to establish it—and the periodic attacks on it—continued for decades from the early twentieth century until at least 1940, when the American Association of University Professors (AAUP) prevailed in its long attempt to ensure this form of faculty protection. Then, the vast expansion of higher education after World War II required, as we know, an enormous increase in the nation's faculty ranks—a development that strengthened tenure as an established principle of employment (assuming that an individual was granted it after a stipulated trial period).

Soon after it was firmly installed, however, tenure began to be trimmed nationally as a percentage of existing faculty positions, beginning with the era of "stagflation" in the 1970s. The most selective and well-known institutions held their own for a longer period of time, but the national average for tenure/tenure-track positions slipped from about 56 percent in 1975 to about 47 percent by 1989, to roughly 32 percent in 2005.

The 1990s witnessed an increasing tightening of the available tenure positions, especially, but not only, in the humanities. This phenomenon happened to coincide with difficulties in two other areas of faculty hiring when I arrived at Harvard in 1991. I soon learned, for instance, that there was a serious struggle taking place in the Law School between a radical group of faculty committed to "critical legal studies," and the more "centrist" faculty.

It is difficult to summarize the concept of critical legal studies briefly, but it was in effect a descendant of the legal "realist" traditions, of the so-called Frankfurt School of Thought, and of modern deconstructive theory. It rejected the concept that "objective" interpretations of the Constitution (or previous case law) were possible and declared that interpretations were subjective (and ultimately ideological) in nature. In his book *That Noble Dream*, Peter Novick cites Professor Sanford Levinson's view on the subject of interpolation:

> it would be nice to believe that *my* Constitution is the true one and
> therefore my opponents' versions are fraudulent, but that is precisely

the belief that becomes steadily harder to maintain. There are as many plausible readings of the United States Constitution as there are versions of *Hamlet*.

In short, if interpretations of the Constitution—and the law—are highly variable and even subjective, and if they often reflect an individual's ideological (especially political) views, then it follows that those who "control" the law—especially in universities and the courts—are really at bottom exercising political (or other personal) points of view rather than deriving them from a study aimed at reaching disinterested "objective" conclusions.

The conflict at Harvard Law School was fierce and the debate focused intensively on faculty tenure (as well as junior) appointments: Which "side" would each new candidate represent? The tone became so virulent, and the situation so difficult, that virtually every proposed new appointment was blocked. Things reached such a pitch that, by the end of my first academic year, the Law School's student newspaper produced a scandalous lampoon, attacking and ridiculing individuals and the school itself.

At that point, I put everything else aside in order to learn as much as possible about the situation. I spent much of the summer interviewing many senior members of the Law School (and some junior faculty) asking each of them to diagnose the problem, and to suggest ways that might help to solve it. This exercise absorbed dozens of hours, and although it failed to produce explicit answers to the school's problems, it did seem to have a therapeutic effect. At the end of the summer, the dean and others decided to form a special faculty committee led by a scholar in dispute resolution and compromise. This and other actions initiated by the dean managed to make a difference, and the tone of the school began to change, slowly but steadily, during the next few years. High tensions remained, but during the passage of time it became possible to begin to make appointments again. Not long afterward, the "moderates" were in control, legal crit studies were in decline, and a positive way forward was underway.

The Law School problems made clear to me how much I would have to depend on others to do much of the work that I myself instinctively did at Princeton. There, I could directly intervene in many situations, but now I would have to rely on the capacity of each dean and his or her faculty members to solve problems that I could only affect indirectly. This meant learning to live more patiently—and to some degree more helplessly—than ever before. I could assist and advise, but I would often have to watch and wait, hoping that time would help resolve situations, while recognizing that it might take the passage of even a few years (as it did at the Law School) before matters were at all settled.

This point was driven home for me when difficulties concerning Radcliffe College first arose. Radcliffe was located mainly in a handsome "yard" not far from Harvard Yard. The two institutions were—as suggested earlier—entirely separate. Radcliffe was incorporated with its own trustees, its own president, and—for a very long time—its own resident women undergraduates. Even after its students began to live in Harvard residence halls, Radcliffe continued to exist as an independent entity, hosting some noncurricular events for women undergraduates. This situation was obviously awkward because of Radcliffe's ambiguous role: It theoretically still had its own undergraduates, and the Radcliffe administration and trustees continued to maintain their technical role as an entirely separate institution.

None of these matters had ever surfaced in my discussions with the Harvard presidential search committee—not because anyone deliberately side-stepped the issue, but because it was, from the Corporation's point of view, no longer a problem for particular discussion or debate. When Jeremy Knowles and I arrived to welcome the new freshman class at Opening Exercises in 1991, however, we were joined by the president of Radcliffe (who also participated in the ceremony). In her talk, she emphasized the importance of women at Harvard, urging them to be assertive, and then she suddenly invited all the first-year women to Radcliffe College for a special reception—leaving the men out. Jeremy and I looked at one another, not precisely wide-eyed, but surprised, taken aback, slightly embarrassed: What could we possibly devise—impromptu—to entertain the men students? This was only the first of several Radcliffe wonderments. We soon began to discover that a corps of Radcliffe alumnae and others were ready to respond to any number of Harvard happenings. The fusillades were sometimes thunder-like, and they provoked some uninhibited reactions, especially from Harvard's robust dean of the College, Harry Lewis. Within a year or two, the drum beat about the paucity of women on Harvard's faculty (and in its administration) became constant, yet there was very little that could be done to speed up appointments, given the slow pace of faculty departures now that mandatory retirement age had been legally banned. Meanwhile, Radcliffe's new president said that she looked forward to a "partnership" with Harvard and added: "We are not competing with Harvard, nor are we merging or submerging our identity. Merger has not happened and it isn't going to happen."[1]

Events at the Law School and at Radcliffe inevitably raised the entire issue of faculty appointments, especially regarding tenure. I set out to add more women (and African Americans) to the Harvard faculty, but I was no less committed to keeping the standard of appointments absolutely high. These twin objectives sometimes conflicted in complicated—even at times tempestuous—ways.

Awarding tenure to an individual is one of the most important decisions that any college or university can make, because (as already suggested) an institution's excellence in research and teaching depends on its faculty—and the faculty is the institution's single most important indicator of its quality. If the faculty is not extraordinary, there is little one can easily do to change the situation, given the length of time that tenured faculty members tend to stay in place. That is one reason why, among the very best institutions, comparative university rankings (whatever the system of measurement) change so little: It takes a very great deal of effort (over a long period of time) for an institution to "move up" into the top-ranked universities; and, similarly, if a tenure system is working well, it also takes a great deal for an excellent institution to "fall."

At the moment, the idea of tenure remains under considerable pressure, not only because of attacks on the conception itself, but also from the simple fact that more and more universities and colleges—in the financial difficulties of the last several decades—are awarding tenure to fewer and fewer young people. Tenured faculty are expensive: They are paid comparatively high salaries and tend to receive excellent retirement and health benefits. As a result, part-time teachers ("adjuncts") have come to occupy more than half of all academic positions in the nation, and many full-time junior faculty do not have "tenure-track" positions—which means that they are not eligible for future tenure at their universities. In short, the number of "permanent" positions has been dwindling, and the trend has not yet come to an end. This change is one of the most consequential developments of the last three to four decades, and it represents a crucial alteration in the nature of the professoriate, as well as in the nature of residential college communities.

Quite apart from those consequences, it is important to raise the question (often asked): Why have tenure at all? To my mind, the answer is straightforward. Tenure is the only way of protecting freedom of inquiry and speech at a level—and in fields of study—where the conclusions of research scientists, economists, philosophers, political scientists, religious thinkers, psychologists, sociologists—indeed any faculty members—may be immensely controversial, and may become the source of fierce criticism, anger, and even enmity among people outside (or inside) the university. Today, faculty who study climate change, reproductive health, euthanasia, African American studies, and other subjects could certainly be at risk in some universities were it not for tenure—a system that guarantees they cannot be removed from their positions if their views are disturbing or offensive to some or many people. The idea (proposed by some people) that five- or ten-year renewable contracts may offer sufficient protection is short-sighted. Once the contract is nearing an end, and before it is renewed, there can easily be a pitched battle about whether or not it should be extended. And such battles can easily become a continuing—and highly disruptive—feature of university life. As a result, full tenure is essential, which is one reason why one must have an appointment process that is as rigorous, searching, and impregnable as possible.

Many people seriously wonder whether fears of "retaliation" against faculty who express unpopular views are exaggerated—whether there are in fact any real dangers attached to the expression of freedom of speech by faculty members. But during the McCarthy period, a number of faculty members were denied tenure for failing to cooperate with the House Committee on Un-American Activities (or not signing "loyalty" oaths); during the Vietnam period, there were incidents at Princeton (and elsewhere) calling for the dismissal of faculty members who strongly and publicly expressed views against the war; and when Anita Hill testified against Clarence Thomas's nomination to the Supreme Court, it was only a matter of days before members of the legislature in her home state called for her to be fired from her public-university post. More recently, faculty members are under assault in Florida's universities, thanks to the attacks by Governor Ron DeSantis. These are only a few of the most obvious examples in which tenure can make all the difference.

The United States is a politically volatile society, and our vast state system of higher education has many institutions that are often controlled by "regents" who are politically appointed. And because state legislatures—political bodies—are one source of funding for all public colleges and universities, some legislatures may be under great pressure to remove particular faculty members because of their views. Nor are the private universities and colleges altogether free from such forces, especially when the nation is strongly divided on certain issues. In those (and indeed other) circumstances, tenure is vital.

A university serves several important purposes, but none is more significant than its capacity to enable faculty and students to inquire freely into the world's store of knowledge—and into spheres where sufficient knowledge does not exist—in order to test theories, explore new ideas, and discover truths that can increase our understanding of reality. To seek, to search, to teach, and to publish one's beliefs are activities integral, not simply to the university, but to the very concept of a free society. No less important is the need to protect the ability of faculty (and students) to exercise their rights as *citizens*, speaking out when they wish on controversial issues, precisely as other citizens are—theoretically, but not always practically—able to do. In short, it is essential in a university that knowledge be advanced, that inquiry remain free, and that those who dare to express what they believe—either as scholars or citizens—can do so without fear. The changes in national tenure practice are therefore not incidental or insignificant: They represent a serious shift in the academy's capacity to carry out its fundamental purposes, and if carried much further, will represent a critical threat to the very mission of many colleges and universities.

UNIVERSITY-WIDE CAMPAIGN

As I looked ahead following my first year at Harvard, I quickly realized that if I were not very forceful in planning an agenda for the university, I could easily be swept up in the process of trying to solve one successive local—even if important—problem after another, with little or nothing to show in terms of a coherent pattern of events that expressed an intelligible plan or design. Seven to ten years could simply slip by with nothing to show except a series of firefights that were (or were not) resolved, often in a reactive way. So I soon began to define the main components of what I hoped would be an assertive set of actions intended to address major challenges: First, the clear need to bring the university closer together. Second, the identification of several individual initiatives that seemed to be significant and would—whenever possible—also be consistent with making the university a more powerful single institution. And next, the goal of undertaking a major fund-raising campaign, especially because the university was in considerable deficit, and the endowment needed an absolutely major thrust forward if Harvard were to be in a position to keep pace with the new intellectual challenges facing it.

At the time, Harvard's endowment stood at about $4.7 billion, and I calculated that we would need to triple or quadruple that figure in the next decade. That would be a formidable task, but it would be essential if we were to respond to all our needs in the biological, medical, and other sciences; in student financial aid; in information technology and its science; in the new "global" realities that were confronting us; in the humanities and arts; and in our libraries and museums. Moreover, Harvard's smaller professional schools remained chronically underendowed, and could not press vigorously forward without more capital to help them. Other new ventures also needed seed money. In short, financial resources were everywhere required, and everywhere in demand.

In my discussions with the presidential search committee before I was appointed, I suggested that one of the best ways of bringing Harvard together was to make the forthcoming campaign university-wide in nature, so that all the schools and faculties would be engaged in a common cause. This would not only focus everyone's energies on a single purpose, but would make each part of the university more knowledgeable about the others, inspiring them—one hoped—to help one another. Harvard had never before in its modern history launched a university-wide campaign, so there was a serious element of risk in attempting to do so. But I felt certain that the power of the university as a whole, with everyone working together, would be far more effective than simply having a few individual "detached" campaigns trying to raise as much as they could (which had been the previous pattern for Harvard fund-raising). In 1991, there were about 150,000 alumni. I thought they were likely to respond and work together to make all of Harvard stronger, rather than would be the case if only a number of individual units went forward on their own.

This must seem like common sense, but one must remember that each "school" or unit had been accustomed to cultivating its own donors for its own projects, reaching far back in time. Suddenly, one was asking them to let their individual donors think about the entire university, and to give—perhaps—to other parts of the institution rather than simply their "own" part. So there were anxieties on all sides, although everyone eventually agreed to sign on.

As we began to outline the priorities for the campaign, several goals emerged: some university-wide objectives common to all the schools (such as new faculty positions and student financial aid), new interfaculty collaborative programs, important school-specific needs, and some projects that I myself identified as central to Harvard's future. Among these were the effort to endow more formidably our various global, international, and regional "centers" (such as the Center for European studies, for Russian studies, for Near Eastern studies, etc.) and to make some new regional centers where none existed (for example, Asia, and Latin America). In addition, I wanted to create "homes" for departments whose elements were scattered throughout the campus (especially in the humanities and in international affairs). By doing this, one would hope to bring significant scattered parts of the university much closer together.

Finally, I was committed to help build African American studies to the point where Skip Gates wanted it, to become the most populous and distinguished department possible. That would certainly not be achievable from the president's office alone; one needed a leader in the field who was also a master recruiter capable of attracting the best faculty from other institutions, and of helping to groom junior faculty. Although the focal point of this initiative would be the Faculty of Arts and Sciences, Skip—the magnetic chairman of African American studies—and I wanted to spur other parts of Harvard to move ahead, so that the total number of African American university faculty would grow exponentially beyond just FAS. I would somehow provide financial resources and help with recruiting, but in the end, Skip made the whole enterprise move forward to the point of unequivocal success. By the end of the decade, more than thirty new African American appointments had been made across the university.

There were of course other projects that were important, but could not realistically be identified as campaign goals. One of these was to find a constructive way to "solve" the Radcliffe question. This was not at all entirely in our power, but later when an opening did finally present itself, I wanted to seize it—and to invest a great deal of money in it if necessary.

Some of our campaign "review" meetings gradually began to help define specific university-wide campaign priorities more clearly, which our development office (together with some consultants) turned into substantive documents. Five prominent alumni—from different parts of the university—were then chosen to be co-chairs of the Campaign, to symbolize the unity of the whole institution. Finally, a few months later, we created a steering committee of about forty additional alumni—all strongly committed to the entire university—to serve as a group who would be knowledgeable ambassadors from different parts of Harvard. In short, everyone was finally ready to launch.

I had never led a campaign before and had hardly ever asked anyone for money. Nor was I certain I could do so successfully. But I had a superb development staff—including Fred Glimp, Tom Reardon, Bill Boardman, Susan Feagin, Jack Reardon (in alumni affairs), and other leaders. They were always there to lay the groundwork and carry out the mission. So we went forward—not without some deep apprehensiveness on my part—committed to an enormous enterprise that would absorb about one-third to one-half of my time for the next several years.

Chapter 6

A Different Future:
Change and the 1990s

The 1990s were a comparatively benign decade with respect to overt student protests. At Harvard—and most institutions of higher education—speakers of many persuasions were invited to give talks, and few if any were shouted down. The tumult of the 1960s had given way to greater quiescence in the 1970s and beyond, moving toward the end of the century. Nevertheless, the era was not entirely without dissension. During the 1980s at Harvard and elsewhere, there were major protests concerning divestment from corporations doing business with apartheid South Africa. In addition, the expansion of the concept of diversity led to the presence on campuses of different groups of students that were frequently at odds with one another. For example, Andrew Schlesinger's book *Veritas* chronicled a number of such events that occurred in my own first year as president at Harvard (1991–92). Rudenstine, he wrote,

> needed all his folksy talents and wisdom with the demands of diversification shaking the foundations. During the night of November 11, 1991, stealthy messengers carried copies of the latest edition of *Peninsula*, the conservative student magazine, to the campus residences. It was a "Special Double Issue" on homosexuality with an exploding

pink triangle on the cover and articles attesting that homosexuality was a "bad alternative" and un-Christian and undermined society. There was a section listing groups "dedicated to helping homosexuals who wish to change their lifestyle."

The Bisexual, Gay and Lesbian Students Association held a protest rally on Friday, November 15, in the Yard, drawing several hundred people. The Plummer Professor of Christian Morals, the Reverend Peter J. Gomes (B.D., 1968), stunned the crowd by announcing that he was a homosexual. "I'm a Christian who also happens to be gay." ... This was a revolutionary statement by the minister of Memorial Church, one of America's seven greatest preachers, according to *Time* magazine.

These tensions flared when the Black Students Association invited Professor Leonard Jeffries of the City University of New York to speak in Sanders Theater on Jewish complicity in the African slave trade. Jeffries was a notorious racist, anti-Semite, and homophobe. Hillel Coordinating Council Chair Shai A. Held (1994) organized an eight-group coalition against the event. ...

In April, *Peninsula* posted flyers advertising a forum entitled "Spade Kicks: A Symposium on Modernity and the Negro as a Paradigm of Sexual Liberation." The flyer was adorned with the image of a black woman stripping for a white audience. ... The BSA, led by Zaheer R. Ali (1994) and Art A. Hall (1993), then issued a flyer entitled "On the Harvard Plantation," condemning the hostile atmosphere. ...

Rudenstine confessed to the Undergraduate Council in April, "Watching a fair number of events on campus this year, I would say that I have been sometimes surprised and sometimes disconcerted to see the extent to which people have been hurt and people have hurt others ... and the extent to which certain kinds of speech, certain kinds of behavior have really been bruising. ... I think that on any long-term historical view, whatever our problems may be, and they are many, we're as a society and as an institution in a far better place because we're more inclusive than we used to be, by far. ... But the pain and the human cost of that is a real cost, and you can't help but be sobered by that, I think. But I don't think we can give up."[1]

So diversity itself began to produce tensions and antipathies that threatened in serious ways the effort to create a campus community that might be constructive in its effort to bring together differences in backgrounds, attitudes, and intellectual convictions. The hope that students might learn—in positive ways—from one another's differences—seemed at moments a forlorn one, although no violence occurred in the 1990s and no invited speakers at Harvard were prevented from giving their talks. Nevertheless, the possibility of imminent or future contentiousness remained—and would be intensely realized within the next two to three decades.

In my final commencement speech as president (2001), I reflected on part of our university situation:

> Our university—as well as others—has recently taken upon itself an even more challenging role: to maintain the values of diversity and free expression while also attempting to create a humane community in which people respect one another's differences, and seek to understand and know one another well. Defining this complicated task—this task of living together—is relatively easy, but finding the means to achieve it is far more difficult. Indeed, it is a task that has never, to my knowledge, been tried before on anything like the scale that we are attempting.
>
> Why, then, should any of us ever have thought that the job would be easy? When the populations of the world have quarreled and fought for millennia in order to protect their religious, ethnic, national, linguistic, and other characteristics or symbols of group identity, why should we expect thousands of younger people to create easily or swiftly the kind of community that virtually all of humanity has tended to resist?

In turning now to review several main episodes of the Harvard decade 1991–2001, I touch on a number of the disruptive events and significant changes that occurred, but will do so by placing them in the context of the relative benignity of those years. Only at the end of the decade was there a prolonged sit-in that seemed to preview what would befall much of higher education in the years to follow—not in terms of future sit-ins but of other types of disruptive actions.

LGBTQ+: CHANGE BY ACCIDENT

Looking back for a moment, June 1969 witnessed the end of another year of antiwar and antiuniversity protests, and most of the academic world was mainly relieved to occupy itself with nothing but momentary release from the campus convulsions of the previous several months. But June

29 marked the beginning of another series of quite different protests that very few people expected—and not so many people noticed. The Stonewall Inn, in Greenwich Village, was home to a congregation of gay and lesbian people (most of them young) who sheltered there during many evenings, often dancing, in apparent shuttered freedom until New York City's police decided to raid the premises, arresting much of the crowd and destroying the Inn's bar and other furnishings.

But the raid led to fierce resistance by those inside: a battle raged all night, and then for several days. In the end, the police were forced to withdraw in the face of a "revolution" that paralleled—in effect—the existing Black Power movement. The Gay Liberation Front was born, and although there were many battles still to be waged, something fundamental had changed—literally almost overnight—in American society and culture.

I myself was scarcely aware of what had happened. I was fully occupied with what the SDS might do in the coming autumn. And I certainly had no idea how quickly—through the AIDS crisis and afterward—the new sexual revolution would affect (and change) attitudes toward so many people who had recently been social outcasts and indeed legal criminals.

In fact, I was still completely unprepared years later when one of my best Harvard staff members asked (in 1991) to see me. When we met, he said that he wanted me to know he was gay, and if that was a problem either for me or for the university, he was very willing to leave. I had been in administration for nearly twenty-five years by then, and (perhaps remarkably) had never confronted such a situation before. But I had no difficulty reassuring him that I did not want him to leave. Indeed, quite the opposite: I badly needed him and his talents, and I did not imagine there would be any institutional problems if he simply carried on.

And indeed, there were no problems. But I did not suspect at the time that the entire movement, not simply toward greater openness on the part of gays, but toward equal rights and full acceptance of them, would very soon gain unusual increasing strength and visibility in universities. Nor did I imagine it would quickly become a contentious issue on campus. Another major college and university change was underway—with profound effects, not simply for higher education, but for the nation as a whole. It began, however, in this accidental way—at least for me.

The next event seemed to me to be quite uncontroversial. I received a recommendation from the head of human resources to extend the health and other benefits enjoyed by married couples to gays and lesbians who had entered into legal "civil unions." But when I brought the issue to the Corporation, I immediately sensed unease and, on the part of Robert Stone, something close to opposition. I had certainly not expected this. Bob Stone was as sympathetic and well-disposed a Corporation member as I had. In the meeting, I gave him—and everyone else—as much time as necessary to discuss and consider the issue. No one spoke out openly against it, but I found myself buttressing the case by referring to our general university nondiscrimination policy (which at the time did not yet specify sexual orientation as one of the "protected" categories). There was some sentiment in favor, but also indecisiveness. After more discussion, I asked whether or not we could approve the recommendation. Bob Stone shook his head—not to register a no vote, but rather to signal disbelief. He had never, he said, expected that he would be asked to vote for such a policy. Then Ron Daniel stepped forward with a "yes." In time, Bob also came aboard—still incredulous.

This quiet affair was nothing, however, compared to what soon happened. A group of conservative students founded—as already indicated—a new campus magazine called *Peninsula*. It was far from subtle in its editorial policy, and went openly on the attack against everything from diversity, "affirmative action," the presence of Black students on campus, and the great threat that homosexuality was said to pose to the university's student body. There had of course been previous incidents: periodic slurs against gays, and times when they had been made to feel uncomfortable in dormitories. Disturbing as these events had been, however, they bore no resemblance whatsoever to the direct and vicious onslaught from *Peninsula*. Homosexuality was said to be un-Christian, as well as a serious psychological disorder that should be "cured" through counseling and therapy.

As Andrew Schlesinger stated in *Veritas*, there was a strong, immediate response on the part of gay, lesbian, and bisexual students who called for a rally in Harvard Yard, not far from my office in Massachusetts Hall. Several speakers attacked *Peninsula* but, even more, others affirmed their right to be treated as all Harvard students are—on equal terms as full members of the university community.

What was a forceful and even brave rally, however, soon became a sensational one. Peter Gomes, the popular, respected minister of Harvard's Memorial Church (and the Plummer Professor of Christian Morals) showed up to demonstrate his support for the beleaguered students. Gomes was an extraordinary campus figure. He was also an African American Anglophile, an honorary member of Cambridge University's Emmanuel College, and a sartorially elegant pastor who could hold his own with virtually anyone.

So it was with a sense, not simply of surprise but near disbelief when Peter took the microphone and said that he himself was gay and he wanted to express his solidarity with all those at the rally, as well as others. His statement set off immediate cheers and applause, but it proved—later—to be inevitably disturbing to many members of the university, to alumni, and to some members of Memorial Church. I was completely taken aback, but I also felt the courage and passion that had motivated Peter.

Within a day or two, I began to receive phone calls and letters from people on and off campus, including a "demand" from *Peninsula* that I should fire Peter immediately, since he could not possibly lead Memorial Church any longer, or preside over Christian services. I actually had no trouble coming to a conclusion on the issue and made a public statement saying that any matters regarding sexual orientation should be discussed and resolved between Peter Gomes and his Church authorities. My job was to evaluate his performance as a preacher, pastor, and academic, and I found him to be exemplary.

To my surprise, the statement immediately began to stifle the debate, mainly because Peter was so greatly admired. But it did not stop *Peninsula*. The magazine continued to publish, and to embolden extreme conservatives. Peter, however, stayed happily and serenely at Harvard for many years afterward—eloquent, witty, and beguiling to the end.

Thomas Cabot was an imposing person who was a direct descendent of the Cabots, who—along with the Lowells—were at the summit of Boston's Brahmin social hierarchy. But Tom, though fully aware of his lineage, was a fine, direct, unpretentious person who was deeply devoted to Harvard. He was also, however, the product of a much earlier era when it never occurred to anyone that there could be "open" homosexuals who were accepted as members of the university. Tom asked to see me privately, to register his great concern and unhappiness—in fact, disapproval—about what was happening on campus, and he was visibly upset when I appeared to be condoning the direction in which matters were moving. This was one of the most awkward and uncomfortable conversations of my entire decade at the university. I did not want to offend or alienate Tom, but I also felt I could not be less than candid with him. I did my best to explain why we could not—and should not—discriminate against individuals or "categories" of students, so long as they were people of unusual ability who contributed in many positive ways to the university.

He was far from persuaded. He moved restlessly in the chair just opposite me. At the same time, he was obviously reluctant to challenge the authority of a Harvard president—a reluctance that was also part of the habits of his own earlier era. We talked hesitantly. Tom clearly could not understand my position, but he also knew me well enough to assume I was not intending to subvert Harvard's moral standing. In time, we realized that neither of us was likely to change his own (or the other's) mind. Yet neither of us wanted to part on anything but good terms. Slowly, and obviously unhappily, Tom stood up and then withdrew, upset but nevertheless courteous to the end.

It never occurred to me that when Harvard decided (in 1993) not only to award Colin Powell an honorary degree but also to ask him to be our commencement speaker, that the invitation would quickly lead to a large and explosive protest. In theory, Powell was the ideal candidate: an African American who, by his sheer talent, commanding presence, and leadership capacity had arrived at the highest position that could be achieved by anyone in the military: chairman of the Joint Chiefs of Staff. He was not only an American icon and an articulate spokesman, but a hero to African Americans everywhere.

Once the Powell announcement was made, however, members of the LGBTQ+ group began to organize against the invitation, and it was only a matter of time before other members of the university joined them. The reason: as head of the armed forces, Powell was ultimately responsible for the notorious and hopelessly inadequate policy regarding gays: "Don't Ask, Don't Tell." The policy was seen, not only as evasive, but obviously one that failed to accept gays as equal members of their profession—as individuals who should be judged according to their abilities.

As the end of the year approached, it was increasingly clear that, without some firm ground rules, the entire commencement address and ceremony could well be disrupted: something unacceptable in itself, and doubly so because a national Black hero would have been shouted down while speaking at Harvard.

My general counsel at the time was Margaret Marshall, whom I had only recently persuaded to take the post. And Margie was no stranger to protests, because she was a South African who had—in earlier days—been the leader of the national student anti-apartheid union. To my immense relief, she willingly took charge of the situation, and began to meet with the demonstrators. Margie soon made it clear to the LGBTQ+ group that if Powell's speech were actually disrupted, it would do far more harm to their cause than any satisfaction that might be derived from it. Fortunately, the students were intelligent enough to realize what was at stake. They then created—with Margie—a plan that would give their group (carrying signs and banners and pink balloons) great visibility at commencement, in exchange for their willingness to keep from interfering with Powell's talk. There was one more agreement: that I would meet with and address the group (including alumni) at a major dinner they were holding on commencement evening in Cambridge.

And that is what happened. Powell spoke uninterruptedly, the demonstrators were highly visible but could nevertheless be ignored, and I talked that evening to the group and assured them that the university was firmly behind a policy that treated all members equally and respectfully. It turned out to be a harmonious gathering—even amicable—and I left in good spirits, more than ready for bed.

Unfortunately, Margaret Marshall remained my general counsel for only four years. I had not been the only person to recognize her talents, and she was soon (in 1996) asked to become a member of the Supreme Judicial Court of Massachusetts. At the time of her appointment, I gave the public "oration" in her honor. I mentioned that while one aspect of the law was intended to restrain human beings from doing harm to one another, there was in fact a corresponding view—embodied by Margie—that saw

> the law as something that cherishes central human values and potentialities: liberty, respect for other individuals, and for the importance of allowing people to find their different pathways in pursuit of happiness. ... Margaret Marshall understands wonderfully the importance of the liberating capacity of the law to help and sustain people, to persuade them that freedom is a reality—that individuals will be fairly treated, that societies and their laws can be equitable, that the aspirations and ideals of people are in fact part of our very conception of justice.

It was not long before Margaret became chief justice of the Supreme Judicial Court of Massachusetts and it fell to her to decide a major case of national significance: whether, under the constitution of Massachusetts, same-sex marriage should be legal. Margaret proceeded in her all-encompassing, unstinting, logical but sensitive way, and finally rendered an opinion declaring that, in Massachusetts, same-sex marriage was in fact constitutional. It was the first case in the United States to endorse such a view, and it provided enormous momentum to what became a successful national movement.

Finally, near the very end of my years at Harvard, the mastership of Lowell House (one of the grandest and most prestigious of the university's undergraduate residential "river-bank" houses) became vacant, and a new person had to be appointed. In making such appointments, the dean of the Faculty of Arts and Sciences usually consults with the president, as well as with student members, faculty, and administrative staff of the house in question. After an exhaustive process, Jeremy Knowles discovered that virtually everyone in Lowell House favored appointing co-masters: two women who were living together as partners. Jeremy was in favor, but also sensitive to the possible explosion. "But, Neil—*Lowell* House!" He and I talked for hours about the potential backlash, but it was clear what should be done. Before long, the two women—Professor Diana Eck and Dorothy Austin—were appointed: the first such instance in Harvard's history. There was scarcely a visible ripple in response, and unsurprising, they were superb masters for many years to come.

Unlike my work to help build African American studies at Harvard, the steps I took with respect to the LGBTQ+ community were completely unplanned, even accidental. I had never confronted the issue directly during my twenty Princeton years, and had no considered policy views on the question. But the initial incident with my excellent staff member suddenly crystallized matters: Would I really let him go because he was gay? In effect, I learned about "equality" as I made my way, confronted by surprise after surprise, issue after issue. Chance led me to create policy, and—in the end—individuals like Peter Gomes, Margaret Marshall, and even Tom Cabot were those who made the difference.

Although these particular incidents concerned a "local" Harvard matter, they were—as I have indicated—no less part of a much larger movement toward university—and national—acceptance of a change that few people would have imagined could take place in so short a period of time. And the change was itself part of a much larger movement toward a broader conception of "diversification" beyond the traditional categories of geography, religion, race, and others. In the early 1990s it was difficult to grasp all the dimensions—and the extraordinary implications—of this movement, but it would clearly alter the nature of student (and other) populations (and interactions) across the nation. We would become even more diverse, more complex, more tolerant as well as less tolerant at the very same time.

TRANSFORMATIVE SKIP

The drive to enroll more African American students at most colleges and universities began mainly in the 1960s. Programs and departments in African American studies were also initiated at many colleges and universities. They rarely had more than a few faculty members, however, because the supply of available African American (or other) scholars in the field was still very small.

Even in the 1980s, the situation was not very different. Harvard, for example, had a demoralized department with few members and without strong leadership. Henry Rosovsky, as dean of FAS, decided to change the situation dramatically, and he persuaded Henry Louis "Skip" Gates to move from Duke in order to reignite African American studies at the university.

Skip was arriving in Cambridge at exactly the same moment that I was coming from the Mellon Foundation. I wanted to work closely with him to see what could be accomplished. Happily, we were quickly drawn to one another as friends, and I asked him to make a plan for what he wanted to achieve—in particular, a list of faculty whom he would like to recruit. Skip insisted that any new African American faculty members should be *joint* appointments. He wanted to ensure that his choices were accepted by *other* departments, not only his own. This was wise: There would be no "Black ghetto." Indeed, part of the goal was to include White faculty as well as Black, and to make *all* students feel welcome in the department and its courses. The hope was not only to build a major local enterprise, but to help provide impetus for other initiatives in African American studies.

Skip promptly made his faculty list, and it included "stars" who were based in a number of other universities, as well as some younger people (and part-time visitors). I agreed to try to find resources for his new team, and also to help with recruiting—although Skip himself was the main (and remarkable) recruiter. His list had (at least) William Julius Wilson, Leon and Evelyn Higgenbotham, Cornel West, Larry Bobo, Jamaica Kincaid, Anthony Appiah (who was arriving with Skip), and several others. This would be a major challenge: Most of these faculty were already very happy at universities such as Chicago, Princeton, and similar institutions. Moreover, Skip wanted to sign up several scholars already at Harvard, including Susan Blier, Barbara Johnson, and Werner Sollors. These would work part time in the department and would offer occasional courses. In total, the entire group numbered at least fifteen—many of whom were among the best scholars and teachers in their disciplines.

The effort began—purely by circumstance—with Leon and Evelyn Higgenbotham. Leon was at the time the most distinguished and visible African American judicial figure in America, and should have been appointed to the Supreme Court but was passed over so that the dubious Mr. Thomas could be placed on the bench. Skip and I had several conversations with Leon, who was a wise and unpretentious person, and he and Evelyn finally agreed to come. From the beginning, Skip also made it clear that Cornel West should be among the earliest appointments we could make. At the time (1991–92) Cornel was one of the best known African American faculty members in the nation, and had a distinguished professorship at Princeton, where he was altogether happy. Skip was convinced that if we could appoint Cornel—given his particular kind of magnetism—it would help to create a cascade of other appointments (and of students interested in studying in the department). It would also assure, because of Cornel's exceptional ability to attract undergraduates of all colors and creeds, that the department would indeed be completely open to everyone. In fact, Cornel's introductory course in the African American department regularly enrolled at least two hundred to three hundred students and helped to bring a good number of them as majors into the field.

In the end, a friend of Skip's decided to endow a professorship in the Divinity School, because the dean was very anxious to appoint Cornel. So Cornel was given a major post with a joint appointment in African American studies. He would not come, however, unless he was promised a university professorship in due course—a commitment that I later fulfilled.

It was not long before Skip then lured Larry Bobo from the University of Chicago, then Jamaica Kincaid, and then, after a *very* long struggle, William Julius Wilson (also from Chicago), who was generally perceived to be one of the nation's best scholars in his discipline. Other appointments soon flowed, and Skip ended up with something very much like the department he had hoped for.

Closely related to the recruitment of African American faculty was the entire issue of affirmative action—and diversity—in college admissions. This policy had gone unchallenged until a Caucasian (White) student brought a legal suit that was heard by the Supreme Court: the so-called Bakke case. The issue was whether a White student—who was denied admission by a public university—would have been enrolled if preferential treatment had not been given to purportedly less able Black students. In June 1978, the court decided (by the slimmest of margins) that certain forms of action in admissions were permissible insofar as they advanced the *educational* purposes of institutions. A diverse student body—with different kinds of students bringing their divergent points of view to the table—had long been recognized as an integral part of education, and the Court upheld this view in a 5–4 decision, with Justice Lewis Powell writing the determining opinion.

I was of course a strong advocate of this point of view, and Harvard continued its work to identify and accept talented Black undergraduates. But the battle to sustain the program was a long and highly controversial one. At a meeting of the American Association of Universities (AAU), an invited speaker made a strong speech against the policy. I replied, but was so angry that I literally walked—actually stormed—out of the meeting. I also then began to write a long statement supporting the policy and, after much discussion, several of us managed to revise it and then have it adopted unanimously (and published) by the AAU. This was not easy for a number of presidents. Some were from Southern states and were at odds with their trustees or regents over the issue. But in the end, they nevertheless signed. It was an act of considerable courage on their part, and a moment of real triumph.

Since the time of the Bakke case, diversity in admissions has been strongly and persistently attacked. Indeed, the very constitutional amendment that was first adopted to guarantee African Americans equal protection under the law was being used to argue that White students should also be assured that they too were equally protected. At the time of this writing, the current Supreme Court has overturned the view of Justice Powell in the Bakke case: The ability to take race into account in admission decisions will no longer be legal. This will almost certainly lead to a dramatic decline in the admission of Black students to many colleges and universities. There will be less diversity, and the potent American enterprise in African American education will suffer a terrible blow of irreparable harm.

UNWIRED: THE COMPUTER SCIENCE REVOLUTION

Some of the most far-reaching changes in postwar higher education had some of the most inconspicuous beginnings. In the late 1970s and early 1980s, few of us had ever heard of DARPA (the Defense Advanced Research Projects Agency), but it emerged in time as the founder of what eventually became known as the *Internet*. The breakthrough had of course worldwide implications, and quickly began to enable computer-driven connectivities that led to forms of global communication unsuspected by even bold and imaginative earlier technologists. I myself had barely heard of DARPA and certainly did not expect it to change, in a revolutionary way, the university's entire manner of going about so much of its work and life. For me, the new age announced itself in a highly unassuming guise. One day, early in my first year in office, I was visited by Sid Verba, head of all the university's approximately ninety libraries (the number has since been reduced). Sid was an excellent scholar, and someone who mainly by his good-natured manner, his quintessential decency, and his tone—constantly flew beneath the radar. Anyone in charge of the university's multitude of dispersed libraries clearly had to be astute, adroit, humane, and sufficiently urbane to manage an enterprise that always has the potential for either petty squabbling or patrician contentiousness. Sid was precisely the right person for the job.

When Sid arrived, he had what appeared to be a clear if also complex idea: He wanted to create a single on-line catalogue that would include all the published materials from all of our libraries. This seemed timely and—in 1991—even bold, so I immediately said yes, of course. But there was only one problem: The "big" schools thought that the amount of money they would have to pay (because each unit would necessarily contribute to the cost) seemed inordinately high, whereas the "little" schools felt they had scarcely any money at all for such an undertaking. The problem could be solved if I would contribute the $11 million required to pay for half the project.

I was faced with an all too frequent problem: scarcely any flexible money of my own, and a consequent need to amortize the project by borrowing against the Center's "bank," hoping that more money would become available in the future. After several meetings and hours of discussion, Sid persuaded me that the new catalogue was essential, that it would for the first time bring all the libraries together, that the cost was really very modest, and it would be an another way for the deans to work collaboratively together. How I would find the money remained an interesting question. But we went ahead and Sid was correct—it was obviously the right thing to do.

Thus began one of the early steps in what would eventually lead to the university's complete involvement in the age of information technology, moving well beyond libraries to the continuous invention of new computer models and then hand-held devices with their multitude of apps, to social media, to the advent of MOOCs (Massive Open Online Courses) and other innovations. Some of these latter developments did not take place until the years between 2001 through 2019, so I witnessed them only after I had left the Harvard presidency. But enough was underway by 2001 to make obvious the fact that, in our effort to connect the different parts of the university, information technology would provide us with previously unimaginable means of doing so. Even the most simple process—email—made it possible for individuals and units in the Faculty of Arts and Sciences to communicate continuously and to work fruitfully with distant Harvard colleagues in medical science and public health. Tying together the university in this way constituted a completely new and extraordinarily effective means of achieving many goals that would otherwise not have been possible. Indeed, communications not only within Harvard, but with colleagues around the world, soon became easy and routine. Thus began, not simply at our own university, but in higher education altogether, one of the most profound changes—affecting research, aspects of teaching and learning, communications, and other fundamental processes—that we had ever experienced.

In 1991, however, Harvard was barely at the beginning of this development, and it seemed to Jeremy Knowles and me that we were already in danger of falling very seriously behind in several key areas: computer science, where we were scarcely underway, and the Division of Engineering and Applied Science (DEAS), where the "divisional" faculty seemed to have little or no coherence or sense of common direction.

Harvard had actually made very early major breakthroughs in computer science, but they had not been followed up. As early as 1944, Howard Aiken—then a navy lieutenant—was in charge of Harvard's Bureau of Ordnance Computation Project, and he persuaded IBM to build what became the world's first computer (which he initially used to compute the coefficients of the arc tangent).

The machine was fifty-one feet long and eight feet high, and it could carry out (with its five hundred miles of wire) five different mathematical operations—three per second. This cumbersome giant was outstripped in 1946 by the Mark I computer. Aiken then became the world's first computer science professor, and he started an MA program in CS at Harvard in 1947. But years later, when Bill Gates entered Harvard (in 1973), he found no rich or large expanded treasure hoard of computer science courses, and dropped out of the university in 1975 to start Microsoft. Much later, in 1991–92, Harvard still lacked the facilities and faculty necessary to be a player in the field.

Computer science, therefore, became a major priority in the Campaign, but our only real prospects were likely to be Bill Gates himself and Steve Ballmer (who had remained at Harvard for his full four undergraduate years). Both of them were running Microsoft, still a comparatively young (but already very successful) company.

When I visited the West Coast, I had a meeting with Bill Gates. His office was unpretentious—very much a business office. When I arrived, he seemed preoccupied. He periodically turned to his computer to stay abreast of things. Meanwhile, I did my best to outline our needs. But there was little apparent rapport and our conversation ended inconclusively. I left feeling worried and discouraged.

To my surprise, however, I heard some months afterward that I would (with Jeremy and our fund-raising leaders) be participating in a tele-conference session across the country, in which Bill Gates and his father would be "present." In our tele-meeting, we talked further about our pressing needs in computer science, and this time the rapport seemed far better. Our leading development staff members followed up, and in due course we received unexpected news: Bill and Steve Ballmer would together provide the funds to build a new computer-science building, to be named, not for themselves, but for their mothers. Our only problem then—which was soon solved—was to recruit a chair of the department and sufficient excellent faculty to move the program ahead. One major, indispensable step had been taken, but it was only a bare beginning. When we dedicated the building, however, Howard Aiken's widow was present, and hanging on the wall in the downstairs foyer was the first computer program that Bill Gates had created when he was still a Harvard undergraduate.

The DEAS presented an even more formidable challenge. Here, there were a few dozen faculty—most of whom were excellent—pursuing their own research projects with little connectivity among them, and no common agenda. There were no departments within the division, and it was difficult for students who wished to pursue a coherent program of study. If anything seemed to need more "unity," this was surely a welcome candidate. But the question before us was hardly a simple one: How to give shape and articulated purpose to a group of individuals who largely followed (and valued) their own pathways in their own work?

Then, quite suddenly, the head of the division—an excellent but not well-organized person—decided to step down, and that gave us the opportunity to search for a leader who was capable of bringing about major change. After a good deal of tribulation, Jeremy found exactly the right person—someone who was at the University of California. He was a distinguished scientist, but most of all he saw the problems within the DEAS immediately, and he had exactly the right personal as well as scientific qualities to fix them. He was gentle, persuasive, firm but with a light touch and great clarity of vision. These characteristics were perfectly fitted to solve the DEAS difficulties that were all too evident. We offered him the job, and he accepted.

Our new dean—Venkatesh Narayanamurti, happily known as "Venki"—immediately began to work along two lines: seeking more faculty who could be strategically placed, and beginning to form small groups that were working in similar research fields within the DEAS. No university of any standing could afford to operate *without* an effective applied science and engineering program, and finally Harvard was in the midst of achieving what was needed. The final problem—the question of whether one should try to create a free-standing engineering school—was something that we knew would have to be considered carefully and solved later. Engineering (as we have seen in the Princeton context) was quickly becoming a more central area for university research and education. Student enrollments in engineering had already begun to grow—across the nation—in the 1970s and 1980s. By the 1990s, they had increased even further. This was partly because the subjects themselves had become more and more important in an age when technology—in all its manifestations—was critical, but equally because student job opportunities continued to flourish.

Any shift from a modest-sized DEAS at Harvard to a full-scale modern engineering school would be very substantial. Significant new resources would have to be found for new facilities and faculty. And the question of whether Harvard should—given its proximity to Massachusetts

Institute of Technology—leap to a full-scale enterprise of this kind still needed further study. Indeed, sometime after I left in 2001, the leap was precisely what took place under President Faust: A very large gift from John Paulson made possible the creation (in 2015) of an entire new School of Engineering, and Harvard then began to achieve even more in the applied as well as basic sciences.

In 1996, a group of faculty in technological and related fields decided to have a national conference that was called *The Internet and Society*. There were to be several keynote addresses, led by Bill Gates, Larry Tesler from Apple, and leading figures from Intel, Sun Microsystems, and other organizations. The proceedings were published in a 500-page volume that was largely (but not exclusively) technical in nature. The conference gave me an opportunity to find out in some detail what was happening at Harvard, and in my opening talk I summarized what were (for some) surprising recent student developments:

> A year ago, the Arts and Sciences websites experienced about 150,000 hits in the month of March. This March, just one year later, the number increased to 2.3 million. There is no sign of a slowdown.
>
> A year ago, the volume of email traffic on the Arts and Sciences network was about 80,000 a day. Twelve months later, the number had grown ... to about 215,000 per day—or about 6.5 million per month. ...
>
> So if I am asked whether something unusual ... is under way, the answer is a clear "yes." And we are only at the beginning.

I and others discussed how the new technologies might change teaching, learning, and—very obviously—research. But there were, I thought, serious worries as well. I was concerned about everyone being flooded with an infinite amount of information (and chat), much of it trivial, and so I talked briefly about the problems confronted by everyone when larger and larger libraries began to be created in the late eighteenth and nineteenth centuries. The eighteenth-century French "encyclopedist" Denis Diderot once remarked that "a time will come when it will be almost as difficult to learn

> anything from books as from the direct study of the whole of the universe. ... The printing press, which never rests, [will fill] huge buildings with books. ... [Eventually,] the world of learning—our world—will drown in books.

The fear of being overwhelmed with volumes and volumes of "information" was real, just as was the fear that individuals would become lost in a vast landscape of books, wandering in stacks for hours or days on end, alone and increasingly unsocial. Robert Darnton, the master historian of eighteenth-century France, quoted (in discussing this topic) a 1795 German treatise on public health, warning that excessive reading induced

> a susceptibility to colds, headaches, weakening of the eyes, heat rashes, gout, arthritis, asthma, apoplexy, pulmonary disease, indigestion, nervous disorders, migraines, epilepsy, hypochondria and melancholy.

Historical parallels are never exact, but in 1996, Columbia's Center for Research on Information Access reported that an increasing number of students "drift off into the [Internet] world, at the expense of everything else." Some of these students had already flunked out. And this was occurring long before the era of Facebook (not to mention Instagram—and others) arrived.

The conference was a success in heightening awareness of what was happening digitally, and pointing toward an unknown future of novel happenings that, everyone hoped, would benefit education and the larger world in untold ways. We were only beginning to be vaguely aware of what might, in social media and international politics, go awry. Mainly, the view was still Panglossian and the results far from Fox-like or Trumpian. The total transformation was barely begun, and hopes were high. Within a decade or more, however, it became clear that the ability of individuals to lead "digital lives" that were highly enclosed in terms of the limited information—and news—they might absorb, would lead to political (and other) divisions in society that were deeply inimical to the sense of a unified nation. One had reached a point where "facts" were no longer shared, and where "alternative universes"—in terms of beliefs, convictions, views—existed in highly divisive ways. The politics of the nation, and to some extent of higher education, were deeply transformed in previously unsuspected ways.

MAJOR PROBLEMS: PRIVATE AND PUBLIC HIGHER EDUCATION

During the early 1990s, I began to be increasingly aware of serious budgetary problems involving a great deal of American higher education beyond its well-endowed selective institutions. One difficulty concerned the long-standing (and worsening) situation related to small liberal arts colleges that were not nationally well known, and had little in the way of either endowment funds or annual-giving revenues. Another problem was also beginning to be a matter of major concern: it had to do with the plight of public-funded colleges and universities in most states.

If the costs of attending Harvard seemed shocking and newsworthy to many people, they were nevertheless cushioned by generous financial aid for more than half of each entering class. But at institutions that were truly under duress, fees were relatively high (and rising), and financial aid (except for loans) was often nearly nonexistent.

I first heard about these difficulties from colleagues, but then I read—in 1994—David Breneman's excellent little volume titled *Liberal Arts Colleges: Thriving, Surviving, or Endangered?* Breneman studied 212 less-well-known and quite small liberal arts colleges, most of which had been in existence for many decades—some dating back to the nineteenth century. The crisis they faced began, in effect, during the stagflation decade of the 1970s, when fees rose rapidly and students (as well as their parents) were becoming more and more job oriented and career conscious. What Breneman discovered was that his group of 212 colleges had begun to change their curricula in order to introduce more pre-professional subjects (in business, health sciences, education, pre-law, communications, etc.). The liberal arts subjects alone no longer seemed to offer potential applicants enough in terms of a secure future—especially when the financial investment was so high, and the payoff so uncertain. Breneman discovered that the curricula of his 212 colleges had pre-professional courses representing about 33 percent of all their offerings in 1972, just as stagflation was beginning. By 1988, however, the percentage of pre-professional courses had risen to 54 percent. Were the institutions any longer liberal arts colleges? He wondered—and rather doubted.

Since Breneman's study, the situation of such colleges has grown worse. Many have gone out of business and one can easily see why their collective future is so precarious. Here, for example, are two relatively recent case studies:

- One college had about 300 students and an annual operating budget of $14 million. Its endowment was very small ($36 million) and its alumni gifts were modest. It existed, in short, almost entirely on student fees, which were approximately $50,000 a year. Its total financial aid budget was barely $21,000. Because of high fees, it was having trouble attracting enough students to continue operating.

- A second college had about 3,700 students, but the number of applicants had recently been declining. It had virtually no endowment and little annual giving. Its cost: $47,000 per year, *excluding* all miscellaneous expenses (such as books, travel, or similar items). It managed to keep fees slightly lower than some of its competitors because its faculty–student ratio was not so favorable, and its faculty salaries were comparatively low.

These examples are not untypical. Moreover, while creating more pre-professional courses had been the main defensive strategy of such colleges, other ideas had also been tried. For example, one college (to boost enrollment) increased the number of admitted foreign students, but the experiment failed because so many of the overseas students were underprepared (especially in English) and could not finish their course of study. Another example: many institutions—to save money—increased the number of adjunct faculty, who are part time and are paid low wages with no benefits. Other colleges introduced a good number of online computer courses, even when the quality was not high. One college, faced with bankruptcy, attempted to drop several departments and their associated faculty in order to save a great deal in annual operating expenses. It chose for elimination those departments that were most seriously under-enrolled. These were nearly all in the humanities: French, Italian, philosophy, piano, art, graphics, art history, and—surprisingly—business. The outcry from almost all quarters was so great that the plan was soon dropped in favor of other short-term emergency measures. Finally, some colleges have very recently considered merging with another institution, so that the combination might lead to larger enrollments (and cuts to avoid duplication). But it is of course not easy to find appropriate partners, or to actually consolidate.

A *New York Times* article (January 13, 2018) pointed out a similar but different problem involving *rural* public liberal arts institutions, especially when their neighboring towns have diminished in population. The University of Wisconsin at Stevens Point—founded in the nineteenth century, in a Wisconsin farming area—was planning to drop its history, French and German departments in order to create career-focused programs. Tenured faculty would lose their employment, and further cuts might well be needed in the future. Applications for admission (and enrollments) had steadily dwindled. Without some dramatic move, bankruptcy would be virtually certain. But it was not at all clear that the proposed new model— if achieved—would actually solve the fundamental problem.

One senior at a nearby high school was planning to major in history at the college, and was quoted in *The Times* as asking, "What is a university without a history major?" But the town of Stevens Point had in recent decades lost thousands of residents to urban areas, and now only had a total population of about 26,000. Most students tended to apply, not to their local institution, but to larger campuses in cities such as Madison and Milwaukee. The projected two-year deficit at Stevens Point was $45 million in 2018, and the state's governor placed a freeze on tuition, so no further funds could be expected from that particular source. The only alternative, therefore, was defined by the state's vice-president of the Higher Education Executive Officers Association: to open up "different markets and [offer] different services."

Not only was the university's mission in the process of being radically redefined, but the language used by the officer was obviously not the language of higher education. *Business, markets, services,* and *sales* were becoming the new nomenclature. Budget cuts, said a member of the American Association of State Colleges and Universities are really not an alternative: They "will give the flagship university a bad cold, and the regional public colleges pneumonia."

Finally, an article (February 2019) in *Boston Magazine* began with the headline, "These Days, Being America's College Town is Starting to Look Like One of Our Greatest Liabilities." It reported that on April 6, 2018, the president of Mount Ida College in Newton, Massachusetts, announced over the loudspeaker (at lunch) that the college (of about 1,000 students) would close permanently after graduation in June. Panic set in, but the situation was in no sense unique. High tuition, doubts about the value of a liberal arts degree, and diminishing applications had combined to lead to bankruptcy, and similar factors were affecting dozens of small colleges in Boston's environs. Eight colleges in eastern Massachusetts had recently gone out of business, and two others in the area (besides Mount Ida) were also likely to close in the spring of 2019. The estimate was that, in a few years, "30 to 50 percent of private colleges [around Boston] will close or merge with another school." The rest of the article suggested some of the ways that small Boston-area colleges were competing for students: new student centers, new media labs, upscale new dormitories, more on-line courses. Although economists were projecting the possible loss of approximately 165,000 jobs in Boston-area higher education, the worst has not yet come to pass, although the future is far from clear.

If many small liberal arts colleges are facing one set of profound problems, publicly supported colleges and universities were beginning (especially by the 1980s) to confront very different but scarcely less obstinate difficulties. Following the student "revolution" of the 1960s and the disastrous economy of the 1970s, more and more states began to invest less and less in their institutions of higher education: sometimes (as in California under Governor Reagan) for ideological reasons, sometimes (especially in poorer states) for financial reasons, and sometimes because of what they believed to be higher priorities. Across the country, legislatures were less and less willing to invest in their colleges and universities, and the only remedy was for institutions to begin raising fees and seeking more private funds—to keep pace with rising costs.

A snapshot of what occurred can be gained if we follow, for instance, the pattern at the University of California over several decades. In 1959, tuition was actually zero—the university was literally free (except for room and board); by 1977, it was $49 a year; by the 1990s it had risen to about $3,000, and it kept moving steadily upward. When the "Great Recession" arrived, however, state funding for public higher education (not simply California) was *cut* in all states—an *average* cut of 20 percent from 2008–9 to 2013–14, with some states as high as 30 to 40 percent, and even the lowest in the 5 to 10 percent range.

This action had a devastating effect, and led to an average national tuition increase of about 27 percent beyond the 2007 level. Some increases were of course very much greater than 27 percent. The result: Literally millions of undergraduates were affected. About 75 percent of all US students were by then (2013) enrolled in public institutions, and approximately four million of them were in research universities. On average (with considerable variation) *each* state enrolled about 80,000 undergraduates in its *research universities* alone. In some individual states, such students totaled about twice as many as *all* the undergraduates attending *all* the eight Ivy League universities combined.

In 2012–13, the average in-state total cost of attending a public research university had reached about $23,500. The data from 2022 show that some of the best-known public research institutions (including Michigan, Wisconsin, California, and Illinois) were in the range of about $38,000 for tuition, room, board, and other fees. If we ask what these same institutions charged out-of-state students, the range was near $60,000, a figure not much lower than that of the best-known well-endowed selective private universities.

Of course, there is need-based financial aid at many of the public institutions, and there is federal aid as well. There are also major loan programs. In the end, some students pay little in the way of tuition and fees. Many others pay far more, and many cannot afford to attend at all. The main point, however, is that the cost of public higher education has increased extraordinarily, and the reasons for this continuous growth lie mainly outside the control of the institutions themselves—and in the hands of public officials and state legislatures. Unfortunately, there is no solution to this problem, unless the institutions can raise even more private money, or the states begin once again to invest heavily in their universities and colleges. Otherwise, the situation is simply destined to become worse: far less money, significant expenses, a need to "cut," and about 75 percent of the nation's students virtually stranded.

A financial reversal, therefore, seems anything but possible. Nevertheless, New York had decided (before the pandemic) to take the step of offering free tuition at two-year state colleges. This was obviously a hopeful sign—a significant move that might have led others in thinking freshly about higher education. Until now, however, the cost of attendance at most institutions has been so high that many students work at odd jobs for long hours to earn money; they borrow very large amounts, which they find difficult if not impossible to pay back; they take more years to complete their degrees; their drop-out rate is very great; and recent media reporting has indicated that some undergraduates are actually eating less to save money. In short, we have a far-reaching crisis, but there is no obvious, realistic remedy available to the colleges and universities themselves. Expanding the search for increased private funds is one alternative, but available to mainly the "elite" public institutions. When we discuss the subject of change in American higher education since World War II, fewer situations have had a greater and more profound impact—affecting the vast majority of all our students—than what has happened in the "public sector" of our complex system.

THE ARRIVAL OF *GLOBAL*

Gradually, during the last decades of the twentieth century, the word *global* began to rival and even replace the word *international*. The Guggenheim Museum, for example, heralded its global outreach, with major installations in Bilbao (designed by Frank Gehry), Venice, and elsewhere. One began to hear the term *global health* and similar phrases.

At the same time, some universities began to consider whether their own futures ought to take account of these new ways of thinking and acting. Now that technology enabled worldwide instantaneous communications, now that the world's economies were increasingly interconnected, now that air travel to nearly all parts of the globe was easier and even pervasive, should universities consider expanding abroad in various ways? If so, did such ideas imply new programs, new "installations," or various forms of undergraduate studies to be undertaken in foreign countries? Expanded research opportunities—and the need to fund them—were only the most obvious of possible activities. What else should one do, if anything?

This was a complex issue and it represented major opportunities under changed conditions for higher education. Different universities soon began to define a variety of ways to move ahead. Some of them considered creating actual satellite campuses abroad, which would admit undergraduates and confer degrees in the name of their home institutions. Others opted for exchange programs, or else accelerated efforts to recruit and enroll a far greater number of foreign students at their home campuses. There would very likely be no single pattern, and indeed there might well be a mix of different initiatives at a particular institution. New York University, for instance, created a new campus for undergraduates in Abu Dhabi, and Yale in Singapore (since discontinued). Our own discussions at Harvard led to different conclusions. First, we decided not to undertake the creation of a degree-granting campus abroad. We were concerned about the costs of doing so and, most of all, we worried about the capacity to sustain such a venture over a long period of time. Would the institution's quality be sufficiently high? Could one find exceptional faculty who would want to teach abroad for sufficiently long periods of time—for years to come? Depending on where the campus was located, could one count on a foreign government to support or tolerate indefinitely an American-like university, with its unfettered freedom of inquiry and expression (and its various forms of diversity)? Would the foreign government conduct its affairs in such a way that we would want to be associated with it?

Our preference was to create a large number of "outposts" in key cities around the world. They would be capable of helping faculty and students undertake research and limited educational missions in different countries. Our own staff (and help from local alumni) could maintain these sites. Several such places could serve as the locus for limited-term midcareer courses (mainly created by our professional schools) because of the strong desire on the part of many foreign professionals to have such education and training available to them. In short, the "outposts" could advance several important purposes, and their activities might well change and evolve over time. Indeed, different professional schools (and FAS) would undoubtedly fashion their own approaches as they ventured abroad.

As it turned out, the Business School, the Design School, Environmental Studies, the Kennedy School, the newly created Asia Center, and the Latin American Studies Center began very quickly to formulate their own distinctive plans, and the School of Public Health and the Medical School soon joined in this general effort. Meanwhile, it was obvious that if these new initiatives were to succeed, they would need considerable resources. As a result, we designated support—in our fund-raising campaign—for international or "global" institutes: Additional endowment funds (ranging from $5 to $10 million each) were in time raised to help such projects. Much more needed to be done, but at least a worldwide agenda was beginning to take shape, and one more piece—at least in the 1990s—needed to be put in place. That involved the attempt (mentioned earlier) to bring all the relevant programs together in one or two buildings so that individuals and groups involved in different ventures would come to know one another, thereby increasing the chances for greater collaboration abroad and at home. Eventually, this took place, under the patient guidance of the fine architect Harry Cobb.

Ironically, one of our first global initiatives began in New York City, not overseas. David Rockefeller was a Harvard alumnus who was deeply interested in Latin America, and he and I soon agreed that Harvard's programs in the study of Latin America were far from strong. In time, David decided to help begin a new Center for Latin American Studies, with ample funds to endow it. The Center was to be "university-wide" insofar as it would involve faculty and students from the professional schools as well as from the Faculty of Arts and Sciences. In this way, any number of subjects and problems might be explored: issues related to public policy, urban design, architecture, literature, health, fine arts, the environment, law, education, human rights—and so on. In addition, this would be yet another way to bring disparate parts of Harvard closely together.

With sufficient endowment, the Center could underwrite graduate as well as undergraduate courses and—equally important—offer fellowships to faculty and students to undertake two- to three-month research projects in Latin American countries. No less significant, we could invite faculty and students from Latin America to spend periods of time at the university. Finally, there could be a full menu of noncurricular activities, such as lectures, conferences, films, readings, exhibitions, and symposia. One would capitalize on the intellectual resources of all the university, bringing together individuals from many of the schools to take advantage of the combined power of their varied talents.

The Center was eventually named after David, and this very early effort made an enormous difference to my own level of confidence near the beginning of our fund-raising campaign. What I learned from this encounter was one simple thing: The quality and significance of a proposed project are what ultimately matter to most potential donors. If there is a genuine demonstrable need, and a chance of achieving something that is important and excellent, then people are very likely to respond. Having a "case" to make, and making it with conviction was, more often than not, largely what was required to stimulate people's interest, enthusiasm, and generosity.

In fact, one of the least understood—to the outside world—aspects of fund-raising is that it is at bottom intellectual and educational in nature. In a campaign, one sometimes asks faithful graduates to give money open-handedly out of sheer loyalty. But many potential donors, certainly major donors, must be convinced that the purposes of a campaign are not only necessary, but that they will sustain and improve the quality of the institution—that their gifts will really matter in significant ways. And to achieve this, those who are asking for funds must know in some detail what is needed, and why. As a result, fund-raising cannot be divorced from educational goals. Unless the two are strongly bound together, a campaign may have a difficult time reaching or exceeding its goals.

There were certainly many moments when I wondered whether our own Campaign would succeed, and so Angelica and I began to travel frequently across the country—and abroad—to bring alumni and friends closer to the university. In the United States, we journeyed to Chicago, Los Angeles, San Francisco, Florida, New York, and elsewhere—something that began to help create a national alumni "community." The original target set for the campaign had been slightly less than $2 billion, and several deans felt this was as high as we should go. No institution had raised even $1 billion at that time. The Princeton Campaign, for instance, had reached just $400 million in the late 1980s. But some of our deans felt that we should try to break the $2 billion number, so we ended up with a figure of $2.1 billion. This seemed more than enormous. In the end, we actually reached $2.6 billion and, equally important, the endowment quadrupled—from about $4.7 billion in 1991 to $19 billion in 2001. This success was due partly to the Campaign, but greatly to the leadership of Jack Meyer, who was head of our team of investment managers, and Ron Daniel—our superb treasurer. The money allowed us to realize essentially all of our individual projects, as well as our broad university-wide goals.

The Campaign involved not only travel in the United States, but many journeys abroad, including China, Hong Kong, Korea, Taiwan, Japan, Berlin, Paris, London, Mexico, Brazil, Argentina, and other destinations. Our voyages were not only part of the Campaign but also an effort to bring the larger, dispersed Harvard community closer to the university. An even more general reason, however, was the simple fact that the institution was now very obviously a global university with many thousands of alumni scattered around the world. In addition, access to officials (as well as to scholars and members of the public) was far greater in the 1990s than earlier. As a result, the simple ability to learn about the reality of life in many countries was vastly increased, and we wanted to take as much advantage of this change as possible.

I gave talks in dozens of cities, and Angelica and I met a wide range of people, including "rulers," political figures, academics, cultural leaders, students, and ordinary citizens. For instance, when we were in Japan, we spent the better part of a day with modern Japanese architects, especially Tadao Ando, with whom we had an immediate rapport—such that he brought us to see some of his Tokyo buildings, including fascinating residences "hand-crafted" in poured concrete.

When we shifted to Beijing, we were whisked through customs and two days later were taken to meet with Chairman Jiang Zemin of China. His quarters were not luxurious, and he greeted us cordially. He gave us a tour of the residence, and—among other things—showed us the room where Mao Zedong had stayed, in bed and ill, during the last months of his life, still running all of China in spite of his condition. There were certainly some awkward and some amusing moments in the visit. At one point, Jiang and I together had to endure the traditional formal Chinese way of greeting and hosting: the two of us sat next to each other on a dais at one end of a long hall. All of Jiang's dignitaries sat (in order of importance) down a row on his side, while my small retinue was visible on our own side. What to do, or say? I was completely perplexed. Then

Jiang leaned over and asked me (in English), what was my favorite movie? I said that I didn't really have just one. "What is yours?" "*The Titanic—* I've seen it five times!"

The visit was doubly important because Jiang had been the first Chinese ruler who decided to travel abroad very visibly to "open up" China to the world. He chose to go to the United States in 1997 and had a major "welcome" and meetings in Washington. He also decided that he wanted to make a full visit to an American university and he decided on Harvard. We extended an invitation immediately, and it was arranged that he would give an important address in Sanders Theatre (located in Memorial Hall). At that point, matters became unexpectedly complicated.

First, there were many students and townspeople who were strongly against the visit. Why give special treatment and a major podium to the leader of a nation that trampled upon human rights and whose values were completely antithetical to our own? Protests quickly began to be organized. But many other people, of course, wanted to see and hear the leader of China. Already, one could see the possibility of clashes between the two groups—and possibly a disruption of the entire event.

Fortunately, two of our own major faculty in East Asian studies— Bill Kirby and Ezra Vogel—stepped forward and helped to organize a series of forums to which students and others were invited, to discuss why an "open" university should be willing to hear speakers of different points of view in order to listen, learn, and either find points of agreement— or radical disagreement. These "educational" sessions had a major effect on the tone of the entire situation. In addition, it was agreed that those who wanted to protest the event could gather on one of the streets near Memorial Hall. If others wanted to show their support for hearing the speech, there was yet another street where they could gather! Nothing was assured, but now at least some semblance of possible order was beginning to emerge.

We soon learned that our contact person would be the Chinese ambassador to the United States. He immediately laid out a series of "demands": There could be no visible protests or demonstrations; Jiang was to be met in a traditional way, by a group of Chinese children bearing flowers; and there could be no question-and-answer period following Jiang's speech. All of this was totally unacceptable to us, and it was not at all apparent what we should do next. My notes report that the Chinese ambassador was self-important, bureaucratic, shrill, trying to be imposing—always reacting in a dogmatic-authoritarian way. "The President does not stand for questions"—"Of course it is the President's decision to do whatever he chooses," I said. "But questions and responses are part of our tradition, so if he does not want to answer questions we on our side will have to ponder that, because it represents something out of keeping. ..."

I was essentially stalling, hoping that Ezra and Bill would call Beijing that evening. They had many important contacts in China and they were soon in communication. By next day we had an answer: "yes, etc. OK."

The entire event was pressured from beginning to end. It (as my notes say)

Involved very intensive day-to-day planning for two weeks in ad-vance—plus a great deal before. There were always tensions. Ezra (who was marvelous and invaluable) wanted the visit to take place, not surprisingly, almost (not quite!) at all costs. Several issues. Making the most of the educational chances, which the faculty undertook. ... Making sure that non-disruptive protestors outside could be seen. ... Also, that those in favor of the visit could [demonstrate]. ... Secu-rity—outside and inside; a huge challenge, given the nature of an open university. Ezra tense; Rick Hunt present; Marc Goodheart helping; Bill Kirby, steadfast as always; police, etc.

Part of the problem was that Sanders Theater (in Memorial Hall) is at the intersection of several main streets, and noise could possibly travel from outside to inside. So we had a special university group attack the problem:

Transformed and sound-proofed Sanders Theater, where the lecture would be, in 24 hours!

On the day of the speech, I stood at the appointed hour

Just outside Sanders—Jiang's car drove from the "tunnel" [next to Memorial Hall] over to Kirkland Street. He got out under the "canopy" near the door. Crowds were massed outside the perimeter of Memorial Hall—far down the streets—and no flower girls!

Jiang greeted me with a cordial handshake, and we then walked together into Sanders Theater, which was absolutely packed to capacity.

After a brief introduction, Jiang walked to the microphone and began to speak (along with an interpreter). I sat listening, but also tense. I could not help but think about the possibility of a disruption from members of the audience. As we have already seen, it only takes several well-placed individuals shouting—from different parts of an auditorium—in an effort to stop a speech, or to make it very difficult to hear. And the process of trying to remove protestors can only add to the total disorder. But as Jiang's talk moved steadily forward, it seemed more and more clear that the audience would mainly listen, and we would almost certainly make our way to the end without serious interruption. The speech itself was friendly, and the audience was in fact appreciative. Three questions were to be answered and had been carefully prepared by our faculty members: they were challenging (having to do, for example, with China's intentions concerning Taiwan), but were asked in a straightforward way. Jiang answered them in very general terms that offered no specific answers. Before we knew it, the entire event was over. There was a good deal of applause. Jiang and I slowly made our way to the door. We shook hands. Then he left, and Angelica and I were whisked off in a limousine with America's ambassador to China. He was very happy about the day's success—which was certainly welcome, but seemed to me to be largely symbolic. A helpful speech, a possible shout-down, another close-call, averted largely by Bill Kirby and Vogel, another event that seemed—almost—to foretell a different future for invited speakers.

There is no question that the most celebratory and deeply moving day of our decade was the moment of Nelson Mandela's visit to Harvard in order to receive an honorary degree. This was not only thrilling in its own right, but was an extraordinary event because the university had rarely given honorary degrees to a single individual—*not* with others at commencement, but at a special ceremony: once to George Washington, once to Winston Churchill, and now Mandela.

Fortunately, the day was brilliant in sunshine—an impossibly perfect spring day, and the Yard was more than filled with crowds standing as far as the eye could see from the platform that had been erected next to Memorial Church, facing Widener Library. Everyone had come to see South Africa's heroic president and be part of a truly historic moment.

Mandela arrived with his wife, and they were open and warm in their greeting: It was clear that, when they saw the Yard brimming with vitality and a sense of history, they too were moved. But before going to the platform, they and Angelica and I went—with several others—to a room in Memorial Church, and we sat together in conversation for more than half an hour. Mandela was full of energy despite his years and the trials of his life. We simply talked, not about major problems or issues in the world, but about the pleasure of the moment. When we emerged onto the platform into the sunlight, there was a prolonged roar and cheer from the assembled crowd, and then—quite suddenly—a stunning group of African drummers, in full bright color-filled regalia, began a "greeting" that, in its powerful rhythm, lasted for minutes. Then a choir of students sang both the South African and American national anthems—a hushed moving tribute that brought a deep solemnity to the moment.

The program had of course been very carefully prepared, and two speakers—one White, and one African—offered greetings to the president. I followed with a somewhat longer introduction, and then Nelson Mandela spoke for about twenty minutes—about freedom, about forgiveness, about some of his own experiences: sometimes witty, sometimes blunt, sometimes modulated: *not* seemingly read, but delivered with apparent spontaneity. At one point, however, he said that

> We constantly need to remind ourselves that the freedoms which democracy brings will remain empty shells if they are not accompanied by real and tangible improvements in the material lives of the millions of ordinary citizens of those countries.

And he concluded by stating that

> We enter this new millennium in the hope that the rich fruits of learning will in this coming century be truly shared by all in this global village in which we live ... and that this institution, of which we are now a proud member, will play a leading role in achieving that.

The main impression—in addition to what President Mandela said—was made not by the speech itself, but simply by watching—and being in the presence of—this heroic figure who had united and healed the terrible wounds of a country that had been tragically divided, and that continues to struggle in an attempt to overcome its past. When the speech was over, thunderous applause, music, drums—and then the four of us walked out of the sunshine to a final rendezvous before Mandela and his wife departed. Everyone was exhilarated, and everyone felt a sense of awe as a result of what we had just experienced. I suddenly thought how strange and yet perhaps appropriate that the century's great leaders of nonviolence—in the face of terrible violence—should have been people of color: Gandhi, Martin Luther King, and Nelson Mandela. All three had brought major forms of freedom and diversity into their worlds, with positive but also tumultuous results that were formidably progressive and simultaneously divisive. Indeed, only one of the three figures escaped assassination.

RADCLIFFE INSTITUTE FOR ADVANCED STUDY

Radcliffe and Harvard began—as we have seen—very early discussions (in 1960) about a possible eventual merger, and only a very few other institutions were in a similar "co-ordinate" situation. Although coeducation was achieved de facto in Cambridge during the 1970s, the awkward governance predicament that I found in 1991 continued to exist until late in the decade. At one point, however, I began to hear rumors that Radcliffe was experiencing difficulties, but it was some time before we realized that the college might be in a weak financial position, and that its effort to launch a number of new midcareer programs for women was not succeeding. Two or three Harvard alumni—who knew some Radcliffe trustees—intimated that the difficulties were real, and that the trustees were concerned. It was not until the academic year 1997, however, that the president of Radcliffe called me and asked whether we might have some conversations. I quickly agreed and we began a series of discussions that stretched over a number of weeks and then months. But the president spoke in veiled terms and I had difficulty understanding exactly what she was proposing—or not proposing. I reported this to the Corporation and Ron Daniel asked whether he could join me in one or two of these sessions. I could not have been more pleased. Ron came to our next talk, but he quickly begged off, because he too confessed that he did not know what Radcliffe seemed to be saying.

The conversations continued without visibly progressing. I felt certain, however, that they would sooner or later lead to a conclusion. Why else would they have been initiated, and why else would the president of Radcliffe have persevered? Nevertheless, I decided that we should open up a second front to see whether some clarification could be achieved by another route. Al Carnesale had just been recruited to become the next president of UCLA, and I had asked Harvey Fineberg—dean of the School of Public Health—to succeed him as provost. Harvey agreed, and he turned out to be exactly the right choice. I immediately asked him to see what he could discover about Radcliffe's situation. He soon enlisted the help of a Radcliffe alumna, Susan Wallach, and they in turn forged a relationship with other members of Radcliffe. In time they learned that Radcliffe's financial problems were in fact serious, and that the moment was coming when we might be able to see whether a new Harvard–Radcliffe alignment could be achieved. How to bring this about, and what the alignment might be, remained obscure. But soon afterward, the excellent chair of Radcliffe's board of trustees—Nancy-Beth Sheer—began to take part in the discussions. Others, including Hanna Gray (whom I had recently asked to become a member of the Corporation), also helped greatly in making a real difference. Indeed, Hanna proved to be exceptionally perceptive from every point of view on the Corporation, and she also took a personal interest in addressing the Radcliffe situation. As a result, we all began to see whether a new Harvard–Radcliffe relationship could in fact be created.

It took months to decide what this future relationship might be. It was obvious that the current Radcliffe mission would have to be changed dramatically, and that another completely new conception was needed. That conception would have to be intellectually compelling, and would have to give special recognition to Radcliffe's historic role in championing the education of women. This was a complicated set of objectives and there were very few alternatives—so far as I could see—that would be adequate. After a great deal of further analysis and discussion—helped immeasurably by Hanna—we finally reached a conclusion: We would bring into being a Radcliffe Institute for Advanced Study (RIAS). It would be multidisciplinary in keeping with our larger university goal of bringing different intellectual fields of study together, and it would be part of Harvard. We would need an extraordinary woman to lead the RIAS as a full Harvard dean on a par with all the other deans, and we would pay special attention in admissions to ensure that a good number of women would be working on projects related to some aspect of women's studies. There would of course be other fellows—including men—who were engaged with a variety of topics, but the special role of women would be acknowledged and honored.

From a practical point of view, Harvard would have to provide the initial money for the new institute, and the university would in exchange receive title to Radcliffe's land and buildings. Thanks to the university fund-raising campaign, we had the necessary resources to underwrite the start of the new venture, but more fund-raising would have to be carried forward by the institute's new dean. The outcome was as positive as we could have hoped for, but many Radcliffe graduates were understandably angry and disturbed. Their own college was suddenly extinct, and their degrees no longer represented anything tangible in existence. There was obviously no way to remedy this, and it created unhappy—even bitter— feelings among some alumnae for years to come. At the same time, the institute gradually gained a Radcliffe following when it began to demonstrate how invigorating and intellectually stimulating it could be.

Once the actual arrangements were agreed to, I wanted to move ahead as quickly as possible, and the late Mary Maples Dunn—the former president of Smith—agreed to be the acting dean for the first year (1999– 2000). That initial year was critical, and Mary carried it off with great skill and spirit. The task of finding a permanent director was formidable, however. The person would have to be someone with exceptional academic credentials as well as all the personal qualities and abilities to enable a new—and far from proven—institution to succeed. I appointed a search committee (of nearly twenty FAS faculty) to help.

Thus began a long, tortuous journey that constituted the most complicated and difficult search of my career. I began by visiting deans and provosts at a number of universities, hoping that the right person would suddenly appear. But she didn't, and after two months I began to wonder whether the entire effort might simply fail. Surely there had to be someone capable (and willing) to take on the new position? Finally, the name of Drew Gilpin Faust was suggested to me. Drew was a preeminent scholar of the American South, and she was firmly installed in the University of Pennsylvania's history department. She had been approached about administrative positions before, but had never ventured forth. Moreover, her husband was also a distinguished professor at Penn, and I was told that the likelihood of their moving was approximately zero. So I immediately travelled to Philadelphia to meet Drew, and see whether she would indeed be the right person for the new deanship. I went—and she was.

Then began a long courtship that lasted several months, simply because Drew was clearly very deeply ambivalent about assuming a major administrative role. She did finally agree to visit Harvard in order to discuss the idea, but she left without suggesting in any way that she would conceivably leave Penn to come north. At the same time, I felt that the very fact she agreed to talk indicated she must have been at least partly intrigued by this new prospect, so I decided not to give up. After more notes and telephone calls, Drew visited again, and this time she asked more questions—and seemed somewhat more engaged. But there was no obvious indication of a "yes." Meanwhile, some of Drew's Harvard friends were strongly urging her to come. Then, finally and unexpectedly, she agreed. The search committee was pleased. I was jubilant.

Drew proved to be everything—and more—than we had hoped for. She was a natural leader, and the RAIS thrived in a marvelous way while she remained in the deanship. In a brief time, however, her talents were more and more obvious to everyone: So much so that she became, within a few years, the twenty-eighth president of Harvard.

So Radcliffe and Harvard were finally united, although the new union—and the new institute—had little impact on the university as a whole. The previous friction between the two institutions had mainly affected the president, the administration, and the deans of FAS. Consolidation affected virtually no one because the institute's fellows would mainly come from the "outside," not from inside Harvard. Nevertheless, two significant institutional "parts" had finally been joined together, making a larger whole four decades from the time when discussions of a merger had first been broached.

SITTING IN: BEGINNING THE NEXT AGE

In my eighth year as president—in 1999—a new issue (and what I began to believe was a new age) began to emerge among a number of students: the concept of a "living wage." It was an issue that had already been raised and addressed—in different ways—by several institutions. Moreover, in the Cambridge area, at least three townships had accepted the idea, and it seemed to many people that Harvard should adopt such a policy for its nonacademic workers.

Part of the reason for the Harvard dispute arose from the fact that some of the less well-endowed professional schools had recently decided to "outsource" their janitorial services to private companies that could do the job less expensively (and might or might not pay benefits). This helped to relieve the considerable budget pressures of some of the smaller underfunded schools. These actions (plus the fact that a committed group of students believed that Harvard paid many of its workers too little) led to a steady, growing, and more outspoken campaign on the living-wage issue.

When I was asked my views, I said that the university should be seriously concerned about its pay scales, making certain that they were fair, but that I was not in favor of the concept of a "living wage" because it was—at the time—really impossible to define. In fact, the few local communities that had already endorsed the concept had arrived at completely different conclusions about the actual pay level that constituted such a wage. Some were noticeably lower (or higher) than others. That seemed completely irrational to me. If the issue were a *minimum* wage, that was eminently discussable, and if we were paying too little, we could find a way to raise the pay scale.

My response was—I thought—a reasonable one, but it did not have any effect on those who were now publicly and more intensively committed to having Harvard adopt the new policy. Moreover, they demanded that the lowest-paid workers at Harvard should receive at least $10 per hour (which was a much more significant figure in the 1990s than it would seem to be now). Most of our schools or units could well afford this (and paid it), but a few might face deficits if the new level went into immediate effect. Nevertheless, it was a reasonable—and definable—goal that we could at least address.

The response of most of the university was revealing. I received hardly any letters or messages from faculty on the issue, although a large number of them later signed a full-page advertisement in the student newspaper, advocating adoption of the proposed new policy. Meanwhile, the main organized union on campus let it be quietly known to us that it would not support a student-led campaign: It had its own distinct agenda and concerns (although some professional-school union members later came out in favor of the students). I continued to feel confident, however, especially because so many Harvard workers were unionized, and we continued to have very good relations with the union leadership. Indeed, a survey of Harvard workers also revealed that more than 90 percent of them were already paid $10 or more per hour.

Then, in the very last months of my final year as president, a group of students, led by Progressive Labor (and SDS) members, became more strident. One day they suddenly took advantage of our building's open-door policy and entered en masse, taking over the ground-floor offices, setting up a "command-post," and essentially filling most of Massachusetts Hall.

I was taken totally off guard, and told our staff that we should continue with our work as much as possible. The students, however, were a different breed than I had known from my days at Princeton: This was mainly an angry and bold group and they paid—for example—absolutely no attention to the plight of the Mass Hall secretaries, treating them rudely and impatiently. The irony of how they acted in the presence of "real" workers was not lost on us, and my assistant—Beverly Sullivan—quickly made her way through all our offices, warning the students to change their behavior. This actually had an effect, but did nothing else to alter the basic situation.

Meanwhile, in part of the Yard (in front of our building), many students had begun to set up small tents, creating a kind of camp in support of their fellows inside. This complicated the entire situation, and the two groups communicated regularly by two-way radio. Food was brought to the protestors through our downstairs windows—something that we decided to allow.

The entire action was far more organized, determined, and impervious than anything I had ever before encountered. I immediately convened all my senior staff, including the head of security. What were our alternatives?

I began with two main points: We would not accept the idea of a "living wage," and we would not call the police to break up the sit-in. The last thing I wanted was to emulate Grayson Kirk of Columbia or Nate of Harvard by having police batter students and throw the entire institution into turmoil that would last indefinitely. That left us with two main options: Wait for the students to exit (because we were approaching the end of term, with exams and then graduation); or ask the courts to intervene, ordering the students to evacuate the building or be held in contempt.

We did not come to a conclusion in our first session, but meanwhile the entire situation began to take on even greater proportions. The national leaders of two major unions flew to the university; the elected Cambridge City Council walked through Harvard Yard in a show of support for the students; and Senator Ted Kennedy made a statement, urging the students to continue, stating that Harvard should immediately adopt a living-wage policy.

So the university had suddenly become a national target: If we were to accept the proposed new policy, the decision would be used to initiate similar actions on other campuses and communities. If Harvard changed course, that could help enormously to legitimize the living-wage policy, and other places would be pressed to follow suit. Our options—in terms of actions that we might take vis-à-vis the sit-in—were suddenly much more complicated, with national union leaders and Ted Kennedy in the battle.

I met with the labor leaders in a long, tense session. They were in one sense respectful, but there was no way that we could possibly agree. By this time, a few days had already passed. My senior staff and I had essentially reached the conclusion that we should wait until the sit-in eventually dissolved. Given the media interest, the national attention to the situation, the national union leaders, and the tent camp on the lawn, I was reluctant to bring in the courts, because there would almost certainly be riot police in attendance—with very unpredictable consequences. If even a few tent-camp students tried to interfere with the court officials or the police, the results could be disastrous. Meanwhile, some alumni and other hardliners were calling for police action and wondered why I did not forcefully move ahead.

It turned out that the wait was very long, and stretched beyond one week into a second, and then beyond. Tempers flared on all sides, and several of us moved to offices outside the building to get our work done. The students showed no sign of being worried about their academic obligations, and I began to seriously doubt myself—wondering whether I had made a major mistake in not going to the courts. The tent camp outside grew larger and I made certain that our security guards would not attempt to physically remove or interfere with anyone who was there. The media kept up their coverage, and what had begun as a local sit-in was now a major public event.

I decided not to change course, even though it was obvious that the students were far more committed and forceful than I had initially imagined. There was not much time before the end of term, however, and in spite of everyone's growing frustration, it still seemed right to carry on as planned. I remembered that President Ed Levi of the University of Chicago had once waited out a sixteen-day sit-in, and that gave me a modicum of comfort!

At that point, I was surprised to receive a phone call from Larry Summers, who had recently been elected to succeed me as president. Larry suggested that we should announce the creation of a faculty-led committee to study the entire living-wage issue over the course of the summer into the autumn. This would provide a legitimate process to help resolve the issue, and I immediately agreed with him. The students would be given a form of victory, while I felt confident that a thorough examination of the issue would not lead—given the unpredictability of defining a "living wage"—to such a major shift in university policy. Outsourcing was a somewhat different issue, and could be dealt with on its own terms. But the living-wage matter had far-reaching implications, and could now be addressed squarely in an orderly, probing way. Meanwhile, a superb committee was established, with Sid Verba, Tim Scanlon (from the philosophy department), Larry Katz from economics, and other equally thoughtful and exceptional people.

Once the announcement of the planned committee was made public, the students felt victorious, leaving Massachusetts Hall to the cheers of their fellows outside. So my last sit-in ended almost exactly thirty years after my first one. That evening, Angelica and I were having a small dinner for some friends at home, and I arrived in good spirits. We had not called the police. We did not agree to the "living-wage" issue. There were no injured students. There would be an excellent committee in place. Margie Marshall and Tony Lewis were at the dinner, and everyone was convivial. The entire experience had in its way been harrowing, but the finale seemed to justify the "harrow," despite the obvious difficulty of it all. Meanwhile, established disciplinary procedures would move ahead to hear the student cases.

Looking back, I was struck again by the fact that the student protestors had remained steadfastly "detached." They did not occupy any building related to the Faculty of Arts and Sciences but focused only on the president's isolated domain. That in itself separated them from any direct relationship with (or influence from) their dean and his staff, quite apart from their teachers. In addition, they were—as suggested—highly organized, with radio connections not only to other students but also to the media. In other words, they allowed themselves no real human contact that might influence them. No one in Massachusetts Hall, including myself, knew them personally. In all these ways, I felt once again that the scale of Harvard and the idiosyncratic nature of its structure made it difficult to try to build a university community or a unified single institution. If that were true in Cambridge, I thought, what must it be like at larger institutions—or at the "multiversities" described nearly four decades earlier by Clark Kerr?

The sit-in was revealing in another way: It suggested that the future might involve, not only problematic issues and protests related to student diversity, but also to major societal problems (such as the wages of workers). A new era was awakening, and it was to be a time when various social issues would come into play—and into contention: a subject for the last chapters of this volume.

FUTURE CONSIDERATIONS: GOVERNANCE CHANGE?

Throughout my decade at Harvard, the Corporation was unfailing in its support and in its oversight of the university. During the late 1990s, however, the task of identifying excellent new Corporation members became more and more difficult. We had been very fortunate to add Robert Reischauer, Hanna Gray, and then Conrad Harper, but because we met for the better part of a day almost every other Monday, the role of being a Corporation member was exceptionally demanding. People in midcareer could rarely if ever give that much time to the position, which meant that we were more and more restricted to having a "pool" of mainly retired people to draw from. We were not tempted to ask people simply because of their wealth—indeed, we had no one on the Corporation who was identifiably in the *Forbes* category. So it was increasingly clear that the size and complexity of the university might ultimately require a change in governance. Something would almost certainly have to be done—in terms of Corporation scheduling, size, and structure—during the years to come. We would have to be less of a small, consultative, collaborative group of seven, and something more like a "board." In August of 1997, I wrote to the other members of the Corporation:

> in the movement from the ... concept of the Corporation as a form of copresidency to the Corporation as a form of Board, we should perhaps think of ourselves as being in a transitional state that is still susceptible to more analysis and possible modification. We are too small, as a Corporation, to undertake the many tasks (usually involving specific committees with appointed Chairs) of a traditional Trustee Board. ... These areas might include (1) physical plant and planning, real estate, and future land usage; or (2) academic planning including information technology; or (3) human resources, "diversity," and labor relations; or (4) federal/state/local community relations ...
>
> There are other possible designs involving, perhaps, the appointment by the Corporation of periodic advisory groups ... to assist

the Corporation on particular topics. ... In short there are various possibilities ... as we think about the future.

When we considered these issues, it became clear that it was too late for me to undertake any action on this front. I had already decided (privately with Angelica) to announce my forthcoming resignation before long, so there was no time to finish the Campaign and put programs in place, while also embarking on so complex a matter as the possible restructuring of Harvard's governance system—especially when the entire subject was barely beginning to surface. Fortunately, thoughtful action on the subject, with a happy conclusion, was finally reached under President Faust several years later.

While the Provost's Office had made a great difference to the strength of the central administration, it would clearly need more capacity in the decades to come. We had continued to function as a team of three academics in Massachusetts Hall: myself; the provost; and Dennis Thompson, our single excellent associate provost. But if one really wanted to interconnect, "integrate," and continue to unify the university—including the attempt to deal with problems raised by student diversity—a number of changes would simply be essential.

Harvard's endowment—with moderate growth—would soon be in the range of $30 to $40 billion, given its compounding effect once it reached about $19 billion in 2001. In addition, its annual operating budget would soon be well above $3 billion moving toward $4 or $5 billion. To oversee and manage such an enterprise would require at least some more than the three of us who were currently the only academics in the central administration.

Ron Daniel and Bob Stone lived relatively near Cambridge, and as both of them were part of the Corporation during my entire tenure, they became close advisors and friends. They remained steadfast—as well as patient and wise—during the various crises of my decade, and they also carried out key assignments during that time. Ron was chair of the Harvard Management Corporation—which oversaw all of Harvard's investments— and Bob was the acknowledged leader of the fund-raising campaign. Without these two Corporation members, I doubt we could have accomplished more than a fraction of whatever was in fact achieved.

The final year at Harvard was devoted to completing as many projects as possible. My original arrangement with the Corporation had been a seven- to ten-year commitment, and ten years turned out (for many reasons) to be exactly right. I was nearly 67 and, in my last year, I could already feel that the institution should begin to enter another major planning cycle, to be followed by another campaign that would require at least a decade to complete. So it was obviously time for a new president who could begin the next chapter in the university's history. If the Harvard years came to an end, however, American higher education did not, and the following pages offer my thoughts about the past two decades, as well as some further observations about the entire period from the 1950s to the present.

Chapter 7

Toward the Present Moment and Its Protests

LEARNING AND ITS PROBLEMS

The following pages focus initially on several large-scale developments in colleges and universities that have occurred gradually but steadily during the past two to three decades. They have made many of our institutions larger and more complex, and often more difficult to run as coherent, unified entities. These institutions are also more controversial, more subject to sustained media criticism, as well as to campus protests. The list of such developments is potentially large, but I have tended to concentrate here on a limited number that seem to me to be highly consequential.

Universities and colleges have several purposes, including promoting the idea that learning has the capacity to enlighten individuals and to free them to live examined and fulfilling lives of thought and action. Henry Thoreau (who deplored his undergraduate years at Harvard) hoped that mankind would aspire to be "Awake"—open to experience and capable of responding to it fully. Emerson wanted his "American Scholar" to be the embodiment of creative "Man Thinking." Henry James (who inexplicably attended but then quickly dropped out of Harvard Law School) valued people who were so alert that "nothing would be lost upon them." These three figures were of course radically different from one another in their personal journeys, talents, preoccupations, and actions. But they shared one significant value: their conviction that the individual—apart from organized groups, political parties, or religious sects—has the capacity to discover significant truths in the face of unfolding experience.

Thoreau sought (in *Walden*) to track down and corner "nature" in order to discover whether it is at bottom "mean" or not. Emerson's American Scholar would be courageous and if need be alone, determined to discover truth by following his own perceptions and convictions above and beyond inherited doctrine, religious sectarianism, or established scholarly tradition. And it was James who confessed that he had "wriggled" and "foundered and failed" until he found at last "a general lucid consciousness which I clutched with a sense of its absolute value." Consciousness could lead to a form of receptiveness and responsiveness in persons "upon whom nothing would be lost" as they encountered reality. So each of the three turned to the *individual*: to the single being "awake" or "thinking" or "conscious," committed to discovering truth itself in order to live a life worth living.

Such journeys—such quests for meaning and knowledge that do not necessarily lead to tangible "applied" results useful to society—have always been rare, but they are more so today because of three main pressures. First, we are obviously a much more organized, structured society—with many defined pathways for individuals to follow as they mature. Next, as we have seen, there is a desire on the part of today's students to pursue professional opportunities, intensifying the phenomenon of careerism among university undergraduates (and their parents). Finally, there has been a steadily growing expectation that our universities will devote themselves more and more to the solution of practical problems useful to society, whether in health, technology, public affairs, the environment, or a myriad of other fields. In short, the modern American university has become more "instrumental"—more pragmatic at all levels—than it was in the decades immediately following World War II (as well as in some earlier eras). The student or scholar who studies primarily to gain more knowledge about a subject that may seem impractical is rather less in evidence. In retrospect, it seems ironic that the 1950s and early 1960s should have been so persistently criticized for being "silent" and politically quiescent, because that was a moment when the search for knowledge that had meaning—but not necessarily any immediate use—seemed a rewarding and worthwhile pursuit.

In a 1991 talk given by Bernard Bailyn of Harvard's history department, he wondered what—in the "pragmatic" world that seemed dominant—could be the "value of studying the early Greek epic" or "Byzantine iconography"? Why bother with "the transformation of politics in ancient Rome"?

Bailyn answered his own questions in the following way:

> Because these are significant passages in the development of our civilization, because they are achievements of the human mind, because they stretch one's imagination and intellect, enlarge one's views of the world, extricate one from parochial environments, and lead one to think about the character and meaning of human experience.

In effect, Bailyn was speaking on behalf of the liberal arts and sciences—especially but not only the humanities—and their decline, and he made the point that those who pursued such subjects now often felt "marginalization and above all ambiguity." Such subjects in the American university "remain respectable, and they are honored in abstract ways, for their contribution to civilization. But as the calls for action grow louder, these efforts seem increasingly old-fashioned." Those who call for more university commitment to solving present-day problems often disparage any different conception as being "ivory tower" in nature, but that is a major misinterpretation. The most searching universities have long been committed to studying the "liberal" arts and sciences for reasons that Bailyn described—sometimes to solve pressing problems, but often to enlarge and help open the mind in pursuit of many different forms of knowledge.

Bailyn's analysis seems a reasonable summary of the situation today, nearly three decades later. Indeed, as the world continues to be turbulent and even violent beyond any immediate remedy, as the environment becomes swiftly more endangered, as technology becomes more pervasive and our politics more adversarial and importunate, the future of humane "liberal" learning seems clearly to be far less bright, and the need for practical "instrumental" solutions more urgent. It is difficult to imagine many leading figures in our present society echoing words that might resemble those spoken more than a century ago (in 1902) by Oliver Wendell Holmes, Jr. in a speech when he was dedicating the new Law School building at Northwestern University. In response to hypothetical questions about the purpose of the building, Holmes acknowledged that students might come in the hope of ultimately having a successful business career (or even a career in law!), but he insisted that the building and the university had much more to offer. It offered the chance to think philosophically about all of one's studies, in a way that enabled one to consider problems and issues far more deeply and imaginatively than would otherwise be the case. A university, Holmes said, is "open to all idealizing tendencies" and is "above other institutions the conservator of vestal fire." It inspires some students not simply to study their "subjects," but also to advance their understanding of life—even to paint works of art or to write poetry. In these and other ways, "those who come to the university want to press philosophy to the uttermost edge of the articulate, and to try forever after some spiritual ray outside the spectrum that will bring a message to them from behind phenomena. They love the gallant adventure which yields no visible return. I think it the glory of that university which I know best, that under whatsoever reserves of manner they may hide it, its graduates have the romantic passion in their hearts."

Perhaps no one was more insistent and even vehement than Robert Hutchins—president of the University of Chicago—in continuing to defend (during the 1930s and 1940s) the liberal arts, and his chosen foe was the "vocational-informational philosophy of education that is coming to prevail" as a result of the apparent advances in Italy (and Germany) where efficiency and "useful" science had apparently created modern "successful" nations with tangible, pragmatic results:

> The trains, we are told, ran on time. The beggars had disappeared. There was less crime than there is in the United States. Italy had gained power and prestige. ... [But] the Italian state is not a state at all. It is an organization of force ... It denies the proper end of the person.

As an antidote, Hutchins proposed "the communication of our intellectual tradition and training in the intellectual disciplines":

> This means understanding the great thinkers of the past and present. It means a grasp of the disciplines of grammar, rhetoric, logic, and mathematics; reading, writing, and figuring.

Hutchins was both extraordinary and fiercely headstrong—one of the (young) "giants" whose ultimate legacy was certainly ambiguous. Nevertheless, he had a conception of the liberal arts that was emphatically rational, ordered, and disciplined (rather different from Holmes's more romantic notion). It eventually expressed itself in Chicago's general education program and was also—in a somewhat different form—a view that prevailed when I was an undergraduate at Princeton. I and most of my colleagues tended to study quite broadly across the liberal arts and sciences, relatively free from the pressure of preparing for a career. We were in no sense superior to today's students—indeed, I think that the best of today's students are more intellectually capable, more sophisticated, and more aware of political and international affairs than most of us were. And it is impossible to criticize current undergraduates for being the product of family, social, economic, and other circumstances that bear on them to be "professional" or career-minded at a much younger age than we were. But the fact remains that we live in a new reality and it affects, not simply undergraduate majors, but also the nature of research, professional education, problem-solving, and the very disposition of the university itself.

Some research, for example, can and should be directed toward the solution of identifiable practical problems (such as the cure of diseases, or the effort to improve certain technological processes, or the remedy of particular social ills); but it can and should also be aimed at the understanding of far more basic problems that are important but have no immediate uses. And here the change has clearly been in the former direction—toward "instrumentalism." The results, moreover, are quite measurable. For example, federal agencies funded more than 70 percent of basic research in the 1960s and 1970s; then, 61 percent in 2004; and then below 50 percent after 2013—with 44 percent in 2015. This "flattening" and reduction of the *proportion* of federal basic research has been debilitating. Moreover, the total basic research figures would be even lower if it were not for the surprising rise in some *corporate* basic research since 2012 (largely by the pharmaceutical industries seeking breakthroughs that would lead to new drugs and larger profits). Drug company basic research rose from about $3 billion in 2008 to $8.1 billion in 2014. In one sense, these new grants have been welcome, but they have of course clear "applied" ultimate ends in view and they are highly restricted in terms of the subject areas they cover. Basic research now represents only about one-sixth of the nation's spending on research and development (R&D). Indeed, two-thirds of all federal spending is on the "development" of products.

This diminishment of basic research in many sciences has been "invisibly" expensive to the nation because many of the most crucial discoveries—with the most consequential implications—have historically resulted from basic research that had no useful end immediately in sight. The discovery of the structure of DNA by Crick and Watson is one such example. They knew that the discovery would be enormously significant and would lead to a myriad of applications, but they did not undertake the effort to solve a specific practical application—all that came soon enough. And Robbert Dijkgraaf, director of the Institute for Advanced Study in Princeton, recently wrote:

> It took [many decades] for Einstein's theory of relativity, first published in 1905, to be used in everyday life in an entirely unexpected way. The accuracy of the global positioning system (GPS), the space-based navigation system that provides location and time information in today's mobile society, depends on reading time signals of orbiting satellites. The presence of the Earth's gravitational field and the movement of these satellites cause clocks to speed up and slow down, shifting them by thirty-eight milli-seconds. ... In one day, without Einstein's theory, our GPS tracking devices would be inaccurate by about seven minutes. Again, a century of free-flowing thinking and experimentation led to a technology that literally guides us every day.[1]

Ideally, the university should be constituted in a way that enables it to engage with the practical problems and challenges of the present while it also avails itself of, and makes vitally available to its students, the apparently "useless" knowledge and insights of the past and present. The university must in this sense be multifaceted. From one point of view, the best institutions attempt to remain so. But much of what has happened in recent decades—whether in terms of new courses, new programs and departments, and even new professional schools—has been motivated by the effort to find solutions to immediate problems. In this sense, many universities are simply less concerned with truth—in all its different manifestations—than in some earlier eras.

Nor does this movement show any signs of reverting to a time when higher education maintained a reasonable distance from the world of current affairs, just as it simultaneously engaged—in other respects—with the pragmatic world of "action." Indeed, nearly sixty years ago, Clark Kerr observed that "knowledge is now central to society. It is wanted, even demanded, by more people and more institutions than ever before. The university as producer, wholesaler and retailer of knowledge cannot escape service."[2] This was uttered partly as something admirable, and partly as a lament. Of course, Kerr's university was publicly funded, so its service function was in certain respects intrinsic to it, but even Kerr was concerned about "slavishly" fulfilling so many tasks. Private institutions, however, clearly have had a somewhat different—and broader—mission which, for many reasons, has simply been attenuated.

Another salient difference between the post-2000 American world, and earlier eras, has been the immense growth in personal and corporate funds, and one highly visible result has been the sudden leap in the enormous size of some gifts to at least a few universities (as well as to some other not-for-profit organizations). Before the early 2000s (and especially the pre-2010 years), it was rare for an ambitious university campaign to exceed more than several hundred million dollars; then, *single* gifts of about a hundred million dollars began to appear. Indeed, the need for larger and larger sums to support or create new or existing programs, or even entire professional "schools," led to intensive and nearly perpetual efforts to raise more and more money. The results were at times stunning, and the effects often admirable. One difficulty, however, was the growing perception on the part of many people that some institutions were becoming more corporate in financial terms: more money; more staff; more vice-presidents and vice-provosts; more prominently written "names" on academic programs, schools, centers, structures, or parts of structures. There was a growing impression that much more seemed for sale—and that board members were beginning to be chosen as much or more for their wealth as for their wisdom. When the central iconic building of the New York Public Library on Fifth Avenue, for example, was given a single individual's name, and when the name was added here and there on one doorway after another—and on *all* the building's stationery—a symbolic line seemed to have been crossed. Philanthropy was rather dwarfed by nomenclature, and it was in fact the case that similar lines were being crossed at other institutions. Egos and institutions seemed to be wed without noticeable embarrassment. In effect, there was simply too much money in the hands of too few people, for the health of our increasingly disequilibrated society.

Were there no precedents? Of course. The difference was mainly in the scale, the frequency, and at times the nature of the "named" enterprises that began to appear in the 2000s. By contrast, when President Charles Eliot created a business school at Harvard in 1908, he later asked his friend Bishop William Lawrence to approach the extremely wealthy George Baker to fund new buildings at the school. Baker is reported to have said no—but then added that he would either give *all* the money needed, or nothing at all. He then gave the full $5 million, but did not ask for a Baker School of Business. Instead, Eliot and Lawrence dedicated the large Baker Library to him, the prestigious Baker Scholars, and the Baker Foundation.

The tendency to give larger and larger amounts of money to universities ultimately led, of course, to the feeling on the part of some donors that they were entitled to play an exceptionally large role in the governance of their institutions—either a positive approach in helping to guide matters, or a negative one in criticizing their institutions—and their institutional presidents—when matters appeared to go awry. The results were unfortunate on all accounts: overweening executives bludgeoning their universities, and universities appearing to be pressed by wealthy individuals in irresponsible ways. By the 2020s, this phenomenon was not only more than unhappy in its effects, but led to fierce attacks on individuals as well as institutions.

In his book *Troubled Times for American Higher Education: The 1990s and Beyond*, Clark Kerr quoted John Gardner discussing other changes in higher education:

> The historical trends have been toward larger scale organizations— and this puts more emphasis on "leadership teams"; toward fractionalization of constituencies.[3]

Meanwhile, other offices—vice-presidents, directors, provosts, and vice-provosts—have grown in number and authority. Kerr singled out the provostship for special comment:

> within the administration, the role of provost has grown greatly in importance—presidents were once their own provosts. The creation of the provostship (or academic vice-presidency) and the rise of provosts or the new persons of power on campus is one of the least recognized but most significant changes of all. Presidents seldom teach anymore ... and administrative staffs have grown much faster than academic, often twice or three times as fast.[4]

Not all institutions have by any means followed a similar pattern— and provosts have proved to be a blessing!—but the over-riding tendency has been in the direction that Bailyn, Kerr, Gardner, and others have charted, beginning thirty or forty years ago and then accelerating after the turn of the century. I was provost at Princeton from 1977–88, and introduced the provost's office at Harvard in the early 1990s. My only defense is that there was only one vice-provost throughout my Princeton and Harvard years.

In addition to the large-scale developments already described, other important changes have also had an impact on the functioning of many private colleges and universities. For instance, their slow but steady increases in size (often as a result of fund-raising campaigns) have led to the creation of more quasi-independent programs, institutes, centers, professional schools, and other units. The addition of more discrete parts— as suggested earlier—means less institutional unity and coherence, and more institutional dispersion. Individual units tend to operate as relatively autonomous units on their own, cultivating their own donors and "friends groups," while determining their own strategic directions. This can lead to exciting results and substantial successes—but also to unexpected waywardness and unmonitored or unchecked excesses of various kinds.

Next, although many colleges have suffered in the past several decades from a decline in applicants for admission, many others have witnessed a continuous surge in applications, such that the entire undergraduate admissions process has become a source of frequent complaints about arbitrary or unfair decisions, as well as constant debates about the nature of appropriate admissions criteria. By contrast, at the graduate-student level, the situation has become dire. Even much-reduced numbers of enrolled students have proven to be too many for the extremely small number of jobs available—especially but not only in the humanities.

We have already noted that "tenure-track" and tenured positions have steadily declined in colleges and universities, whereas part-time "adjunct" faculty positions have greatly increased in number: They now represent about half of all academic posts. The academic profession has simply become a less and less desirable (or feasible) career since the boom days from the late 1940s to about 1970. And adjunct faculty are now beginning to unionize at many institutions.

When Clifford Geertz delivered his Haskins lecture in 1999, for instance, he described his own experience studying the liberal arts at Antioch College in the 1950s (my own era at Princeton). He wrote:

> I simply took just about every course that in any way looked as if it might interest me, come in handy, or do my character some good, which is the definition, I suppose—certainly it was Antioch's—of a

liberal education.... The result of all this searching, sampling, and staying loose... was that, when I came to graduate, I had no more sense of what I might do to get on in the world than I had when I had entered.

What one was supposed to obtain there, and what I certainly did obtain, was a feeling for what Hopkins called "all things counter, original, spare, strange".... One might be lost or helpless, or racked with ontological anxiety, but one could try, at least, not to be obtuse.

Geertz became, of course, an academic and—rather later, in the 1990s—he found himself wondering whether his own undergraduate experience, and his own kind of academic career, was feasible any longer. He noted that there was "a fair amount of malaise about, a sense that things are tight and growing tighter"—that it was no longer "wise just now to take unnecessary chances, strike new directions, or offend the powers":

The question is: Is such a life and such a career [as mine] available now? In the Age of Adjuncts? When graduate students refer to themselves as "the preunemployed"? ... Has the bubble burst? The wave run out? ...

[Until] a few years ago, I used blithely, and perhaps a bit fatuously, to tell students and younger colleagues who asked how to get ahead in our odd occupation that they should stay loose, take risks, resist the cleared path, avoid careerism, go their own way, and that if they did so, if they kept at it and remained alert, optimistic, and loyal to the truth, my experience was that they could get away with murder, could do as they wish, have a valuable life, and nonetheless prosper. I don't do that anymore.

More recently, an article by Charles Peterson drew on current data to discuss (in particular) the extent to which the PhD labor market had reached disastrous proportions, partly from "over-production" of candidates, but mostly because the number of tenure-track openings has shrunk steadily—even precipitously. In history, for example, there were an average of 122 applications for every available tenure-track position in 2017–18.[5] The chances of becoming a tenured faculty member were about as remote as becoming a rock star or an NFL starter.

Not only did tenured openings decrease, but adjunct positions surged in number. Salaries were so low (perhaps $20,000 a year) that individuals were forced to live at the margin's edge (or work at two or three jobs). As Peterson wrote:

> According to the UC Berkeley Labor Center, 25 percent of part-time faculty nationally rely on public assistance programs. In 1969, 78 percent of institutional staff at US institutions of higher education were tenured or on the tenure track; today, after decades of institutional expansion amid stagnant or dwindling budgets, the figure is 33 percent. More than one million workers now serve as nonpermanent faculty in the US, constituting 50 percent of the instructional work force at public PhD granting institutions, 56 percent at public masters-degree granting institutions, 62 percent at public bachelors degree-granting institutions, 83 percent at public community colleges, and 93 percent at for-profit institutions.[6]

These conditions helped to lead to another set of difficulties in American higher education: the plight of graduate students seeking academic positions, when virtually none were to be had. This has led in some situations to the advent of graduate student unions in *private* universities, where job opportunities were very scarce, and where many students (some who were married) stayed on for years, with little or no further fellowship support and low wages for teaching courses led by senior faculty. At Harvard, for instance, the UAW helped to organize university-wide graduate students in search of better wages, child-care benefits, and other "demands." The new union and the university were unable to agree on terms, and the graduate students went on a brief strike just before the end of the autumn term in 2019. The strike inevitably disrupted a great deal, given the role that graduate students play in undergraduate teaching and grading. Fortunately, a settlement was reached, and a contract signed, in 2020.

If we continue to examine what has happened in American colleges and universities during the past two to three decades, we have already noted that the concept of diversity is one that has not only entered—pervasively—the vocabulary of higher education, but has steadily expanded its meaning beyond previously imaginable bounds. The new term of choice is *inclusiveness*: that (or *diversity*) has infused undergraduate admissions, and its effects have led to forms of mutual student learning as well as forms of student tension, conflict, misunderstanding, and problematic behavior.

From the 1960s through the 1980s, diversity tended to be defined by the movement to include Black students in previously all-White colleges and universities. Simultaneously, many all-male (and all-female) colleges began to admit students of the opposite sex. More high school (rather than boarding school) students also came to private selective institutions; quotas on Jews dissolved and kosher kitchens became common at many colleges and universities. More Catholic students were also admitted. Later, and quite suddenly, the emergence of openly gay students took place—a shift that eventually included members representing the entire spectrum of the LGBTQ+ population. So by the 1990s, *diversity* was already a term and a reality that was far more expansive and complex than even a decade or two earlier. It was then only a short step to the inclusion of more minorities and a great range of international students. Then, in the 2000s attention turned to more students from low-income and "first-generation-college" families.

Could such a mix conceivably co-exist with many or all of the different members and groups actually learning from their counterparts—or would they simply avoid one another or be antagonistic? We have already seen, in earlier chapters, some of the complexities and disruptions that student diversity introduced on many campuses. This development was a daring adventure: the socioeconomic and heterogeneous cultural, geographical, religious, racial, ethnic, economic, social, and sexual mix constituted an altogether new and unpredictable phenomenon.

In the field of education, meanwhile, media articles attacking institutions "of privilege" are now commonplace and are far more frequent than those recognizing the educational and research achievements of these institutions (or the steady and growing number of scholarship students attending them). Indeed, a recent *New York Times* article by David Leonhardt (March 24, 2021) reported that "negative" media news outweighs news about "positive" accomplishments because that is what readers prefer—and is therefore often given to them.

If we now turn from some of the university changes just described, to more specific recent protests against—and attacks on—our universities, do we find a common theme that unites what has been happening from about 2000 to 2020?

A few points seem to me to be helpful in attempting to explain what has occurred. First, there has obviously been no single overriding issue or theme to recent protests, and they have in this sense been very different from the 1960s primary focus on the Vietnam War (with its purported relation to college and university "support" for the war) and on issues related to civil rights.

Second, although many of the recent protests have concerned campus diversity, many have also focused on major societal and political problems that have been growing steadily in serious (and sometimes threatening) ways. They began to be more evident after the turn of the century, and gradually provoked not simply students but also adults to engage in various protest actions.

For example, the formidable threat of climate change has become more dire—and more evident to larger numbers of people—in the past fifteen to twenty years. The vast maldistribution of American wealth, similarly, became a matter of major concern during the past two decades. Moreover, well-publicized mass high school shootings—and shootings of Black individuals—occurred in the period 2005–23; as a result, the issues of gun control and policing have been more and more pronounced. In addition, some political problems (such as Israeli–Palestinian relations and antisemitism) are now far more divisive than they were in the 1990s, when Yitzhak Rabin seemed to hold out the promise of a "two-state solution." Since Rabin's assassination, Israel has moved forward to claim more Palestinian territory for itself, and Donald Trump shifted the US embassy to Jerusalem—a highly provocative decision. Then the October 2023 Hamas invasion of Israel was utterly explosive in its effect on campuses.

Third, unlike the Vietnam War (or even apartheid in South Africa), there is little hope of solving—in the near future—most of the problems that students are protesting today. Recent gun violence (and policing), or the maldistribution of wealth in the United States, or tensions concerning race relations or climate change, or the crisis in Israel are clearly major— in some cases international—difficulties that are highly resistant to major change. There are not likely to be any ready solutions to these problems, and no amount of shouting-down of speakers (or analogous actions) is likely to be effective. In the 1960s, it was possible to think that ending the Vietnam War could in turn bring an end to most student protests. But no end is in sight with respect to many of the current issues, and the future of campus protests concerning them is therefore simply uncertain.

Finally, it is obvious that groups who were previously discriminated against—Blacks, women, gays, "trans," and various minorities—have in the past two decades often asserted their recently found rights in potent ways. There has been obvious pressure, in many fields, to have more individuals from underrepresented groups promoted into conspicuous institutional positions; to make certain that there is equal pay for equal work; to ensure that verbal slurs are avoided by people in authority—or else they should be protested; and to demand that those who are in power be punished if they are associated with activities judged to be discriminatory, or if they appear to be deficient in responding to major political events that can have an effect on all those inside the institution.

Examples of such incidents are legion. For example, there was recently a prolonged struggle at a major New York museum because one of its trustees owned a company that manufactured tear gas, and tear gas was being conspicuously used against immigrant groups and minority protesters. The museum battle raged for months, virtually paralyzing the institution, until the trustee eventually left the board. Examples from higher education are multifarious, and some will be cited later in this chapter.

One result of this phenomenon has been a heightened sensitivity to all potentially discriminatory actions or remarks in colleges and universities, with calls for apologies or dismissals (or demonstrations against the offenders). Another result has been the rise of an "anti-woke" movement by the political and religious "right": White supremacists need no longer be silent; people in schools need no longer say *gay*—or *trans*; Jews, in a "Christian nation," may be more openly attacked—and so on.

Governor Ron Desantis of Florida is only the most recent conspicuous figure to make a major political point of such views. Donald Trump has of course been espousing some of these ideas for years. And, of course, we saw earlier that Allan Bloom's *The Closing of the American Mind* expressed a longing for a "dominant" past American society that was said to be Protestant, implicitly Caucasian, male, and traditional in its "supervision of the language"—and that kept "minorities" in check.

As part of our recent contentiousness, some *adult*—not only student—protests have been an important factor in swelling campus difficulties. Although it is not possible to gauge their effect on students, it does seem unlikely that the adult actions have had no role whatever in spurring similar university events. For example:

- The Occupy Wall Street movement (in October 2011) was directed against the so-called 1 percent of wealthy Americans (and similar people in other countries). For many days, there were large groups protesting economic inequality, not only in the United States but in London, Montreal, Zurich, Frankfurt, and elsewhere. Thousands of people (including students) occupied parks and other public spaces—actions that attracted worldwide attention.

- In February 2012, a young Black man—Trayvon Martin—was shot and killed, and the murder led to the creation of the Black Lives Matter (BLM) movement (following the acquittal of the assaulter).
- In June 2016, Representative John Lewis led the Democrats in the House of Representatives in a sit-in that lasted more than 24 hours, over the issue of gun control. Lewis had of course engaged in similar actions half a century earlier, and was now accused of creating "chaos" in Congress. After the sit-in, more than 170 lawmakers followed him out of the chamber and down the Capitol steps, where a large crowd of supporters greeted them. (I myself happened—by sheer coincidence—to be there at the time.)
- In February 2018, Republican lawmakers attempted to limit important provisions of the Americans with Disabilities Act. Citizens in wheelchairs and on crutches flooded hallways of the House of Representatives, and disrupted a meeting of the House Rules Committee to prevent changes related to the ADA. Photographers and televisions news broadcasters displayed shots of police arresting the protesters as they were dragged out of the building. One person in a wheelchair was handcuffed and the police arrested ten others.
- In June 2019, Al Gore—in a Class-Day speech at Harvard—called for the university to sell its stock in fossil fuels. During the next several months, Harvard's Faculty of Arts and Sciences voted to have the Corporation sell the stock, and students were inevitably involved in the action.

In short, a number of serious societal problems have been prominent, especially in the past two decades, and adults have responded to them in ways not altogether different from students, although student tactics—borrowed from the 1960s—have involved an even broader range of actions.

Indeed, the great variety of issues that have engaged students is extraordinary in its breadth. If we were to examine, for instance, a list of speakers who were shouted down (or "disinvited") on various campuses in recent years, we would find a group so multifaceted that (unlike the 1960s) no small number of identifiable issues binds them. They would include (as a selection) Christine Lagarde, Condoleezza Rice, Charles Murray, Milo Yiannopoulos, Ben Shapiro, Nicholas Dirks, Anita Alvarez,

Bassam Eid, Acton Bronson, John Brennan, and many others. Very recently, law students at Yale and Stanford shouted down speakers—and in neither case was any disciplinary action taken. Some of these speakers were repudiated because of anti-Palestinian views; others for anti-Israeli or anti-Black views; others for reputed misdeeds in public office; others for their purported lack of concern about a range of other issues (such as climate change, or specific legal decisions).

We currently have a highly variegated student population, attuned to a highly variegated set of personal and political issues, and equipped with ready-made tactics. Some of those tactics were used occasionally in the 1980s and 1990s—indeed, they never entirely disappeared. For example, during my own relatively benign decade at Harvard in the 1990s, we were constantly concerned about disruptive protests—especially shout-downs—two of which (concerning Jiang Zemin's visit and Colin Powell's commencement speech) nearly materialized, and one long sit-in did in fact take place. Indeed, the different nature of the potential protests at Harvard in the 1990s—one concerning politics (China's Jiang Zemin), one concerning the LGBTQ+ community and Colin Powell, and one concerning a social issue (the "living wage")—heralded the greater differences to come in the 2000s.

Moreover, one of the most deleterious effects of our current situation is the threat posed to faculty members. If "trigger warnings" are not given, there may be protests by students who claim that they should have been warned about one possible hazard or another. And there have of course been recent well-publicized instances when faculty members have been discharged (or denied appointments) for purported missteps.

At Hamline University, for instance, a faculty member was recently let go for presenting an image of the Prophet Muhammad in an art history class, despite many warnings to students about what was to be shown. At NYU, an accomplished part-time teacher of organic chemistry was fired when students complained that his grading was too harsh. At Harvard's Kennedy School, a potential visitor was denied a fellowship for an alleged bias against Israel—and so on. In short, not simply invited speakers, but teachers and scholars, are far more an endangered species than was the case not many years ago.

Firing or disinviting specific faculty members was not, of course, the only unhappy effect of the situations just described. Each event of this kind inevitably discomforted many other faculty members in the same institutions who often felt potentially vulnerable in the face of such actions.

Moreover, student complaints about the statements and attitudes of certain faculty members were almost predictably disconcerting: What could one safely teach, or say, or discuss without repercussions? The effects could be more than unsettling and obviously demoralizing.

As one looks to the future, it is far from easy to predict whether the current level of distress in American higher education will increase or lessen. Part of the difficulty is that most of the issues facing society— or that are inherent in student diversity—are not (as suggested) readily amenable to solution. During the late 1960s, it was possible to think that the Vietnam War might be ended—and with that, much of the protest movement. But it is not likely that many local campus protests will lead to the solution of international climate change, revive the two-state possibility in Israel and Palestine, solve our national gun (and policing) problems, or relieve the complexities that are part of a diverse student population.

So the current state of higher education remains problematic. As I suggested in the introduction to this volume, we may have reached a point where the nature and substantial number of changes that have occurred in our system of higher education have finally combined to create many institutions that are not only comparatively large in scale, but are considerably more decentralized, characterized by a large number of quasi-autonomous parts and power centers. Given the current nature of these institutions, it may well be that some level of conflict, protest, and "contentiousness" is now inherent in them. They are simply difficult to administer, and rather resistant to a sense of shared felt unity.

A good number of colleges and universities have not been subject to many of the changes just described. They have remained relatively modest in size, as well as more coherent in the nature of their commitment to the liberal arts mission. As a result, they may well be able to weather many of the difficulties that confront more variegated institutions, although some recent events (such as at Hamline) would suggest that no one is entirely immune from the current range of difficulties.

It is also possible, of course, that in a few years, a new generation of students will see the futility of (for example) constantly shouting down speakers—or that universities will finally begin to invoke disciplinary penalties against those who resort to obstructive tactics. In short, exhaustion bolstered by discipline may prevail, and some protests—probably not all—may subside if not disappear. In addition, we should, moreover, take note of some very recent movements—on both the political left and the right—to counter aspects of our current contentiousness. For example, a group of former Rhodes Scholars recently (2023) created an "Alliance" protesting changes that the Rhodes trustees have made in the past two decades. The Alliance wants to dismantle diversity, equity, and inclusion (DEI) "anti-racism initiatives," including a Rhodes program designed to enhance "the diversity of the selection committees and [give them] unconscious bias training." Another target is a program to instruct "new Rhodes Scholars on racial justice, equity and other issues of conduct."

During this past year (2023), the writers group PEN America created an initiative called *Champions of Higher Education*, which invited former presidents of colleges, universities, and education "systems" to sign a statement "committed to promoting a positive vision of American higher education as an essential guarantor of free expression in a democracy and advocating against attempts to quash academic freedom, freedom of expression, and the right of students to learn." As of June 2023, more than 200 presidents had signed the statement.

In addition, approximately seventy Harvard faculty have created (in 2023) a Council on Academic Freedom, advocating the ideals of free speech and inquiry. The group "will encourage the adoption and enforcement of policies that protect academic freedom." Freedom of expression is decidedly one of those policies.

Meanwhile, these and other policy proposals have suddenly been dwarfed by events following the terrible Hamas attack on Israel in October 2023. At the present moment, the war continues at fever pitch, and its implications—including its effects on campuses—are such that any attempt to make predictions about the future may seem futile. Nevertheless, some analysis of the situation and some thoughts about what might be undertaken are—however tentative—important to consider.

WHAT SHOULD BE DONE?

The turmoil on many university campuses following the October 7, 2023 Hamas attack on Israel was so extraordinary that it raised the question whether there are ways for educational institutions to mitigate the effects of such an event.

Many university presidents condemned the terrorism of the Hamas invasion, but some were criticized for not speaking out soon enough—or unequivocally enough. Then, very soon, a number of student groups moved to condemn Israel for its imputed long-standing actions against Palestinians. As a result, there were many statements and some actions against Jewish students on various campuses. Moreover, Islamic students also began to feel threatened. In the late 1960s, students protested against their *institutions*, but now, groups of students sometimes confronted one another—a new phenomenon in its intensity, and one that was far more difficult either to alleviate or control. A number of threats were made online, but there were also student rallies, marches, and speeches to that effect. Tensions reached exceptional heights, and security was sometimes called to guard Jewish social organizations such as Hillel.

Finally, some wealthy alumni—including CEOs and law partners—began to identify and "blacklist" students who blamed Israel and favored the Palestinian cause. This was an unprecedented campaign that sought to deny future employment to such students. Nothing like it took place in even the worst days of the late 1960s. Simultaneously, some alumni called for the resignation of their respective university presidents and said they would no longer make financial contributions to their institutions. Given the ferocity of feelings, it was far from clear what could be done—if anything—to lower the level of tension and allow people to consider, at a very different pace, the entire situation.

In this sense, technology intervened to make the situation very different from most protest events of the 1960s, when much more time was required to plan actions and to create difficult conditions at universities. In 2023, the Internet and smartphones made instantaneous communications possible, such that protest movements were organized on some campuses in less than a day after the October 7 Hamas invasion of Israel. And once launched, rapid actions continued, making university interventions relatively impracticable.

Indeed, as it turned out, very little could often be done. Individuals and groups sometimes acted fiercely. The ability to listen, discuss, or debate tended to fall by the wayside on many—not all—campuses. Rarely, at universities, have actions and reactions moved so swiftly and categorically. Then suddenly, at the very end of November, the House of Representatives committee on education called three university presidents—from Harvard, Massachusetts Institute of Technology (MIT), and the University of Pennsylvania—to testify about the issue of antisemitism at their institutions.

Many people assumed that, following the Hamas attack, university presidents should make immediate statements, and presidents were—as suggested—forcefully and impatiently criticized when they hesitated or failed to be as unilateral as their critics desired. But knowing when to comment—and how to comment—on major world events is not by any means apparent, and the hasty criticism by individuals was more than unfortunate. I myself think that, ideally, educational leaders should not comment on national or international events in ways that would inhibit faculty and student expressions of free speech. The university president should not take sides, as it were, in situations that are clearly open to discussion and debate, although he or she should feel free to speak out in expressing—for example—dismay at the terrible violation of human life that occurred in the Hamas invasion of Israel.

President Christopher Eisgruber of Princeton adopted this last point of view—condemning the *human costs* of the Hamas attack, while simultaneously recognizing that Jewish or Palestinian or other students (or faculty) should feel free to express their various views about the *politics* of the Middle Eastern situation. Moreover, Eisgruber's statement was made, not immediately, but on October 10, allowing him time to make a thoughtful response. As a result, students were made aware of available counseling services, as well as faculty who were willing to discuss the entire range of issues related to the Israel–Palestine situation in an effort to achieve greater clarity and knowledge.

Of course that desire for greater clarity and knowledge may have seemed hollow to many on some campuses, particularly when students often felt beleaguered or threatened because of their ethnic or religious views and backgrounds. Nevertheless, the nature of the very difficult circumstances should not have obviated the importance of a central goal: Universities are dedicated to a greater understanding of events and situations, and one has to remain firm in ensuring that commitment even during highly divisive times. There were any number of moments in the period 1967–70 when students effectively pressed to the limit—and often beyond—their universities' desire to uphold and realize fundamental educational values, including free speech. One had to resist giving in to such pressure, while moving forward in the hope that calmer and saner moments would at some point prevail.

Such pressure was made even more vivid during the House of Representatives education committee meeting when the presidents of MIT, Harvard, and Penn were recently questioned about antisemitism on their campuses. The session turned out to be neither a "hearing" nor an "inquiry" but an inquisition with clear political attacks on the presidents by representative Stefanik, who attempted to force the presidents to give a "simple yes-or-no" answer to a question calling for the genocide of Jews. Would such a call be legitimate free speech on their campuses, or would it be intolerable?

Unfortunately, the presidents had been "prepped" in advance by highly legalistic counsels, and they replied with minimal statements—that their response to Stefanik's question would "depend on the context." This was clearly inadequate, and the presidents obviously lost the rhetorical and political battle. There was of course no interest on the part of the House Republicans to probe the real issues at stake. Stefanik's only goal was to humiliate the three leaders and have them fired. When Penn's president resigned shortly afterward, Stefanik said, "One down, two to go!" The other two remained in office with the support of their boards, although the Harvard situation was soon clouded by charges of plagiarism against President Claudine Gay—charges brought forward by two opponents determined to have her removed. An outside group of three experts initially cleared Gay of anything serious, but no sooner was that phase of the situation concluded when additional allegations were unveiled. Unfortunately, Gay's position became extremely difficult, and by the end of December, she had resigned.

Not all university situations are immediately "soluble," although many people—perhaps understandably—have difficulty accepting this fact. Commentators have—since the October 7th Hamas attack—been quick to fault universities for any number of reasons: The institutions have "failed to educate" their students, or they are unremittingly "woke" in their attitudes, or they are not sufficiently concerned about antisemitism, or they are simply badly led. ...

I myself do not believe these views take us very far in actually understanding the current scene. In fact, we need once again to remember that "adults" have been in charge of the Middle East for more than a century, and have continuously failed to solve its complex issues. Indeed, a brutal war in Gaza is killing thousands of innocent people at the moment and there is no consensus among the reigning nations as to whether the war should continue remorselessly, or whether there should be another "pause" to release hostages, or whether there should be a cease-fire. A "two-state solution" is discussed, as if it were even remotely a realistic goal in the near future.

So if the best and most committed individuals have been unable to bring peace to the Middle East since at least the 1917 Balfour Declaration, why should we expect today's students to emerge with, not forms of disagreement and even conflict, but wise views, ready agreement, and an assured solution? We must find a way to mitigate the conflict, but the effort will be far from simple.

It is not clear how the current campus problems will be resolved, because they concern a situation that has been intrinsically resistant to any clear resolution and is—in my view—inherently tragic. What we must desire is to do the best one can in the current unmitigated circumstances while hoping that some interim solution to the Gaza conflict can lead to a period of even temporary peace.

Much damage has been done to our universities in the past few months. The actual campus situations have led to significant difficulties, but some of the greatest problems have been caused by individuals who have been quick to condemn and all too hesitant to help. The University of Pennsylvania situation was very unhappy in this respect, with wealthy alumni threatening the institution and its president, instead of offering to give advice and assistance. The spectacle of what happened at Penn will long be remembered, and not in a way that will ingratiate its donors and graduates.

In the midst of the recent spectacle, many if not most people have failed to notice and applaud the extraordinary distinctiveness and qualitative ascendency of our universities. Rankings of institutions are generally not very useful, but it is nevertheless difficult to overlook the fact that in any and all global rankings, eight of the top ten existing universities in the world are American—with MIT, Harvard, Stanford, Columbia, and others in the lead—and only Oxford and Cambridge as competitors. We may choose not to notice or celebrate this fact, but before we neglect it, we should at least remark on how much these institutions contribute to the well-being of our entire nation and indeed to many other nations.

Next, it is clear that, remarkable as our universities are, many of them remain large, decentralized, potentially fragmented, and highly diverse. As a result, they may remain vulnerable, simply because their various "parts"—and certainly their students—may respond in unpredictable ways to events on campus, or in the larger world outside. As one result, the role of the university president has become far more difficult than it was several years ago. The current reality will require much more care from the rest of us before we move to attack our institutional leaders in the wake of national or worldwide events that may be sudden, fierce, and capable of provoking immediate angry responses on many sides.

The present time is one when we all must think, not only in terms of today, but of the long run. We need our universities—and they need us and our support—not only at the present moment, but perhaps even more earnestly in the unpredictable future, with (among other matters) a crucial American presidential election ahead in 2024. Without our universities, where do we believe we will find most of our future leaders, or important new ideas in many fields of inquiry; or intelligent responses to many of the world's most pressing problems; or the sheer capacity to educate many individuals who will lead valuable and helpful lives?

These institutions have been indispensable for centuries—sometimes in the midst of calamitous situations—and they will continue to endure because our society simply cannot function well without them. They and their leaders require, not instantaneous and inflammatory condemnation in the face of contention, but assistance and wise counsel.

If some leaders actually fail in due course, then there are well-tried and appropriate ways to relieve them of their duties. Meanwhile, a form of steadfastness is required of those who participate—even partially—in the world and life of universities, where all must ultimately live and labor together, seeking a degree of concord. That concord, at turbulent moments, may seem utterly elusive, but it must nevertheless be continually sought and perhaps—at moments—even found.

The hope just expressed in these last few paragraphs may seem monumentally naïve, given the way that events have actually unfolded from October 2023 to the end of December. Far from a desire to help universities and their presidents with patience and advice, an increasing number of individuals have been mainly intent on removing major university leaders, while humiliating their institutions.

Indeed, the assault on so-called elite universities has been a planned effort to dismantle as much as possible of their purported "woke" infrastructure: to eliminate their DEI programs, to rescind affirmative action and diversity in university admissions, to somehow reduce the power of the "progressive" faculty and administrators, and generally to bring about a "conservative" revolution in the nation's greatest institutions of learning.

How these purposes are to be achieved is the subject of several chapters in a quite different book. All one can say here is that part of the agenda—such as the end of affirmative action in college admissions—has already been realized as a result of a ruling by a new Supreme Court. The battle to do away with DEI programs—which are undoubtedly problematic—now extends well beyond Governor DeSantis in Florida.

The taming of the progressive faculty, however, is proving to be far more difficult, mainly because very few conservatives choose to follow academic careers—careers that require years of disciplined study leading to highly uncertain professional futures, with mainly modest financial rewards.

For the moment, America's major universities are confronting a time of sustained combat and severe difficulty. Not only are there the problems intrinsic to the very nature of these institutions—their potential inherent contentiousness—but there are in addition difficulties presented by determined adversaries. The test for their future leaders may be even greater than those already experienced. Student protests may continue to grow.

Choosing university leaders will require great acumen and exceptional "vetting." Trustees will be tested severely on their ability to make wise decisions, including vital efforts to help guide their institutions and support their leaders effectively.

Deciding on future academic priorities—given the fact that we now inhabit a world in which so much is unravelling—will require not only exceptional judgment, but also major resources from donors who are fundamentally philanthropic rather than self-important.

Fashioning new aspects of an undergraduate teaching program may well be highly desirable, given the recent serious difficulties that have taken place on so many campuses. It may be that a required course of case studies focusing on the nature and purposes of the American university—and especially the university's concept of "academic freedom" as it has developed in the past century—would help to introduce an element of more reflection on the part of all concerned, so that future divisive incidents might be tempered in ways that recent incidents have not been.

In short, much remains to be done, in a spirit that might recapture, not simply the latent feeling but the actuality of greater unity in our universities. Otherwise, internal stress—including student protests—and external antagonism may together pose the threat of increased discordance, with potential embattled leaders working amid dissociated institutional "parts" or groups, leading to even greater forms of contentiousness and further reputational blemishment. Such a future is happily far from inevitable, but more effective forms of collaboration and greater efforts to achieve commonality of purpose will be necessary to change course.

From 2002 to 2025, Harvard—for example—will probably have had six or seven presidents during a total of 23 years, for an average length of three to four years per person. Different circumstances have been responsible for the situation affecting each leader, but the net result will have been a figure that is not sustainable for a major institution. Indeed—as suggested—presidents of American universities are finding it increasingly difficult to survive for many years. A new day must be found, and new ways of achieving institutional unity must be discovered if American higher education is to prosper indefinitely. Such prosperity is altogether achievable, but it will only come with a new will and a consequent spirit in which individuals and groups care more about realizing a measure of institutional unity and common educational purposes in a mutually respectful way—where a degree of concord is indeed sought, and is to some degree actually found.

October 7–December 31, 2023

* * *

Epilogue

APRIL 26, 2024

Some of the recent protests on university campuses have rivaled many of those of the late 1960s. Fortunately, there have been no massive police "busts" such as Columbia's in 1968, nor any terrible killings such as those at Kent State, but the current level of extreme virulence has nonetheless been remarkable.

It is of course possible to list the reasons put forward by students and others to describe what is happening and why. But rational explanations do not fully account for the extraordinary emotions and actions that we have been witnessing. The current level of apparent antisemitism would, in my view, have been impossible to predict in advance, just as the level of pro-Palestinian passions would have been equally unable to foresee. Together, they have obviously made the situation at many universities more than difficult to manage. And given the great variety of our universities in terms of their scale and structures, their internal and external governance arrangements, and their various degrees of faculty engagement in campus affairs, there is little that anyone can prescribe concerning common responses to highly divisive situations.

If we sift examples from the late 1960s, are there any ideas that might be useful to university leaders and others as they confront today's problems in higher education? Very little seems transferable. I have, however, been taken aback by the speed with which many administrators have moved to call police to break up tent camps. To date, the police have avoided acting as wildly as they did at Columbia and Harvard in the late sixties, but I have wondered why presidents and others have risked potentially unruly actions rather than seeking—for example—court injunctions ordering students to disperse. Such injunctions are difficult to enforce, but are worth considering before police are called. There will always be hard-liners who want immediate action, but they should— barring actual physical dangers in a protest—be put off as much as possible in favor of other means. To date (April 26, 2024), we have been lucky. No buildings have been taken over, and no "busts" have occurred. But one's luck may run out.

During the late 1960s, some universities commissioned reports concerning divestment from stocks that were said to support the apartheid regime in South Africa. Depending on the results of the analysis—and the options available—universities could decide whether to divest or not.

Current demands by protesters (in 2024) for universities to sell stock that is said to be related to Israel's war in Gaza have resulted (to my knowledge) in just one analysis, although Brown University has apparently agreed to let protesters meet with its board of trustees to discuss the issue; that action has led to an end to Brown's protests for the moment. Universities have generally appeared to be unwilling to discuss divestment, probably because that would seem to take sides in the Israel–Hamas War, and might be judged to be inimical to Israel, with no consideration of the fact that Hamas brutally began the conflict. Nevertheless, analysis and discussion—whatever the final decision—are almost always preferable to police action.

Meanwhile, there seems to be no end in sight to the main protest situation. Modern communications have made it possible to create swift protests at universities and colleges across our entire continent—at Texas, NYU, Pomona, Northeastern, Columbia, Vanderbilt, USC, Harvard, Stanford, Emerson, Yale, and elsewhere. Perhaps the only exhortation that might be helpful is too obvious to mention: Presidents and other administrators should work in very close collaboration with faculty leaders (and faculty consultative bodies) as well as with trustees before taking action. If there is a serious split among these, the results can be disastrous.

The more that institutions of higher education function as collaborative consultative bodies, the more they are likely to find better—if not ideal—pathways through the current crisis, avoiding the worst that happened in the 1960s. But the crisis is unfortunately liable to last throughout this academic year into the next.

The problems that began in Palestine a century ago have—not surprising—failed to be resolved, and the current Israeli government has for decades only made matters even more intractable. No two-state (or single-state) solution is even remotely in sight. Given the brutality of the current war, nothing but a very long pause or actual cessation may bring an end to the protests that are now consuming so much of the attention and energy of our universities. Unfortunately, such a pause or cessation seems unlikely at the moment, so the summer break from the academic year will at best give leaders time to consider what approaches to the protests may be possible in the autumn. We should not expect ideal solutions, but any efforts to achieve analysis, discussion, consultation, and greater mutual understanding among the different participants are to be prized above the use of force.

* * *

Notes

CHAPTER 2

1. Richard Freeland, *Academia's Golden Age* (Oxford: Oxford University Press, 1992), 74, 88, passim.

2. Clark Kerr, *The Uses of the University* (New York: Harper Torchbooks, 1964), 36–47.

3. Ibid., 32.

4. David Riesman, *The Lonely Crowd* (New Haven, CT: Yale University Press, 1950), 65.

5. Ibid., 67.

6. Ibid., 346.

7. Ibid., 348.

8. William H. Whyte, *The Organization Man* (New York: Simon and Schuster, 1956), 7.

9. Ibid., 72–73.

10. Ibid., 284.

11. Ibid., 245.

12. Ibid., 247–48.

13. Ibid., 403–4.

14. Ibid., 404.

15. Otto Butz, *The Unsilent Generation* (New York: Rinehart, 1958), 28.

16. Ibid., 129.

17. Ibid.

18. Ibid., 131.

19. Ibid., 173.
20. Ibid.
21. Ibid., 174.
22. Ibid.
23. Ibid., 188.
24. Ibid., 184.
25. Ibid., 187.
26. Ibid., 189.
27. McGeorge Bundy, "Were Those the Days?" *Daedalus* 99, no. 3 (1970): 555.

CHAPTER 3

1. The Cox Commission, *Crisis at Columbia* (New York: Random House, 1968), 17.
2. Ibid., 34.
3. Daniel Bell, "Columbia and the New Left," *The Public Interest* (fall 1958): 95–96.
4. Jerry L. Avorn and Members of the Columbia Daily Spectator, *Up Against the Ivy Wall* (New York: Vintage Books, 1968), 32–33.
5. Ibid., 26–27.
6. Cox Commission, *Crisis,* 60.
7. Irving Howe, *The Radical Papers* (New York: Doubleday Anchor Books, 1966), 286–87.
8. Clark Kerr, *The Uses of the University* (Cambridge, MA: Harvard University Press, 1963), 9.
9. Ibid., 48.
10. Ibid., 103.
11. Seymour M. Lipset and Sheldon S. Wolin, eds., *The Berkeley Student Revolt* (New York: Doubleday Anchor Books, 1965), 462.
12. Ibid., 67–70.
13. Ted Widmer, ed., *American Speeches* (New York: Library of America, 2006), 617.
14. Avorn, *Up Against the Ivy Wall*, 26.
15. Todd Gitlin, *The Sixties* (New York: Bantam Books, 1987), 106.
16. Ibid., 107.

17. Ibid., 285.

18. Ibid., 285–86.

19. Ibid., 286–87.

20. Ibid., 286–87.

21. Gitlin, *The Sixties*, 197–98.

22. Daniel Cohn-Bendit and Claus Leggewie, "1968: Power to the Imagination," *New York Review of Books* (May 10, 2018): 6.

23. Bob Dylan, *The Lyrics, 1961–2012* (New York: Simon & Schuster, 2016), 83.

24. *The Daily Princetonian*, February 28, 1969, 1.

25. *The Daily Princetonian*, February 28, 1969, 3.

26. *The Daily Princetonian*, February 27, 1969, 1.

27. Andrew Kopkind, "Thoughts of Young Radicals," *The New Republic* (1969): 23.

28. Ibid., 23.

29. Lipset and Wolin, eds., *The Berkeley Student Revolt*, 369.

30. Roger Rosenblatt, *Coming Apart* (New York: Little, Brown, 1997), 58.

31. Lipset and Wolin, eds., *The Berkeley Student Revolt*, 552.

32. Ibid., 538.

33. Fritz Stern, "Reflections on the International Student Movement," *The American Scholar* 40, no.1 (1970–71): 126.

34. Ibid., 126.

35. Rosenblatt, *Coming Apart*, 44.

CHAPTER 4

1. Arthur Levine, ed., *Higher Learning in America, 1980–2000* (Baltimore, Johns Hopkins University Press, 1993), 96.

2. Andrew Delbanco, *College: What It Was, Is, and Should Be* (Princeton, NJ: Princeton University Press), 42.

3. James Cuno, "In the Crossfire of the Culture Wars: The Art Museum in Crisis." *Harvard University Art Museums Occasion Papers* (1995): 1, http://www.artmuseums.harvard.edu/professional/occpapers3.html.

4. Ibid., 6.

CHAPTER 5

1. *Harvard Magazine* (Sept.–Oct. 1991): 65.

CHAPTER 6

1. Andrew Schlesinger, *Veritas: Harvard College and the American Experience* (Chicago: Ivan R. Dee, 2005), 250–52.

CHAPTER 7

1. Robert Dijkgraaf, *The Usefulness of Useless Knowledge* (Princeton, NJ: Princeton University Press, 2017), 5.

2. Clark Kerr, *The Uses of the University* (Cambridge, MA: Harvard University Press, 2001), 114.

3. Clark Kerr, *Troubled Times for American Higher Education* (Albany, State University of New York Press, 1994), 41.

4. Ibid., 42.

5. Charles Peterson, "Serfs of Academe," *New York Review of Books* (March 12, 2020): 42–43.

6. Ibid., 42.

Index